BRING NORWAY

LANCE FRIEDMAN

ISBN: 979-8-89079-472-7 (paperback)
ISBN: 979-8-89079-473-4 (ebook)

Dedicated to the dogs who cause chaos, damage,
and mischief – yet bring a smile to your face.

Contents

Introduction

"This is Norway," I proudly announced in an email to friends and family. "And, he's a handful!"

One year earlier, Oscar, my sixteen-year-old pal had passed away. After months of traveling, working, and absorbing the loss of my canine friend, I was ready and excited for the next dog. During my travels, I had spent time in Iceland and Norway, including visiting husky farms in Beitostolen and Tromso. After hiking and riding with the eager huskies, I was hooked. They were enthusiastic sledders and wonderful companions. I loved those eyes and their personalities. I knew my next dog would come from a husky rescue organization.

I monitored the Orphans of the Storm animal shelter website, waiting for a husky to come up for adoption. Also, I looked at Forever Husky, a rescue organization one hour away. Any young adult husky would be a candidate.

When I found a blue-eyed male at Forever Husky, I began their multi-week adoption process. First, I filled out the application. They wanted to be sure I was suitable to take the dog – a unique breed. Did I have high enough fences to hold the escape artist? Did I realize the energy involved? I knew huskies required a lot of activity and attention. I was ready to accept the challenge.

During the husky search, I explored the idea of adopting a senior dog. I always wanted to help an older dog who couldn't find a home. After months of seeing the same sorry dog on the Orphans of the Storm website, I finally decided to check him out on a Friday in January.

The scruffy ten-year-old in the picture had a likable look. Unfortunately, the meet and greet was a disaster. The poor thing was a basket case, and unapproachable; possibly due to years in shelters and prior neglect. Thankfully, it was a no-kill shelter, so he could stay as long as needed. But, for me, it was not a fit. *I cannot save the world.*

While exiting the shelter, I noticed a young female husky, with one blue eye and one brown eye, sitting in the corner. *Where did she come from?* Then, further down the row of cages, I saw a grey husky with brown eyes. *Where did he come from?!* He was not profiled on the Orphans website.

I brought over one of the volunteers.

"What's the deal with this husky mix?" I asked. "I didn't see him on the website."

"He came in yesterday," she said, "with thirty other dogs from Tennessee."

"Really? That many?"

"They didn't have room at the shelter down there. So, we brought them here." A subtle way of saying they would have been euthanized.

"Can I take him out for a moment?"

She opened the cage and handed me the leash. While we walked outside, the husky just looked around. He led me, sniffed a little. Mostly, he simply looked out into the distance.

"Not paying much attention to me, huh?" I said to him.

He stared ahead.

He was not the husky I imagined. He did not have the blue or white eyes typical of his breed. And, his body shape was slim, though he sported a big head. The majestic husky I had envisioned was kind of a funny-looking fella. But he had piercing brown eyes that seemed observant and probing.

While we walked around the grounds, he seemed gentle enough; still, he didn't acknowledge me at all.

"Hey, dude. Gimme something! I am here to find a dog. You gotta sell yourself!" I joked.

Nothing.

But something struck me. I believe in fate and timing – And, then, there was the funny big head!

We returned to the cages, where I asked more questions.

"So, you don't know anything about him? Is he housebroken? How old is he?"

"We figure he is about two years old. And, he seems housebroken. Like I said, we just got him yesterday."

I looked again at the new tag on the cage. "Gus. Siberian Husky mix". *Gus? Really?*

"Let me take him around one more time."

"Sure," the volunteer said. "No rush."

As we did another lap around the area, I weighed my decision. Unlike Oscar, a black shepherd schipperke mix, this guy was a grey and white husky. I was looking for another male dog. Big enough to wrestle and roughhouse with; but, not too big. And, something different from Oscar. *There is only one Oscar!*

"Hey, Gus." He didn't turn around. In fact, he didn't react to anything spoken. "OK, we can throw that name out the window." The name Gus didn't seem right for a husky, anyway.

During our walk, he made a point to step in a massive mud puddle and get dirty. *Definite personality. And, sort of funny-looking.*

"I'm going to take him," I said to the volunteer. *This is impulsive; but I believe in fate.*

It cost me four hundred fifty dollars for adoption, shots, and neutering. Over the weekend, the husky would go to the vet for the procedure. *From Tennessee, to one day in a shelter, to the clinic… and then a name change.* I wrote "Norway" in the adoption papers.

Over the weekend, I prepared for his arrival. And, I learned he had worms. "Of course, he does," I mumbled to myself. More money and more stuff to fix. But I would not be deterred!

* * *

On Monday, I went to the clinic and picked up my dog! We walked outside toward the car. A thought occurred to me: *I wonder if he likes riding in a car? If not, that will be a problem. No more road trips.* I led him into the Nissan. He climbed onto the back seat and sat there. I loaded a bag of medical items, dog treats, and adoption gifts into the car. Then, we took off.

The drive went fine. Norway peered out the window. No car sickness. He seemed good for the road. Ten minutes later, we went to the house. Inside, I placed the pain pills, some treats, and items on the kitchen counter. Norway stood at the entrance looking at me.

"Last week, you were on death row in Tennessee. Then, you were at the shelter for a day. Then, you got your jewels snipped. Now, you are at your new home! Quite the week."

I gave him a guided tour and let him wander through the house. He sniffed the baseboards in the living room, bedrooms, and office. Then, he walked around the kitchen. I led him to the porch and introduced the doggie door. With a treat in my hand, I lifted the flap. He burst through the door. I stepped inside, lifted the flap, and he popped back inside. It was a fun game to him. At the same time, he understood he could enter and exit as he pleased.

"OK, I am going to run and get you some vittles. Then, we'll have lunch."

I put the Elizabethan Cone over his head. The cone would prevent him from chewing his stitches. He sat on the couch and looked at me. Poor guy looked silly with a funnel over his head.

"I'll be quick." I darted out the door. At the store, I picked up a rotisserie chicken to spice up his dry dog food. Then, I raced back home. I hurried inside the house, wondering what I would find. *How did Norway react to being left alone for a moment?*

I stopped short. In the living room, the funnel was torn apart, lying in the middle of the rug. *Where's Norway?*

Through the window, I saw him trotting around the fenced-in backyard. I went outside to check on him. He got excited: someone to play with!

"Norway, you are going to tear your stitches!" I warned. "Slow down." I tried to settle him, but he just kept playing and running away from me.

OK, that is not working. But, at least, he is having fun.

I went back inside to unpack the chicken. As I poured dog food in the bowl – and, topped it with the juicy chicken – I noticed something was missing from the counter.

"His pills!" They were gone. After scanning the kitchen, I went outside and searched around frantically. There on the grass was the bottle of pain pills – open and empty. *Oh, no.*

I went inside and called the vet clinic.

"Hi, I picked up the husky earlier today."

"Yes, how's it going?"

"OK, I guess," I said while watching Norway through the window. "But I think my dog swallowed all of his pain pills."

"All of them? Are you sure?"

"Yeah, he got a hold of the bottle when I stepped out for a few minutes. Right off the counter."

"Huskies will do that," she said.

"I found the bottle in the backyard, but I didn't see any pills." *How did he unscrew the safety cap off?* "I think he ate them. Should I bring him in? Or, is there something I should do?"

The woman asked, "How does he look?"

"Fine, I guess. Right now, he is just running back and forth in the backyard. He looks energized and happy." *Five days of pain pills might do that!*

"Is there any way you could calm him down?"

"I tried. He thinks I am playing with him."

"OK," she said. "Just monitor his stitches."

"I guess." I wasn't sure what I could do. He'd already torn apart his cone. "But the pills won't harm him?"

"We'll see," she answered. "If he seems OK, then they will just go through his system. Just be careful and call us if his behavior changes. And, keep an eye on his stitches."

I got off the phone and watched Norway playfully run back and forth. *What can I do?* He ignored the lure of treats. I couldn't catch and stop him. We would just have to wait and see if the stitches ripped open. But, right then, he was as happy as could be!

That first evening, Norway enjoyed his chicken dinner. Afterward, he wandered around to look for a sleeping spot. He had the backyard, a doggie bed, the couch, and other comfortable choices. Eventually he came into the bedroom and jumped onto the bed. He walked around, climbing over me, and then plopped down beside me, pressing up against me.

"Bonding," I said. "This is a good start."

Then, for a moment, I recognized how trustworthy – or, naïve – I was with dogs. Here was this random stray dog, that looks like a wolf, lying beside me. He could rip off my face in the middle of the night. Yet, I had a sense that he would be a kind companion.

PART 1

EAST

NORWAY WATCHED ME exit and enter the house.

"Going on a road trip," I told him as I passed by carrying supplies. "You're going to like this!" I went out the door, making sure the latch was closed.

After five months, we were going on our first big trip. Having done extensive road trips with Oscar, the planning and preparation came easy. I packed the same items, then loaded the Nissan with a few duffel bags, snacks, and dog supplies.

I spent thirty minutes getting ready, while Norway observed. *Then, he made his move.* When I failed to latch the door completely, he made a dash through the opening.

I put down my box and walked out into the driveway. Norway was standing about forty feet away.

"Come here, Norway," I encouraged him. I crouched, and kindly said, "Come on, boy."

Then, he smiled and darted down the street. *F$%#K!* I had learned from prior occasions that it is terribly difficult to catch a two-year-old husky.

I ran inside and grabbed the leash, along with treats to lure him. I went back outside, and headed down the residential street to track Norway. At 6:00 a.m., the neighborhood was quiet. I found him in the next block, sniffing bushes. I cautiously approached. At one hundred feet away, he saw me and trotted farther. Then, he stopped and sniffed some more. Occasionally, he looked up at me. I tried walking away to draw him closer, but instead of following, he just watched. Then, I called out. No reaction. I waved his treats. He was not interested. Each time I got close, he went farther. It was a game of edging closer and snatching him when he was not looking.

Forty-five minutes later, I corralled Norway.

"Not part of the plan. You are wrecking our schedule," I said to my energetic, eager companion.

EVANSTON, ILLINOIS, to PERRYSBURG, OHIO

THE LAST ITEMS went into the trunk. I set my laptop bag on the passenger floor. Then, we did a final inspection around the house. The appliances were off, the windows were closed, and the desktop computer was shut down. I locked up, and then led Norway to the passenger side of the car. He wasted no time leaping into the seat. I got in, started the engine, and we headed down the driveway. After a two-year hiatus, the road trips resumed!

Waiting for the driver!

As we started east on I-94, Norway enjoyed the ride. It was a cool morning, so I cracked the windows on the way toward downtown Chicago. Suddenly, I heard a sound in the backseat.

"Oh, my god!"

Norway had one front leg through the narrow opening in the back window. His head was outside. *He is trying to jump out!* The next highway exit was one mile away. And, this road section did not have a shoulder to pull over.

While steering the car —moving at forty miles per hour amid the modest traffic -- I stretched back to grab his collar. I couldn't reach. Norway cried out, because he was partially stuck in the gap. When I cracked the window a bit more, Norway tried to get another paw through. So, I rolled the window up to prevent him from squeezing out. He squirmed. I was steering the car, trying not to swerve into the next lane - while glancing over my shoulder to see where Norway was. Then, I pressed the button to lower the window a bit. Norway cried louder.

"Oh, shit." I had accidentally pushed the wrong lever, closing the window tighter.

Finally, I managed to stretch and grab a clump of Norway's fur. Holding tight, I abruptly opened the window and yanked him backward. Then, I closed all the windows.

"What on earth are you doing? You cannot jump out of a moving car!"

Norway just sat back in the seat and thought about his latest caper.

The next hour of driving was smooth. Surprisingly, Norway slept the entire way. *Maybe the morning escape and car incident had worn him out?* We made our first stop in Elkhart, Indiana. I had read about a giant American Gothic statue and wanted to see it. Also, halfway to our overnight destination seemed like a timely spot for lunch.

We found a parking place on the main street. There were several statues and artwork lined along the sidewalks. While Norway stretched his legs, I browsed the scenery, which included several theme-painted elk statues and illustrated hearts. I scanned the area for lunch options, and searched for the giant American Gothic. At the end of the block, we reached a large park, where the massive piece was in the distance.

The farmer with the pitchfork, beside his wife and suitcase, towered about twenty-five feet high. It had traveled to various fairgrounds, museums, and parks around the country. Now it was in Elkhart. Norway and I got a closer look and took photos from different angles.

American Gothic, Norway, and Lance

We left Central Park and continued to browse for lunch spots downtown. Unable to find a place with outdoor seating, we drove toward the interstate and settled for a Subway sandwich shop. I preferred local spots, but this chain restaurant had a wide-open outdoor patio.

Our first road trip lunch went well. Norway seemed pleased with the Subway turkey slices and enjoyed sitting in the shade. After the break, we returned to I-80 East, and continued to northern Ohio.

Later that afternoon, we passed through Maumee and arrived at the La Quinta Inn in Perrysburg. I had been there three years earlier with Oscar, and I liked the spaciousness and large front lawn.

When we entered the hotel room, Norway scouted the new surroundings. Meanwhile, I inspected the room, moving the complimentary shampoo and soap out of the husky's reach.

Earlier this year, I had learned of Norway's attraction to household items. One afternoon, I had come home from work, and Norway was relaxing on the couch. We had a snack, watched TV, and then it was time for bed. When I went to brush my teeth, I realized the entire bathroom counter had been cleared! *Oh, Norway.*

I went to the living room and looked out the window. Meanwhile, Norway trotted through the porch and out the doggie door, into the backyard. I walked outside with a flashlight, and found all my bathroom items on the back lawn!

Beside my comb, now adorned with chew marks, lay my toothbrush and toothpaste. And, my bottle of mouthwash… my *empty* bottle. *Did Norway drink it? Or, did he just rinse and spit?*

Norway practicing good hygiene

I sighed and picked up the items. I wished I'd had a video recording. It would have been amusing to watch Norway move one item at a time from the bathroom to the backyard. It was quite an accomplishment.

After I cleared the La Quinta room of potential trouble, I looked over tomorrow's route. Meanwhile, Norway found a spot to take a nap.

In the evening, we went into downtown Perrysburg. As we walked up and down a few streets, and then along the Maumee River, people stared at Norway. Many commented, "Beautiful dog."

One woman stopped us. "My gosh. He is a gorgeous husky. Where are you from?"

I explained the road trip, that this was our first day traveling together.

"Well, he is so well-behaved," she said. "Mine is very energetic."

"Really?! You have a husky?"

"Yes, she is six years old."

"With blue eyes?" I asked.

"One blue. One white."

"Cool." I love those bright eyes. "What is your dog's name?"

"Iceland."

"Iceland? You're kidding! This is Norway."

She laughed. "Great name."

"Have you been to Iceland?" I asked.

"I have, many years ago," she said. "Have you been to Norway?"

"Yes, last year. Beautiful country. The fjords are magnificent. And, I got to meet some huskies out there."

"Really?"

"Yes, one day, I went hiking with a husky. It was amazing. My canine hiking partner was such a wonderful, social companion." I told her about the Norwegian countryside and the experience. Then, I added, "And, another time, I went summer sledding with a group of huskies. They loved running down the road, dragging me along."

"Huskies are so wonderful."

We talked about their endless energy. She informed me that hers started to slow down after about five or six years. I supposed I was in for a wild ride for the next few years. Then, I explained how I found Norway.

"His name at the shelter was Gus. I considered the name Columbo, but that seemed more appropriate for a basset hound or bloodhound. I had other options, but they were the names of other dogs; and one was the name of my friend's kid. So, I passed on those. Norway just seemed right."

Norway and I had dinner at Zingo's. The patio table was solid, but not large enough to hold the husky. He could easily drag it away. I set him next to a bench that was anchored to the ground. "Wait here, buddy," I told him. "I'll try to be quick with some vittles for us."

He watched me go around the corner and into the restaurant. A moment later, I returned to him. Then, we picked a table. The woman came out with our chicken and falafel. It was as delicious as I remembered from a few years earlier. Norway enjoyed the seasoned chicken chunks mixed with his dog food.

Following dinner, we continued our walk along the river, passing statues and monuments. Then, we circled around and stopped at O'Deer Diner for a giant sundae. A crowd of people sat enjoying the summer evening. Norway got excited when another dog approached. I held on tight to his harness. Then, to prevent a scene, I distracted him with tastes of my ice cream sundae.

After dessert, Norway and I returned to the hotel. The end of a solid, eventful day. I was pleased that traveling on the road would be something I could do with a young husky – just as I had done with old Oscar.

PERRYSBURG, OHIO, to ERIE, PENNSYLVANIA

AFTER PACKING ITEMS into the car, we headed to the lobby. The La Quinta women at the registration desk nicely offered to hold Norway while I grabbed some breakfast items. They even gave him dog treats. *Norway making more friends!*

With breakfast in hand, we returned to the hotel room. After Norway tipped over his entire water bowl, I mopped up and fed him. He picked out the eggs and the dog treats, leaving most of his dog food.

Day two of driving went OK. The Ohio toll road had a one-hour delay due to an accident, along with the expected construction. Otherwise, the Thursday traffic was fine.

We passed through Cleveland and continued east to check out the Ohio bridges I had seen on RoadsideAmerica.com. The Liberty Street Bridge in Geneva was quite appealing. Completed in 2011, at just eighteen feet, it became the shortest covered bridge in the nation! A placard with its history, dimensions, and features was mounted on the side, and a kiosk and little toll booth area added charm. It did cross over a small creek --- so, it wasn't just for show.

At the Plymouth-Ashtabula township line, we visited the Smolen-Gulf Bridge. Dedicated in 2008, it was the longest wooden-covered bridge in the US and fourth-longest in the world. It spanned 613 feet at 90' above the Ashtabula River, offering a pretty view.

It was fun to contrast the bridges, as well as hike around the surrounding park areas. In between our bridge tours, we picked up lunch from Mr. Hero. Wrap and fries for me; chicken for Norway. We ate at picnic tables overlooking the bridge.

Above and below the Smolen-Gulf bridge

An hour later, we arrived at the hotel in Erie, PA. After picking up the room key, we headed out to explore Lake Erie. We started at Presque Isle Park on the sandy peninsula, taking in the beaches, bike paths, and volleyball courts, mixed with restaurants, snack bars, and recreational activities. *What a spacious public space!* Norway had his first water encounter, playing in the little waves along the lake-front. I had chosen Erie, because it was a suitable stopover between

Ohio and New York; but this afternoon excursion was a pleasant surprise.

We returned to the Red Roof Inn, where the dog-loving woman at the front desk gave an incredibly warm greeting. In our hotel room, I surveyed the space and picked up a remote control sitting on the night table. *Too low.*

"Not going to get this one," I said to Norway as I patted him on the head.

During the past several months, I had gone through five TV remotes. The first time, I had come home and couldn't find the remote. Not under the couch. Not on the table. I looked out the window. The device was in the backyard. The plastic cover, batteries, button, and handle were in pieces. Norway had plenty of snacks and chew toys; but he couldn't resist the remote.

The conversation with the cable company went like this:

"Hello, thank you for calling RCN. How can I help you?"

"I need to replace my remote control," I began.

"Is it broken?"

"I'm not going to make up a story," I admitted. "My dog destroyed it. He got to it and chewed it apart."

The woman took it in stride. "Oh, that can happen. Do you want to exchange it at the office? Or, we can send one to you."

A few days later, the new remote arrived at my door. Two weeks later, another replacement was needed. I had tried to train Norway. But he snatched the next remote. I realized I needed to train myself, not my husky. I began placing the remote on a shelf.

One day, I forgot and left it on the couch. When I returned a few hours later, it was missing. Another call to RCN. Eventually, I habitually placed it on the shelf when leaving the living room. *I was trained.*

In the hotel room, I turned on the TV and placed the remote control behind the screen. Norway found a spot on the cool bathroom floor. Meanwhile, I checked Yelp and found encouraging reviews for Tasty Bowl. *Worth a try.*

Dinner was good. At twelve bucks for spring rolls, chicken, veggies, and white rice, there was plenty for Norway and myself. *Ready to dig in!* But I could not find the plastic utensils. The take-out place had forgotten to pack them. I ran down the hall and asked the nice woman at the front desk. She handed me a fork and spoon.

Following dinner, I fell asleep watching *Alone* on the History Channel. Norway was by my side the entire night. *By my side.* Norway the husky did not sleep at the foot of the bed. He did not sleep next to me. He slept *against* me. Sort of *on me*!

Years later, I mentioned to a Russian couple that I had a husky. The man asked, "Is it a Siberian husky?"

"Yes, he is."

"Does he sleep near you?" he continued.

"He does," I said. "Actually, he kind of lays on me. How did you know?"

My Russian friend smiled. "Yes, they were bred that way. In the northern parts, huskies were taught to protect the children while the adults were working and hunting. The huskies would keep the children warm."

"Impressive." It amazed me how domesticated animals can maintain traits in their bloodline. Norway was far from Russia. Yet, he exhibited the characteristics of the breed; and he was great with kids.

Although he hogged the sleeping space, I could at least keep track of him and I knew he wasn't chewing on something. And, I could take him outside if he got up.

Later in the evening, Norway began barking mixed with husky talk. He wanted to play. *Not good in the hotel room.* I tried giving Norway a chew bone, which did occupy him --- for ten minutes. Then, after offering him the rest of the Chinese food, he was content and quiet.

ERIE, PENNSYLVANIA, to SYRACUSE, NEW YORK

I STARTED THE morning with a shower. A moment later, Norway jumped in, splattering water around the bathroom. *At least, there are no paw prints in the room.*

"Are you proud of yourself?" Norway just smiled while having fun.

Outside, it was overcast with bits of rain. But no complaints— it was not hot. After loading the car and packing up, I left a five-dollar tip for housekeeping and wrote a quick "Thank you" on LaQuinta Inn paper. I doubted the Red Roof housekeeper would mind.

The on-and-off rain continued, so we would bypass Niagara Falls. I had seen it on other occasions. Norway could see it another time. It was not worth the multi-hour detour with crappy weather.

After an hour, we paused at a rest area. As I walked with Norway and had a snack, a dozen people complimented the dog. A couple in an SUV drove by; and, a mini-husky poked its head out the passenger window. It looked like a cross between a chihuahua and husky with blue eyes. It yipped, and Norway barked back.

We returned to the I-90 tollway and continued east. Half-way to our destination, we exited to take a lunchtime break. As we pulled up to the window, I searched for my ticket.

"Hello," the toll booth woman said cheerfully.

"Hi," I answered while shuffling through papers and my pile of spare change. *Where is the ticket?*

"Oh, boy. He is handsome." She eyed Norway, perched in the passenger seat. "Quite a road companion."

"Yes, he's great company," I said, "although he hasn't got his driver's license yet!"

The nice woman smiled and waved at Norway. We chatted as I kept looking for my toll ticket.

"I can't find the ticket," I finally told her. "We're coming from Erie. We entered from there."

"That's OK," she said. "You can use that price."

"Thanks."

After exiting the tollway, we stopped for a break at Tim Hortons. We sat at nearby benches in the shade and had lunch. Across from us sat a woman and her husband, a little terrier beside them. They were eating sandwiches, while their dog sat and watched – intrigued by Norway. Then, it turned toward two other pups in the distance.

Norway tried to pull away from the table to play with the little terrier – until I pulled out our snack. Immediately, he refocused and leaped onto the picnic table. *Time for lunch!*

Not the best table manners

"OK, OK," I said to him. "So embarrassing. I can't take you anywhere," I joked while standing face to face with him. The others in the park area watched and laughed. A sixty-five-pound husky can be a formidable lunch effort.

In the afternoon, we checked into the Syracuse hotel and went for a quick excursion. I took the wrong exit and landed in a ghetto with stragglers loitering everywhere. I turned the car around, and with my map, traced a path to downtown.

Syracuse reminded me of an old Eastern US city. A bit run-down, but trying to rebuild. There were many commercial vacancies; yet, sections with new cafes and restaurants. We walked through a few blocks of bars and restaurants, until spotting the twenty-four-second clock. Set up on a street corner, it honored the first basketball shot clock used in 1954. A plaque explained the origin, purpose, and background of the clock. A nifty bit of basketball history.

Ninety minutes later, Norway and I returned to the car. On the ride back, I missed a turn, detoured, and took the long way. *Travel is a learning curve.* At last, we pulled into the hotel parking lot. I collected the bags and bowls, and we headed for the stairs. Our room was at the top; but Norway did not want to go up the stairs. *Ugh.* Instead, I carried the pile of items to the elevator, seventy-five feet down the corridor. We took the elevator up. Then, walked down the long corridor to the room.

Once inside, I dropped off the items. As I started to check my email, I noticed Norway was pacing. Fast! I picked up his leash, and we ran to the stairs. *Nope.* He would not go down. And, he would not let me lift him. So, we trotted down the corridor to the elevator. *Waiting, waiting.* Got in. Pushed the down button. *Waiting, Waiting.* After an eternity, we got to the bottom and trotted to the grass. Nothing. Then, a moment later, Norway found his spot and relieved himself. The lunch, snacks, and all kinds of stuff had worked through him. I bent down to pick up the waste, when I noticed, fully intact, *the white tollway ticket that was missing! When did he eat that?*

We regrouped in the hotel room until dinnertime. The kid at the front desk had suggested, "Joey's is the best restaurant in Syracuse". Also, he said, "Mafia's Italian Pizzeria is a good spot." Both were next to the hotel. I checked online for menus and reviews to pick one. Since Joey's was busy, taking at least an hour for take-out, we walked to Mafia's.

As we approached, a young guy left with a pizza. "Cool dog", he said to me. I set Norway next to the entrance and went inside to order. As I looked at a menu, the owner appeared.

"You can bring the dog inside," he said. "Beautiful dog."

I escorted Norway inside and ordered the eggplant sandwich. It was enormous and filled with fresh ingredients. The owner showed me the huge eggplant he cut. While I watched him make our meal, we had a nice conversation.

I learned the owner had been a chef at many Atlantic City hotels and casinos. Eventually, he moved and opened this spot with his wife about fifteen years earlier.

As they put together the side salad, I requested meatballs for Norway.

"How 'bout a leftover burger patty?" he offered.

"Perfect."

They did not even charge for it. I think they liked the dog!

Mafia's pizza. Another satisfied customer!

A few minutes later, he offered to cut up chicken as well. *A feast for Norway!* We had picked a great place.

Carrying the bags of dinner, we walked back to the hotel room. In the bathroom, I prepared Norway's dinner - dry dog food, topped with the burger and meatballs. Norway sniffed and watched with anticipation. It looked good.

Following his delicious meal, Norway climbed onto the middle of the bed and fell asleep.

SYRACUSE, NEW YORK, to LAKE PLACID, NEW YORK

AT 5:30 A.M., Norway began his "I want to play" barking and yelping, mixed with Husky talk. Luckily, our room 201 was at the end of the corridor, and room 203 was vacant. It was unlikely he disturbed anyone. I took him for two walks, bringing items to the car, hoping to settle him down a bit.

Back in the room, I managed a workout, mixing exercises for thirty minutes. Half the time, Norway watched with interest. The other half, he got involved —wagging his tail and pivoting back and forth while I did jumping jacks, crawling under me during the planks, and climbing on top of me doing sit-ups. *At least, he's not barking.*

After checking out, we sat in the air-conditioned Red Roof lobby so Norway could enjoy attention from two of the hotel workers. Fifteen minutes later, we hit the road.

Yesterday's rain had passed. It was bright and sunny with a cool breeze. We briefly used the I-90 tollway, where I observed another tollway worker doing double duty -- alternating between handing tickets to those going, and flipping to the other side to take tickets and money from those coming. *God bless him for doing the tough active job.* The young man happily greeted us and took time to offer Norway dog treats! This time, Norway ate the treats, not the toll ticket.

We exited onto I-81 north and headed sixty miles toward Watertown, NY. At Route 3, we turned east and continued into downtown Watertown. While passing the courthouse, I noted signs to Route 12. A pizzeria sat next to the currency exchange, tattoo parlor, and monument ponds. Suddenly, I recognized we were criss-crossing the route Oscar and I had taken three years ago!

We traveled east on Route 3 for two more hours. Ten miles short of Lake Placid, we stopped at Saranac Lake. There was a farmers market beside the village. We walked around the area, noting the bars, restaurants, and local monuments. Afterward, we went to the lakefront, grabbed a slice of pizza across the street, and ate a quick snack in the park.

We finished our drive into Lake Placid and found the Crowne Plaza. The location was great -- near the Olympic attractions. The room was disappointing, with no clear view of the lake. However, it provided quick access to the front lawn. Crowne Plaza was much more expensive than the Lake House visit three years earlier. *Perhaps, we had gotten a deal because the Lake House had just opened.*

Norway and I spent a few hours strolling around the village. We enjoyed the open air, view of Mirror Lake, and quaint local shops. Mostly, we visited the outdoor skating rink where Eric Heiden won five gold medals, and the arena location of the "1980 Miracle on Ice".

Wandering past sports history

A woman passerby was extremely sweet, offering to keep Norway company while I went inside to explore the Olympic ice rink for fifteen minutes.

The husky attracted quite a bit of attention. Some were a bit wary of him. But most people enjoyed meeting Norway, especially five young coeds we encountered. We chatted for a moment as Norway soaked up the attention. The females loved him, his name, and the fact that he was a rescue.

The luckiest dog in the world!

We followed the main road up the hill to a synagogue. It was an ornate building with a big blue menorah embedded in the brick face. Interestingly, the 125-year-old synagogue was open all year round, supported by a couple dozen families in the area.

Norway and I turned and went back to the main area. We enjoyed beautiful weather, plus water bowls were conveniently placed at different restaurants. We stopped for a sandwich at the Big Mountain Deli. I ordered a #42 out of forty-six sandwiches -- a tribute to the forty-six Adirondack peaks. The avocado, tomato, onion, and cheddar cheese on fresh bread looked appetizing. And, the young guy serving was super nice and helpful! Meanwhile, a young woman was watching out the window, keeping an eye on Norway.

We walked back to the Crowne Plaza to retrieve Norway's dog bowls, as well as pretzels and soda in the room. Instead of the long way around on the paved route, we tried the shortcut. Thankfully, Norway was OK trotting up the hill and stairs.

Full of energy at the top of Lake Placid hill

He was adapting, starting to go up and down some stairs, and interacting with certain dogs. At the hotel room, we had dinner. After five minutes, he was conked out on the floor.

Following a power nap, Norway was running around the room with a surge of "I want to play" energy. I was exhausted.

"Save it for tomorrow!" I promised.

LAKE PLACID, NEW YORK
(day 2)

AT 1:00 A.M., I followed Norway outside, where he promptly did some business. Afterward, we slept well as the air conditioner cranked. Norway was by my side. Although two beds occupied an enormous room, Norway crowded onto the soft bed with me. He woke up at 5:30, but luckily, he simply repositioned himself and went back to sleep.

At 7:15, Norway was up, stepping on my head, and walking over me.

"Wonderful," I said to him. "Yes, I'm excited for today, too!"

Lake Placid was a town I recognized. With no plans to drive, we could relax, with plenty of time to revisit favorite places. After dressing, I grabbed Norway's water bottle, my headphones, and an extra shirt from the car. This morning, it was sunny, cool, and peaceful.

After confirming directions at the front desk, we began the 2.7-mile loop around Mirror Lake -- the perfect length for a leisurely one-hour walk. The path mostly encircled Mirror Lake

Drive, making it tough to get lost. We walked down the sidewalk, past the small, sandy public beach, around the bend, and up the road past a section of beautiful homes. We went by numerous walkers, dogs, runners, and triathletes swimming in the Lake. The July Lake Placid Ironman competition was a few weeks away.

We stopped and talked to a variety of people, including a New York woman who had traveled in Iceland to see the northern lights and loved huskies. We passed some again on the other side of the lake, as they were walking clockwise while we walked counterclockwise. Encounters were 85-15 positive. Occasionally, Norway excitedly "attacked" another dog. Or, lunged at a runner. Norway loved to play, but he did not recognize boundaries. *And, he is unaware that he scares the crap out of little fifteen-pound dogs.*

In one instance, Norway lunged at a runner. The woman darted aside, as his paw swiped high at her shirt sleeve. I yanked Norway aback, and hoped that he hadn't scratched the woman or torn her shirt.

Twenty minutes later, we saw the same woman! We were unable to avoid her on the narrow sidewalk. In this second encounter, she stopped running and turned to us.

"Hi," she said with a smile.

"Hey, how's it going?" I answered cautiously. I was certain she recognized us.

"Great dog."

"Thanks. He gets a little excited. Sorry about earlier. Did he tear your shirt or scratch your arm?"

"No, it's all good. I love dogs."

After a brief pat on the head, she jogged away.

Overall, Norway followed the path, and people enjoyed meeting him. On the north side of Mirror Lake, we ran into a couple dragging their Labrador retriever our way. Apparently, the lab wanted to go down a road to the water. *He knew the way!* Unfortunately for the pup, the couple had an appointment in the other direction.

Norway and I walked down the road to a boat landing beside Lake Placid. We greeted two young girls working there. As three kayakers with fishing gear were pulling in to the dock, I introduced Norway to swimming. He half doggy-paddled after plunging into the water. Then, panicking a bit, he tried to climb onto the pier instead of just swimming the five feet to the shore! But he was improving.

Morning adventure in Lake Placid

We returned to the path along Mirror Lake, connecting onto Main Street through town. Eventually, our walk ended at the sandy beach where the route had begun. I took Norway over to the lake shore. He still was not enthusiastic about the water and swimming. But he loved darting around in the sand!

During a quick stop at the room, I checked messages and made the Montreal reservations. I spoke to a gentleman named Turgay and booked directly --- which resulted in a slightly better price and free parking.

Norway was impatient, so we headed off to find lunch. I picked up a salad at Good Bites. Then, walked to Big Mountain Deli to see about a chicken sandwich snack for Norway. There was a huge line; so, we returned to the Crowne Plaza to eat on their patio with a view. This plan worked out well until it started raining.

After a brief rest in the room, we went back to the beach. I noticed there were posted "No Dogs" signs. *Hmmm, I hadn't seen them this morning.* No swim lesson for Norway. Instead, we walked around the town.

The sun had come out. While a trail hike was an option, we preferred interacting with the dog-friendly people. Also, it was amusing to see crowds keep Norway company while I was inside a shop getting a frozen hot chocolate.

Norway waiting with his new friends

At dinner time, I spoke with a woman and her family while waiting for a #46 sandwich outside the Big Mountain Deli. She had a female husky. Her pure husky was super mellow, although she had similar habits of laying on the woman when sleeping at night. Her boy loved playing with Norway. And, Norway enjoyed it, howling and rolling around! Others gathered to take pictures with the prominent husky.

Following the public relations, we strolled back to the room and relaxed. I watched TV, and ate half of the sandwich, leaving the rest for a nighttime snack. It was a tasty mix of turkey, provolone, avocado, tomato, and other fresh ingredients. I gave Norway the turkey out of the sandwich. He was pleased with his share.

The laundry room had two washers and three dryers. *How many people at this resort did their laundry on vacation?* After utilizing the available machines, I returned to the room and dumped the clean clothes on the bed. As I folded and placed items in the suitcase, Norway came over. For some reason, he enjoyed watching me fold laundry at home. *Maybe he felt like he was participating in an activity. Or, was he eyeing one of the pieces to add to his collection of chew toys?* Each time, he would hop on the bed next to the clean clothes and sit with a sense of comfort as I folded them.

LAKE PLACID, NEW YORK, to MONTREAL, QUEBEC, CANADA

WE GOT UP at 5:30 a.m. -- thanks to Norway. He began to bark, talk, and run around on the bed. After I showered and stashed a few items in the car, we retraced our path around Mirror Lake.

The thick-coated husky appreciated – and, thrived in -- the chilly morning temperatures. At one spot, Norway got a burst of energy and raced ahead. I tried to keep up; but, the slack in the leash disappeared and Norway's harness jerked him backward for a moment. He got more excited and pressed ahead, digging into the ground and dragging me behind. The more I pulled back on the leash, the more excitedly Norway countered with a burst forward. He was in sled dog mode. If I had another husky and a sled, I could have gotten quite a ride!

After fifty yards, Norway suddenly stopped by a tree. He sniffed the scents around the base, while I caught up. Then, satisfied he darted off again. *This is fun!*

After the morning trot, I handed Norway treats. Then, he passed out on the bed. I checked email and wrote quick directions on paper --- *86E to 9N to 87N to 15--* to Montreal. *How hard could that be?*

I finished packing and clearing stuff out of the hotel room fridge. The slushy Gatorade was pretty good, just like the slushy raspberry iced tea I'd had in the Erie, PA hotel room. *I have not quite figured out these hotel mini fridges.* Breakfast was not included in our hotel reservation; and, we skipped the rather expensive extra option. We were ready to go. Norway perked up as I picked up his leash.

Lake Placid to Montreal was about a hundred and twenty miles of driving. Halfway, we stopped in Champlain, NY for a snack at Nathan's fast-food. I picked up a sandwich for me and beef slices for Norway. After our pit stop, we crossed the border. *Bon Jour.* Welcome to Quebec!

I followed my directions, printed maps, and the giant Montreal skyline into the heart of the city. With little trouble, we reached our hotel. After parking, Norway and I climbed the steps to meet Turgay. The friendly gentleman checked us in and pointed us to room 4.

The accommodations were terrific. We had two rooms, a kitchen, and bathroom. Plenty of space for just me and a dog. The cable TV was minimal - but they offered DVD movies to use with the room's player.

A block away, I found a store to get necessities. *Where would Norway wait if I went inside?* It was harder than I thought to find an outdoor cash machine. A hotel staff member made a great suggestion: find an ATM at a pub. It was an option, assuming Norway was in my sight.

With a list of attractions and a map, we set out to explore. Once I got oriented, it was quite easy to navigate the section we walked. Tour highlights included a very cool matador mural on Blvd. St. Laurent – among other eye-catching street art; and Schwartz's deli with its famous original smoked meat. There was a line, and besides, I do not eat meat. As we walked by, Norway eyed the crowd. At Parc LaFontaine, we spotted the forty-nine-foot, giant slingshot, carved from a dead tree. Surrounding this piece was a nice-looking park with plenty of squirrels for Norway to chase.

People were sunning, biking, and walking their dogs, enjoying a cool, beautiful day. After more than three hours, Norway had grown tired–he even lay at one of the last traffic lights. But he made it!

We took a break in the room until dinner time. Looking at online maps, along with TripAdvisor and Yelp reviews, I chose Cafe Lola Rosa. The Mexican/vegetarian restaurant was five blocks down Rue Milton. On the way out, I got directions to an ATM from Turgay. It was inside the convenience store we had passed two doors down! The ATM was right by the window, so I could see Norway. I withdrew cash and bought a soda on the way out.

We walked down Milton, passing restaurant options for tomorrow. Norway was scouting, tugging, and stopping every three feet to smell scraps and shrubs. Then, he would race ahead. We had walked more than three miles that morning in Lake Placid, and we added almost four hours exploring Montreal. Yet, he had more energy to expend.

We reached McGill University at the end of the road. *Did we miss the restaurant?* I asked a few people, and on the fifth try, I found two students who pointed us in the right direction. I couldn't believe we had passed the restaurant the first time. *Why didn't Norway tell me?!*

As Norway waited beside a tree, I went inside to order take-out. While waiting for service, I could see Norway through the open wall. A young woman was keeping him company, and other passersby greeted him. *Very good.*

A few moments later, while paying the bill, I heard growling --- A little dog had run up to Norway. *Oh no.* I went outside to see the dog and its owner scampering across the street. *Oops.*

"Norway, try to avoid any international incidents, please." I said to him.

He just happily wagged his tail.

With the bag of food, we headed back. The Café Lola Rosa dinner was healthy and tasty. Plus, plenty left over in the fridge. There was a bit of spice, so hopefully it would not upset any stomachs

-- mine or Norway's. I didn't want to have to walk him in the middle of the night.

Where do I walk him? I suppose in the back alley, where homeless people had set up shop. The alley did smell a bit like a urinal.

In the evening, we went for a quick walk to see if Norway would relieve himself and whether the frozen yogurt place was open. The froyo place was closed, and Norway did not go. We did greet three Eskimo/Northern Canadian/indigenous/homeless/drinkers who were out in the back. They were quite polite and had an affinity for the husky and me. Hopefully, they would keep an eye on our car.

I collected dog treats and a sweatshirt from the car. On the way back to the apartment, I picked up an ice cream bar at the convenience store. Then, we headed up the stairs, ending a day of a lot of walking in Lake Placid and Montreal. There was not much on Canadian TV, aside from an *America Ninja Warrior* rerun.

MONTREAL, QUEBEC, CANADA (day 2)

"BOY, YOU RECHARGE quickly, don't you?"

At five a.m., Norway began to yelp and bark, leaving me no choice but to go outside. To his credit, he did his business during our walk around the city block. I led him back inside, up the stairs, and into our room. I tried to go back to sleep, but Norway began jumping on me, yelping, and wagging his tail.

"Oscar would never do this!" I joked, complained, and pleaded.

I relented and got up, showered, and dressed. I drew up our game plan, using the Wi-Fi to scan various spots in the area. Meanwhile, Norway sat on the bed, napped, got up, napped, and chewed through part of a bedsheet. *F$%#k.*

I neatened up the room and dumped Norway's food, just as a few ants appeared. After removing the food, they vanished.

On the way out, I grabbed my headphones, camera, waste bags, the dog water bottle, and map. Outside was sunny and cool—a perfect morning for exploring and outdoor activities. We started down Rue Milton, passed Lola Rosa Café, and on to McGill/University

Road to the museum area. On the way, tons of cool photography, artwork, and sculptures were displayed along the streets!

Norway and the Wolf statue

We turned toward the financial area, walking among people going to work. Strolling down the wide Blvd. Bourassa, past the Bourse, Montreal Exchange, and big banks, was pleasant.

As we turned toward the old city, Norway became a bit sick, hesitated, and almost threw up. At the next corner, just two blocks from the open grass of Victoria Square, he relieved himself on the sidewalk. Thankfully, I had bags and a full container of water to clean up.

We reached the western part of the old city, passed the Centre d'histoire de Montreal museum with its impressive architecture, and strolled by several quaint shops. I stopped at a cafe to get a banana smoothie and try a vegan *pastrie*. The peanut butter/chocolate snack was quite good. Meanwhile, water and a treat pleased Norway.

After the breakfast break, we spent time on cobblestone roads, by the port with views of the river, and back around to the huge palaces, plazas, Hotel de Ville, and Notre-Dame Basilica. *Awesome.* Being a weekday, it wasn't too crowded. I noticed a watering spot, near an outdoor fruit stand. Norway got a sip, and I bought items for tomorrow.

We continued up and down the Old Montreal streets, eyeing potential rest places. When I looked over a wall menu at Creperie Chez Suzette, Norway decided to lie down beside me. He was exhausted. A woman was setting up the patio.

"Excuse me," I said. "Is it OK if we eat here?"

"Yes, it is fine," she said, and offered any of the outdoor lunch spots.

I chose a table off to the side, in the shade for Norway, with a view of the passing people. I decided to try the crepes and Quebec maple syrup. Moments later, a big family took up two full tables beside us. Norway rose to meet our neighbors seated in the adjacent plastic chairs.

"Sorry about that," I said to the boys seated closest to us. "I hope he's not bothering you."

"He's OK," they said. "We like dogs."

"Where are you from?" They didn't have Canadian accents. One sounded Southern.

"We live in Seattle and North Carolina. We're visiting family here in Montreal."

Norway started to nose into their table area. They gave him a pat on the head. "What's his name?"

"Norway."

"Really? Her parents are from Norway." They pointed at their mother.

We continued chatting until the food came out. Norway turned his eyes to my plate of crepes. They were terrific, and the Canadian maple syrup was tasty.

Twenty minutes later, the manager and the cook came outside with complimentary cheese for the customers and snacks for Norway. Also, they agreed to prepare a doggie portion of roast beef for five bucks. Great! Norway made some friends, was fed, and we all got to relax and enjoy Montreal.

After cooling and fueling, Norway and I continued sightseeing, then headed back. We never found the dog park. It wasn't at the listed address. However, we viewed more cool murals and street art.

Then we reached St. Laurent. *Familiar.* That led to Sherbrooke. *Familiar.* And, eventually, Parc Ave. I was getting the hang of the streets. I realized that the street names changed when you moved to different districts, much like Paris. Also, I noted areas with Jewish influence—restaurants with *Kosher* written in Hebrew. Also, the style had hints of New York and classic Europe. I noticed the attractive, chic women. And observed Inuit-indigenous influence and appearances.

When we arrived at the hotel entrance, Norway got excited. I opened the door, and he dashed up the lower part of the stairs. He paused, looked back to make sure I was right behind him, and darted up the upper half. *I guess he's learning how to use stairs!*

When we entered the room, Norway headed right to the toilet and his water bowl. He gulped the water, plopped down on the cool floor next to the fridge, and passed out before I took off his leash and harness. We were exhausted from five hours of walking.

After uploading photos and checking messages, I sat in bed with the pup and watched a DVD. I had picked *Legalese*, a TV movie with James Garner, Gina Gershon, and Mary Louise Parker. *How bad can it be?* Through the window, I watched the clouds pouring in. *Is rain on the way?*

Following the movie, and after lying around, I went to fix dinner. We had the leftovers from Lola Rosa Café. Plus, Norway had dry dog food to mix with leftovers and the wet canned food in the fridge. And treats, in case he didn't like his dinner.

Before turning in for the evening, I stopped at the convenient market next door to grab a soda and a candy bar for later. We greeted two more Inuit people living in the back alley. They loved Norway, probably because he looked like a wolf.

We encountered an elderly lady. When I mentioned I was from Chicago, she commented, "It's dangerous, no?" *Is that the impression of Chicago this Canadian has?* For some reason, a Chicago tourism commercial frequently appeared on the local Montreal station, encouraging people to visit Chicago. Apparently, the television ad had not affected this lady's impression.

Back at the room, I turned on the TV. A television commentator was talking about finding out info about your blind date. "You want to see if they are criminal, transgender, or a Trump supporter." The panel nodded, and the audience laughed in agreement. *Guess the wholesome matchmaking days of* Dear Abby *and* The Dating Game *have ended.* I flipped channels. Then, after an unhealthy dose of toxic television, I tried another 1990's DVD movie from the front desk until I fell asleep.

MONTREAL, QUEBEC, to QUEBEC CITY, QUEBEC

AFTER GETTING CHANGE to leave for housekeeping, we said good-bye to Turgay. The gentleman was very understanding when I mentioned the hole in the bed sheet. Thankfully, he liked the husky. Norway went ahead and started down the stairs.

"Great job, Norway!" He made it to the bottom. Admittedly, once he started, he couldn't turn around midway down the steep stairway. Nevertheless, we were pleased with the accomplishment.

Look out below!

We got in the car and followed Rue Sherbrooke southwest until turning onto Autoroute 15.

"See, I'm learning my way through Montreal!" I proudly said to Norway. He was staring out the window watching the rush hour traffic.

At times, the French signs and roads were a bit confusing. Luckily, I could see a big orange sphere in the distance. I was on the correct path to the Gibeau Orange Julep. Its claim to fame as the largest orange sphere in the world became obvious. The roadside attraction—a fast-food spot with an eye-catching architectural design—was erected in 1964 by the Gibeau family.

Hanging around the Orange Julep

At nine a.m., we parked in the mostly empty, huge, round parking lot. *This place must fill up on weekends.* The orange julep drink was delicious. It tasted like a sweet version of Orange Julius. We sat at picnic tables and listened to satellite radio pop and rock music blasting out of their speakers. I treated Norway to a burger patty for breakfast. I passed on any food, although I was tempted to try the vegetarian hot dogs and their poutine.

After the morning pit stop, we headed back onto the 15 Nord, then connected to the 40 East. Then, in fluid traffic, we entered the QC-25, which was a tunnel toward downtown. Next, we turned onto 20 East. And off we went to our next city.

Norway slept through most of the easy drive. I followed my written directions: *20 East to 73 Nord and connecting to 40 East.* It was going fine, but some of the signs were a bit misleading. *Am I still on the correct route?* I began looking for a gas station to check my directions, when suddenly I saw the turnoff for Route40.

We took 40 East and started looking for the hotel. I noted signs for downtown Quebec and Montmorency—two places we intended to visit. Then, among the city sights, I saw the hotel on the side of the road.

Le Dauphin was a score! First, the price and location were quite good. It was next to a twenty-four-hour Tim Hortons, in case I wanted a snack later. The front desk people were very pleasant. One enthusiastically wanted to pet Norway. Our room was tremendous, with nice features, lots of outlets, and comfortable decor with non-carpeted tiles, so no messes. The curtains opened to reveal an indoor pool. Sadly, Norway hadn't packed a swimsuit.

The hotel staff left a dog kit with a few treats, a blanket, and little dog bed, in addition to a dog bowl and waste bags. It was welcoming and thoughtful. Norway jumped onto the bed to look at the contents. *I doubt that's what the hotel had intended.*

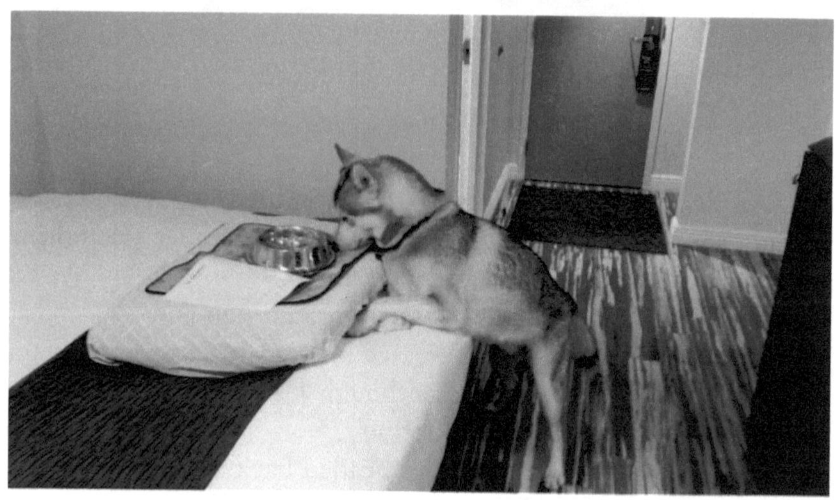

Norway eyeing his goodies

There was another Le Dauphin about one hundred kilometers before Quebec. Was this a Canadian hotel chain? *Will I find others further along on this trip?* I tried the cable TV. There were many French stations. The talk shows looked familiar, but they were speaking French. I changed channels and found *Magnum PI.* Much better!

In the afternoon, we drove twenty minutes to Montmorency Falls. I had learned it was a beautiful place with views and an opportunity for Norway to get some exercise. On the way, rain poured, then it stopped briefly, only to be followed by hail. Undeterred, we continued to the park.

At Montmorency, I learned you could get to the top via the stairways. This worked for me but not for Norway. While Norway showed promise in Montreal, he was still wary of steps. To this point, I had never gotten him to walk down the stairs to our basement. And at some hotels we had to take the elevator when he resisted the stairs with all his might. I wondered about the fear. Had someone pushed him down? Had he been locked in a basement? I hoped it was natural and not trauma from an experience.

We took a back trail, winding up the side of the mountain. Eventually, the shaded, wooded path emerged at the top where the stairs ended. The skies overhead had cleared. And we got a gorgeous view of Quebec City, the St. Lawrence River, and the horizon.

Descending paths are not easy, especially after rain. We retraced the damp trail back down. The pace was brisk as Norway excitedly led the way.

"Wait a sec," I called out as I hurried behind him, holding his long leash.

"Wait." We picked up speed. "Norway! Wait!" I tried keeping up, sidestepping the rocks, trying to maintain my footing on the muddy parts of the trail. But it was not enough.

"F$%#%$K!"

I slid thirty feet down the muddy hill—until Norway stopped and turned to look at me. He was expressionless, wondering why we had stopped.

"Wait," I said emphatically to him.

I gathered myself, wiping clumps of mud off my legs and clothes. "Slowly, please."

He happily resumed his descent down the slope.

Despite the muddy clothes, it was a fun excursion. Montmorency offered cool waterfalls, a nice trail, and glimpses of Quebec in the distance.

An abundance of commercial choices were in the area along Route 40: strip malls, restaurants, stores, and services. Costco, Walmart, and McDonald's were mixed with local places. As we scouted restaurant options, I saw a guy getting into a car with his dog. I asked him if there was a nearby PetSmart. He suggested a similar place just down the road and offered to lead me there.

The pet store was one mile from the hotel. It turned out to be rather good, selling similar items. I did find a slightly different harness that was suitable.

Down the street, we ordered takeout from Scores, a family restaurant with many options. I split the chicken and rice with veggies, giving Norway the chicken kabobs, while I ate the rice and veggies. Also, we had a side of poutine—fries, cheese curds, and gravy—with some ketchup. It satisfied a craving after a full day of driving and hiking. Norway gobbled his food, and after he learned he could not have any of my poutine, he went to sleep.

QUEBEC CITY, QUEBEC, CANADA (day 2)

AT FOUR THIRTY a.m., a paw struck my face. I pushed it aside. Norway moved it back. *Is he doing that on purpose?* Then, he stood up and leapt off the bed. *Ugh, I should have left the paw where it was.*

"OK." I got up and put on shoes and a shirt. Then, Norway led me outside. He routinely marked his favorite tree for the third time in two days. After a few minutes, we went back to check the laundry room availability. The hotel offered free use of a washer and dryer, with detergent and softener. These were usually full of clothes—but not at 4:45 a.m. Good job, Norway!

I put our wet and muddy items into the washer. Back in the room, I set the alarm clock and went to sleep. Forty minutes later, I got up to switch the clothes to the dryer. Back to the room. When I climbed into bed, Norway jumped in. I reset the alarm clock for forty-five minutes and went back to sleep. Got up. Walked a few doors down to the laundry room. I pulled out the lighter fabrics and let the dryer take care of the rest. Back to the room. When I entered, Norway was waiting by the door. Then he hopped back into the bed. I followed, turned on the TV, and waited. Thirty minutes later, I collected the remaining cleaned clothes, sweatshirt, and towels I had used at Montmorency.

After soaking in a tremendous water pressure shower, I went with Norway to the lobby.

The hotel's breakfast room was a bit crowded. I searched for a spot to secure Norway. The chairs and tables did not look like they could hold him if he decided to make a getaway. I settled on an ice machine near the lobby. I darted into the dining hall and grabbed fruit, a banana, and eggs for us. A minute later, I ran back to the ice machine and saw a crowd of people. *Are they adoring him? Or did Norway do something wrong or get tangled up?* I approached to find a guy petting happy Norway. The crowd was watching as they waited for an elevator. I thanked the man for keeping my dog company, collected Norway, and went back to the room.

After breakfast, I picked up my camera and phone from the room's row of charging outlets. Then, at the front desk, I received a map and directions to the old city. We could take our time today. Old Quebec was quite manageable to walk around in a few hours, assuming we did not get hosed by any rain.

I found the parking lot easily. The $18-CAD-per-day rate was a bargain. It proved more economical to stay at the less expensive hotel and drive for the day rather than at a pricier place in Old Quebec.

We walked toward the Parliament Building, a tremendous structure across from the Fontaine de Tourny. On this hot day, Norway was particularly interested in this majestic fountain with water jetting out and surrounded by decorative flowers. To him, it was a drinking fountain. Part of me wanted to let the dog loose. The other part of me wanted to be respectful of the public space. I compromised and let Norway get close and sneak a few sips.

A delicious sip from the fountain

While Norway was taste-testing the Parliament fountain, a couple sitting on a bench watched with amusement. *Oh, what the hell…* There was construction going on, so how bad could it be?

While the area was undergoing renovation until 2019, cranes and crews were scattered across the sites. Nevertheless, the statues and tributes to historical figures were interesting, and, the area was well maintained and clean. Mostly, the fortress walls surrounding the old city were noteworthy.

Among the moderate crowd, touring with Norway was fine, although he kept tugging and lunging at the horses that went by. Although he startled some pedestrians, most people seemed OK with Norway. Countless folks commented, *"Bon Chien."* Several asked to take photos of him. *Norway making souvenirs!*

We proceeded down the main thoroughfares, spotting the ornate Fairmont Le Chateau Frontenac, the St. Lawrence River, and the wonderful Terrasse Dufferin. Not only was it a pretty walkway, it was super-wide for a dog stroll.

Terrasse Dufferin

During the busy lunchtime, it was difficult to find an open cafe to sit with Norway. We wound up at Le Chic Shack. I guessed that *chic* was short for *chicken*, although it could have meant style. The restaurant provided a menu posted outside, and I interrupted one of the workers to order takeout. He kindly went to get a Jardin burger, fries, and a cola-type drink.

While waiting, I noticed maple and pepper fries were on the menu. *I wish I had tried those.* The guy brought my order outside, and I was very grateful for his help during a busy lunch hour.

After leaving a generous tip, we took the boxed meal and found a bench in the nearby plaza. *Bon appétit.*

The delicious veggie burger came with lettuce, tomato, beets, and special sauce on an artisan bun. It was a terrific colorful presentation of a burger. Maybe it was chic after all. As Norway and I ate with a view of Fontaine de la Place d'Armes, many passersby greeted us.

After lunch, we walked to an ice cream shop. We relaxed and had a maple-flavored sundae while watching people walk along the Terrasse Dufferin.

Eyeing the sundae

Eventually, Norway and I began to tire. We headed back to the car and returned to the hotel. We had time to explore the outer parts, but seeing the heart of Old Quebec was satisfying. *Bon chien* and I were very impressed!

QUEBEC CITY, QUEBEC, to EDMUNDSTON, NEW BRUNSWICK

AFTER WATCHING THREE *Big Bang Theory* episodes last night, I turned off the TV and went to sleep. I was back up at one a.m. because Norway was sitting in the bed panting. A cool evening stroll outside seemed to satisfy him.

At five thirty a.m., Norway began pawing at me and stepping on my head. We did a lap around the hotel. Full of energy, he ran around the parking lot. Although I can be a morning person, Norway's schedule was killing me.

Today's drive was a few hundred kilometers on the TransCanada highway. We waited until after nine a.m. to avoid rush-hour traffic. Along the auto route QC-20 Northeast, a view of the St. Lawrence River was on the left side with farmland on the right.

We stopped at an easy pull-off beside a Subway, Tim Hortons, and a gas station. These seemed quite common along the Canadian highways. Following a long walking break with Norway, I used the bathroom in Tim Hortons, then bought a drink and a muffin to repay the favor.

During the next leg of the drive, Norway mostly slept in back. Meanwhile, I missed the Route 85 turnoff, which added thirty-five minutes to our trip. *Bummer.* Eventually, we got on QC-85 east and headed inland. The landscape turned to pine trees, reminding me of Maine or upper New York.

We stopped for gas about forty kilometers out. At the station, we met a cute woman who was selling auto wax for interior and exterior use. It was unnecessary for an eight-year-old Nissan. Still, we had a nice conversation, as she loved the husky.

Upon arrival in Edmundston, we made a quick detour across the border to Madawaska, Maine. Off the US-1 highway, Main Street, we discovered 4 Corners Park. I had been to the Four Corners Monument, which marked the spot where Utah, Arizona, Colorado, and New Mexico meet. This geographic landmark recognized the four extreme points in the continental US.

Established in 2007, the cool attraction provided a good photo op of the most northeastern spot in the United States. Plus, it included a tribute to motorcyclists who had ridden to all four corners of the US: San Ysidro, CA; Key West, FL; Blaine, WA; and Madawaska, ME. There were groups that organized a nine-thousand-mile challenge of covering all four corners in twenty-one days.

I approached two ladies walking around the fountain and granite dedications. One kindly took a few photos as Norway fluttered in my arms. Eventually, she snapped a well-centered souvenir shot with Norway facing the camera.

Four Corners Park in Maine

Across the way, a McDonald's board was promoting their McLobster Roll.

"You gotta be kidding."

I'd had the McRib long ago, during my meat-eating years. And, surprisingly, it was pretty good with the sauce. Out of curiosity, Norway and I tried the McLobster Roll. As fast-food lobster goes, it was *McDecent*.

Madawaska, population under five thousand, was a small town. Norway and I walked up and down the main street for about thirty minutes in search of a card for a friend's birthday. After visiting Rite Aid, the post office, and local shops, I found a suitable postcard.

We returned to the car and drove up Bridge Avenue, crossed over the St. John River, and headed back into New Brunswick. On the Canadian side, we resumed on Prom de Veterans and followed the map to Four Points by Sheraton. There was plenty of parking, and it seemed easy to get around town.

Our room was the size of a comfortable apartment, with a bed and couch, a fridge, and a TV, plus plenty of outlets for recharging. It had wood/tile flooring, so if needed, easy cleaning.

This area in Edmundston provided an ideal start for an afternoon walk. Up the road from the hotel, we passed statues, Cathedrale de Immaculée Conception, Fortin du Petit-Sault, the marina, and finished through the walking bridge and promenade around Parc du Petit-Sault. It was a pleasant tour for Norway and me.

From a street full of restaurants, I chose Frank's Bar and Grill beside the hotel. It had good online reviews and a diverse menu. Since we were exhausted, the convenience was worth the somewhat high price.

After booking tomorrow's hotel, located in the southeastern side of New Brunswick, we headed for dinner at Frank's. The bilingual hostess helped considerably with the French part of the menu and accommodated Norway with chicken penne. Also, the young woman working was very nice. Charged to the room, the meal was one less credit card receipt.

As we waited for takeout, restaurant patrons stopped to say hi to Norway on their way out. *Norway, the canine greeter.* I noted the red Canadian maple leaf flags decorating the lobby and restaurant area. It was a pleasant atmosphere.

It would have been nice to eat on the patio. However, by dinnertime Friday, the empty restaurant became packed. We took the dinner bags and headed up to the room. The meal was quite tasty: penne, cheese, broccoli, and peppers. Norway devoured the chicken with a few pieces of pasta.

While eating, I turned on the TV. The channel guide displayed an hour later than I thought it was. I realized that we had crossed into another time zone: the Atlantic.

I fell asleep in my clothes. At 2:15 a.m., I woke and walked the dog (just in case). Back into the hotel, up the elevator, and back to the room. Norway hopped onto the bed and went to sleep. Meanwhile, I changed clothes and checked the Wi-Fi. Unfortunately, the connection had not improved. I watched the French-Canadian version of *Lip Sync Battle* on TV. *Lip Sync Battle: Face à Face* had the same set design and format. The co-hosts were a French-speaking man and woman. Same introduction, with two competitors going after the lip-sync belt. Each had chosen American rock-and-roll songs.

EDMUNDSTON, NEW BRUNSWICK, to MONCTON, NEW BRUNSWICK, CANADA

CANADA DAY! JULY 1. We passed through the flag-filled lobby and started outside with a loop around the hotel area. We walked by the cathedral, statue, and shops under overcast skies. I hoped for the best, as the forecast predicted rain.

The ninety-minute morning leg of driving was in the rain. Fortunately, when we got out of the car to visit *RoadsideAmerica*-listed spots, the downpour dwindled to a drizzle. We explored the Florenceville area, stopping to see "Noah's Ark." Built in 1993, the three-hundred-foot replica was an ambitious project. At the time of our visit, the structure had tenants and a café.

On the way back to the highway, we paused at Potato World, the New Brunswick potato museum, where I learned about the potato's impact in the region. Apparently, the climate and soil in this area were ideal for growing potatoes. Home of McCain Foods, the largest producer of frozen potato products, Florenceville-Bristol is the "French Fry Capital of the World."

Twelve miles down the road, we made a stop in Hartland to view the "world's longest covered bridge." The 1,282' wooden bridge was a cool structure, spanning over the St. John River. Originally built uncovered in 1901, the harsh weather compelled the town to enclose it in 1922. The structure was amusing, as the width allowed only one car to go through. Since side-by-side cars could not fit, traffic in one direction must wait until the other side cleared. Nevertheless, the bridge has provided a helpful connection to other locales in the area.

We resumed on TransCanada-2 East, until our last stop at the "Largest Axe in the World" in Nackawic. The intriguing site showcased its giant axe, constructed in 1991 to represent the forestry industry. The handle was nearly fifty feet high, and the blade was about twenty feet long. Apparently, musical and theater performances took place on the stage surrounding the axe. *Horror show, anybody?*

I took pictures from different angles, plus, shots of posted history and statistics about the axe. Then, I tried to get a full photo with Norway. I set the camera timer for ten seconds, and we ran down the field and turned to pose. As I led Norway back to the camera, he playfully came along. I looked at the digital image: it was off-center, Norway was looking in the wrong direction, and I looked like a lunatic tackling my dog.

We made a few more attempts, setting the camera timer and running down toward the giant axe. Everything was going well until Norway got free from his collar. He started racing around the park, chasing birds, and stepping into the water. I think he might have waded further into the St. John River if he hadn't been afraid. I watched, followed, and hoped I could round him up. While passing a nearby party boat, several folks on the deck seemed amused by the dog running around and my having to chase him.

Eventually, Norway settled down and came back to me. *Oy vey. An international incident.*

Time for a picture—chop-chop!

We left with a fine souvenir photo to capture the moment. And I was reminded to use the harness, because Husky Houdini knows how to slip out of his collar.

Overall, the three-hundred-mile drive was fine. I snacked on an energy bar, dates, and nuts. Meanwhile, Norway enjoyed his cozy pillow and a treat. At four o'clock, we arrived at the Four Points by Sheraton in Moncton.

In the lobby, balloons, cookies, and snacks were set out in celebration of the 150th Canada Day. Like the Four Points in Edmundston, this hotel offered plenty of space and amenities. Since Halifax and Prince Edward Island were a few hours away, this Moncton location would be a solid springboard. I added two days to the hotel reservation.

Before dinner, we ventured out to see if we could catch the local tidal bore. Twice a day, the high tide from the Bay of Fundy flows into the Petitcodiac River, which runs along downtown Moncton.

The thick wave of water will roll back and raise the river levels as well as create waves. I didn't see much. *Was this site an exaggeration?*

After too much drizzle and waiting for the tide, we bypassed visiting downtown and the Canada Day celebrations. Instead, we wound our way back to the hotel. Mapleton Street ran past a stretch of restaurants and stores. Considering menus and reviews, I settled on the closest places: Thai Zone or Panizzi. I scanned each and picked the Thai place.

Dinner was not bad. The teriyaki Tao salad had a good flavor and consistency. Norway seemed to like the chicken. When I looked over at him, he had flipped his bowl upside down. His dog food was spread on the floor, and Norway was eating it up.

"You gotta explain that one to me."

After finishing dinner, I led Norway out to the car to get another overnight bag. While the dog received three compliments, I got three wicked mosquito bites. We returned through the lobby, where the receptionist greeted us. I got a candy bar at the front desk, collected some treats for Norway, and we settled in the room.

I went online to watch surfers on the Moncton tidal bore. The videos were shot from the same spot where we had been standing. So, right place, but wrong time. *Maybe the rain affected the tide?*

PRINCE EDWARD ISLAND, CANADA

NORWAY PAWED AT me around four a.m.

"Alright. Alright," I complained. "I hear ya."

I put on a sweatshirt, pulled the towels out of my shoes, and put them on. They were almost dried out from yesterday. We went down the elevator and greeted the young man working the night shift. He recognized us with a nod.

Outside, it was drizzling, but, luckily, no mosquitoes. Norway took a leak and did his Michael Jackson moonwalk. He stepped forward and tried to kick up dirt to cover the scent. He smiled and followed me back to our room.

At seven a.m., Norway was not going to let us sleep in. Big day ahead. I showered, ate a snack, and packed up stuff for the day. In the lobby, I used an ATM to withdraw necessary Canadian dollars. And, I spotted a gas station across the street. An ideal launching spot for the day.

I got brief directions from the woman at the lobby's front desk. I went with her suggestion, taking NB-15 instead of TC-2. It proved faster than the online estimate. *It often pays to ask a local rather than an online search engine.*

Less than thirty minutes from the hotel, we turned into Shediac. I followed Main Street toward downtown. We reached the visitor center, which featured a huge lobster and a fisherman. The fifty-five-ton, eleven-meter-long creature certainly defended the town's claim as the lobster capital of the world. I took photos, exercised Norway around the park, and looked at the shops and monuments. Across the street we enjoyed an open view of the water from Northumberland Strait.

Surveying the view beside the world's largest lobster

Highway 15 was an easy feeder into TransCanada 1, taking us to the Confederation Bridge connecting Prince Edward Island. The massive bridge, finished in 1997, took four years, and cost one billion dollars—and eliminated the need for ferries to get to the island. This seemed a better alternative to travel in the icy winter waters.

The eight-mile bridge over Northumberland Strait in the Gulf of St. Lawrence took about ten minutes to cross. The highest point was about two hundred feet over the sea. When driving, it got a little uncomfortable at those heights above the large expanse of water. *Just stay in the middle lane and follow the cars.*

When descending onto the island, we entered Charlottetown. Known as the birthplace of the Canadian Confederation, Charlottetown is where the founders first met in 1864. The road signs led to the heart of the Island, where the original settlers landed on shore. There were 150-year Canada celebrations and maple leaf flags flying everywhere.

It was easy to park in an area packed with artisans and a farmers market on the main strip. We walked around the main streets by the harbor. Snack shops, souvenirs, and sights provided an enjoyable atmosphere. Among the monuments were construction workers and equipment to make the place even nicer.

We stopped at the Chip Shack for lunch. The lobster roll was pretty good, a notch below the ones in Maine. But the fries were excellent, representing this potato area very well. While eating at an outdoor table, we encountered several people who wanted to greet Norway. I had a long conversation with a man who asked to pet Norway. He had just lost his thirteen-year-old lab three days earlier, so he appreciated the comfort from Norway. I could empathize, remembering Oscar's final days.

"My wife and I are from Ontario, about an hour from Toronto," he said. "We visit PEI frequently—flying, not driving."

"Is it always this quiet?" It was a delightful summer day. *Where was everyone?*

"This is very crowded for PEI!" he said happily. "Usually, it's quite empty." He, like I, preferred the tranquility and space. *Hmmm, a scenic harbor and beach area, with lots of restaurants, shops, and activities with no crowd?*

After a post-lunch walk, Norway and I headed north to Brackley Beach. Near the shore, I could view kite surfers in the distance enjoying the pleasant scene. Since dogs were not allowed during the summer, we continued west to Cavendish.

I drove up and down the main Cavendish road, then stopped and asked a knowledgeable local kid where to find "the potato place." Eventually, I pulled over at a random area because I had seen the "Cows Creamery" sign. While exploring the shops, I spotted a restaurant called Red Island Baked Potato.

We walked, took photos of the church, and stopped at a donut shop. The owner, Kip, had just opened the place eleven days ago. He loved dogs and offered donut pieces to Norway! The husky enjoyed that. I learned Kip was from Saskatchewan, and he too had had a dog, which had lived to be twenty-one years old! He missed him. Kip gladly came out to take a photo of Norway and me in front of his shop.

A doughnut with sweet filling

For a late afternoon snack, we circled back to Red Island Baked Potato. I ordered a Tex-Mex potato, consisting of BBQ sauce, chicken, sour cream, cheese, and fixings in a potato. It was outstanding. The flavor and texture were perfect. At the tables outside, I handed Norway the chicken, while I enjoyed the PEI baked potato covered in toppings.

Afterward, we went back to Donuts by Design to say good-bye and order a dozen to go. I chatted with Kip as people passed by and eyed the donuts and Norway. Four girls recognized the husky from Charlottetown three hours earlier. I said good-bye to Kip, and he handed me an extra bag of donuts.

"A snack for Norway," he said. Although off-shaped, the donuts were much appreciated by the pup.

On the way out, we stopped at the creamery. Cows was named "best in Canada" and rated one of the top ten in the world. The ice cream was delicious, using locally sourced ingredients. The blueberry flavor was the best I had ever tasted. And the chocolate, toffee, and caramel concoction was very good.

By late afternoon, the sun finally came out. It was beautiful outside but time to drive back. We started heading toward the south side of the island and the bridge, occasionally checking the map on my laptop, and guessing for the most part. Norway slept most of the way. He seemed pleased with the Prince Edward Island sampler of treats: lobster, chips, donuts, and ice cream.

We crossed the bridge back to New Brunswick. The toll was $46.50 CAD (approximately $35 USD). It seemed reasonable. The New York tunnel was about $15, and this PEI bridge was impressive. We gotta pay for the bridge!

We backtracked past the familiar sights from this morning until we reached the correct exit off the TC-2. Back to the hotel in Moncton.

In the lobby, Norway and I stopped at the front desk.

"Any chance you found two bowls?" I asked. "They're not in the room. And I'm not sure if I left them somewhere."

"We have your bowls." The guy presented Norway's items. We lucked out, finding them just before a trip to PetSmart down the street to replace them.

"I must've left them here after getting directions from the lady at the desk this morning."

We returned to the room, where Norway ate dinner and napped. I uploaded photos and watched TV: more *Big Bang Theory* and *Modern Family* episodes, and bits of '90's movies *Twister* and *Tombstone.*

Overall, it was a great excursion today. Prince Edward Island was impressive with lots to explore! PEI offered a variety of spacious landscapes: ocean, ponds, farmland, beaches, and towns. It provided good food, history, and activities, especially in Cavendish: water park, amusement park, paintball, movies, kids' stuff, jet skiing, and more. I would love to return someday.

HALIFAX, NOVA SCOTIA, CANADA

THE NIGHT OWL was up at one a.m. Norway was panting in the warm room. The strange air conditioner randomly stopped. After I reset it, the unit cranked again … until it stopped. We went outside for a cool stroll. Norway got some relief, and we managed to avoid the mosquitoes. We greeted the two guys working the night shift. I think they liked us breaking up the monotony. After resetting the air conditioner, we went back to sleep.

At 6:40, we prepared for another day. We greeted the dog-friendly hotel crew. The morning receptionist gave him a treat and petted him. This hotel was a Norway favorite.

The sun was shining. Hopefully, that was a good sign! We hopped on the highway, no problem. Excited with anticipation as we neared our easternmost destination, I followed the road signs toward Halifax, Nova Scotia. At the NS border, I stopped for photos (and mosquito bites). Norway got to run around the welcome center front lawn.

Next year's Nova Scotia visitors' brochure?

Inside the Visitors Information building, I received a very helpful map and a suggestion to go to Peggy's Cove. We climbed back into the car. Norway's underside and paws were soaked. And the wet grass had soaked my running shoes. It could be wet socks all day unless I pulled out my extra dry trail shoes and white socks in the car. But they would look awful. *Fashion vs. comfort?*

We continued south on TransCanada-104. At Truro, in the middle of Nova Scotia, the roads branched out in different directions—sort of like the spoke system at airports. We went south on NS-102 toward Halifax and Peggy's Cove. On the way was a "Halfway between the Equator and the North Pole!" roadside billboard. We stopped at the Stewiacke exit to investigate.

A big Tim Hortons cup sat on top of the coffee store, alongside a little shopping mall and mini golf place. I filled the car with gas and got a photo of the touristy sign. I wondered if we were truly halfway. There is some dispute, since the Earth is not a perfect sphere. Still, it was close enough.

We passed Halifax and traveled south on NS-333. The Peggy's Cove road was a leisurely drive along St. Margaret's Bay. It took a bit of time but proved worthwhile. Beside the quaint fishing village was a beautiful walking area and picturesque scene of the lighthouse and the Atlantic Ocean. Understandably, and unfortunately, it was very crowded. But, all in all, a nice visit.

In front of the lighthouse at Peggy's Cove

We circled back to downtown Halifax with the map, guesswork, and some luck. We walked around and climbed up the steep hill next to the citadel, which offered a gorgeous view of Scotiabank Centre Arena and the water behind it. We walked back down to the riverfront. Browsing the nice shops was OK but stressful with a distracted, troublesome husky. He chased birds and dogs, and picked up scraps from the ground, but he did seem to be having a pleasant day. Nevertheless, I was glad we saw this part of Halifax.

During the ride back, we stopped at Oxford, the "wild blueberry capital of Canada." Just off TC-104 stood a friendly, robust blueberry character next to Tim Hortons and Irving Gas. Nearby was a park with kids playing in the water and a family restaurant and motel. Plus, a little ice cream and fresh-strawberry stand. I asked two girls if blueberries were in season.

"No," they told me. "Not until August."

"That's too bad." I would have liked to try them or treats filled with them. "Are there any restaurants in town?"

"This is the town!" They pointed at the diner next door.

I got a chicken garden salad, poutine, and garlic bread. Then, I bought a soda at Tim Hortons and sat in their seating area. The food was good. And, I had plenty to share with Norway. Although we missed the fresh wild blueberries, we were greeted by the smiling blueberry man.

We went back on TC-104 and passed the familiar Nova Scotia exits. At the New Brunswick border, we connected to TC-2 and went by wind farms. At Moncton, we took the 454 exit and Mapleton Road to the hotel.

We reached our turnaround point!

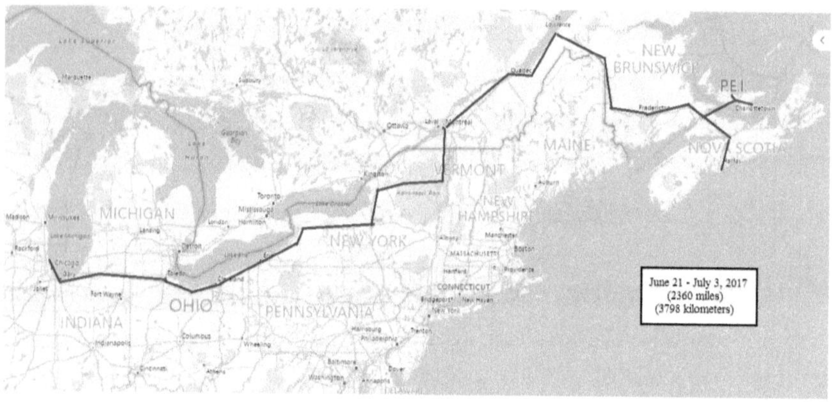

The inaugural road trip with Norway was going well. After a laundry run and a car interior cleanup, we reset for the second half of our trip.

MONCTON, NEW BRUNSWICK, CANADA, to ORONO, MAINE, UNITED STATES

FROM CANADA DAY and flying red maple leaves to US Independence Day and stars and stripes. We were heading back to the States. Just before leaving, we ran up and down the parking lot of Four Points by Sheraton. Norway got super excited, leaping onto a five-foot ledge.

"Holy shit!" I said in amazement. "Great hops, Norway."

A husky rescue organization suggested owners should have fences over six feet high to prevent runaways. *Now, I can see why!*

After finishing his antics, Norway excitedly leaped into the car.

We began our journey westward at the Reversing Falls in St. John. With a bird's-eye view, we watched the whirlpool and waves in the flow of water from the Bay of Fundy to the St. John River, recognizing that, at some point, it completely reverses later in the day. It was an interesting phenomenon. Behind us was Wolastoq Park. This sculpture park offered a history of the St. John area with a cool display of statues. Adding to the spacious pathway was a view of the river and surrounding industries.

We drove forty-five minutes on TransCanada 1 along the Bay of Fundy to St. George. At our last stop before departing Canada, I spent $40 CAD to fill up with gas, leaving $10 CAD and a pile of change.

We encountered another big blueberry display, where we met two nice women who were attracted to Norway. They showered him with attention as I looked at the local items. Although not in season, I bought a few blueberry pastries. Then, through their recommendation, I tried the takeout spot down the road. I collected the coins and $10CAD bill to buy a lobster roll, fries, and a drink. We ate at the picnic benches out front. The lobster roll was OK, and the French fries were terrific.

We backtracked to the main area of St. George. I shot a few photos, specifically a nifty-looking post office building. Then we finished at Pete's Dairy Bar. The family-owned place was fantastic. Three big scoops, stuffed in a large Styrofoam cup, for a couple of bucks. *Screw overpriced Ben and Jerry's.* This ice cream was tasty— arguably the best black cherry ice cream I had ever had.

Norway and I were sitting outside when three girls across the street walked by. "Love your dog!" one of them yelled to us.

"He's a good one!" I called back to them. Meanwhile, Norway kept his eye on the mound of ice cream.

Almost out of Canadian cash, we departed St. George and followed NB-1 until we crossed the St. Croix River. After exiting through Customs, we were back in the United States. We took Airline Road/Route 9 through Maine all the way to Bangor. We spent some time trailing a pack of cyclists who were racing through the winding streets. And with on-and-off rain, the ride was eventful.

We ended at University Inn Suites in Orono. Near the University of Maine, Orono was a nice alternative to neighboring Bangor. The room was filled with a microwave, a fridge, and comfortable furnishings. The internet was slow, so I turned on DIRECTV and caught the end of a *Prison Break* rerun. Meanwhile, Norway chewed through the soap and shampoo bottles. No, he did not clean himself—just spilled it all over. *Never a dull moment.*

I walked Norway around the hotel grounds. Kids were playing in the swimming pool and eating hot dogs, a fitting 4th of July celebration. At five o'clock, we went inside and enjoyed a complimentary cup of wine along with some cheese offered by the inn.

I talked a bit with the kid at the desk; he was a student finishing at the University of Maine. He had family in New Brunswick.

"We were just there," I proudly said. Then, I recounted the places we had seen in the area. A few guests passed through the lobby and greeted Norway and me. A woman and her husband from Halifax were especially delighted to see Norway. They had two huskies at home.

"You didn't want to bring them?" I asked.

"One of them doesn't like the car, so we don't bring them. They like to be together."

I learned the couple had had several huskies over the years.

"Are they always so energetic?" I asked after sharing some of Norway's escapades.

"Don't worry," the lady said. "They settle down when they get to be around seven or eight."

That's five more years!

We spent thirty minutes chatting with them and the desk clerk. Norway was enjoying the attention. While we talked, their daughter showed up. A sophomore soccer player at the University of Maine, she had to return to school early for preseason practice. She immediately turned her attention to Norway.

The group offered suggestions for dinner. On the 4th of July, most nearby places were closed. Down the road, we wandered through the little downtown area. At Tio Juan's Mexican Restaurant I picked up rice, beans, and chicken fajitas. Then we walked back over the bridge to the hotel.

La fiesta con mi amigo

There was plenty of food for at least two meals. Plus lots of delicious chicken for Norway. The fridge and microwave came in handy for a snack later. After dinner, I enjoyed the tasty blueberry pastry for dessert.

ORONO, MAINE (day 2)

I LOOKED FORWARD to the next couple of days. We had extra time in a familiar, appealing area. Plus, my mom and sister—in the middle of their ten-day road trip through Maine—were coming this way.

At four thirty a.m., I gave Norway a quick trot around the lot. Each hotel room had a sliding door, giving quick access to outside grass and the car nearby. After a lap, I tried the television, sorting through an American cable selection of 150 channels, including random retro stations with reruns.

At 7:15, I began a brief workout in the room. In between sets, I raced into the breakfast hall. The inn provided a nice spread, including waffles, fresh bagels, and juices. I picked up a big bowl of cut fruit, as well as scrambled eggs for Norway.

In the room, I dropped Norway's snack into his bowl on a white towel. Norway ate the eggs and the rest of last night's dinner "husky style": dumping the food onto the white towel rather than eating out of the bowl. *Is he inspecting his food? Organizing it?* Sometimes he is a funny, weird pup.

After his strange picnic breakfast, Norway turned his attention to my workout, joining in the burpees and jumping jacks. He was jumping along with me and into me. To distract him, I gave him a Maine University Inn black bear. Baxter the bear cost$19.95, with the profits going to charity. The stuffed animal occupied Norway so that he didn't tear up the room!

After breakfast, we took an eighty-minute hike on the path next to the Stillwater River near the University Inn.

Stillwater Trail in Orono

In the afternoon, we drove to the Bangor waterfront. I proudly recognized parts of Bangor and reached the waterfront parking lot without a map. As I hoped, the Pompeii Pizza food truck was in its spot near the river. After I ordered a margherita pizza and soda, I told the woman about Oscar and our visit three years ago. I recalled their generous help on a hot day, providing water and a car ride home. Moreover, Will, the young man who drove Oscar and me, was working the oven! He recognized me and was glad we came by and brought up the story.

After enjoying a pizza picnic in the grass, Norway and I took a brief walk around the Penobscot riverfront area, then returned to get ice cream from the Wild Cow Creamery vendor. *Wow.* I tried rum raisin and salted caramel scoops. The texture and taste were outstanding. The kid said the creamery had up to one hundred flavors, and they constantly switched them around. *I wish we had time to try the others.*

We drove back to the hotel. An hour later, Mom and Kelly knocked on the door.

"Hey!" Following a few quick hugs, they turned their attention to meeting Norway.

"Norway!" they called out. He got up and excitedly plowed into them, wagging his tail.

"How's he been doing?" They had heard the stories about torn-up property, swiping items, and running all over the place.

"Actually, he's been very good. After the first hour of driving, he figured it out. He sleeps in the back of the car during stretches. Then, when we stop, he pops up, and we do our thing."

"Well, that's good," my mom said.

"I know. For a two-year-old husky, he's quite mellow in the car."

We hung out in our room 110. They told me about their road trip visits along the Maine coast. "We're just down the hall in room 113."

At five o'clock, we went to the lobby for a complimentary glass of wine and chatted with the manager at the front. Then we took a short drive to Orono Bog Boardwalk. Norway was not allowed on the boardwalk, but we were able to walk around the trail together.

Afterward, I found the way back through Orono along the roads and river back to the hotel. We greeted the young guy at the front desk. He reminded me of Eric Forman from *That '70s show.*

BAR HARBOR, MAINE

AT SIX THIRTY a.m., Norway and I went back to the Stillwater River trail. This time, I left the camera and keys; the plan was to jog the entire four miles. We left the inn, started across the bridge, and onto the dirt path. Norway paused and relieved himself. *Ugh, I'll have to carry the waste bag most of the run.* We passed three women doing yoga, a few runners, and a black lab puppy, as well as homes and property along the river.

At our halfway point. Norway soaked himself while taking gulps of cold river water. We trotted back, passing a few runners and the guy with a dog from yesterday. The dog was restrained today. We passed the yoga women, and paused at a spot—the same place Norway had relieved himself. *Good memory! I should have left the waste bag and found it on the way back.* Norway slowed the last quarter of the outing. He'd never learned how to pace himself. We finished strong.

In the hotel room, I showered and picked up a few items. Then, Norway and I joined my sister and Mom. At the front desk, we got directions to Bar Harbor from the young receptionist.

During the drive, I noted familiar sights from a few years ago, including a fireworks store and frisbee golf course. We passed motels and cottages, plus, shops and billboards advertising an endless option of lobster, pies, ice cream, or fruit and berries in season. It is a tough drive if you are hungry!

We started in Acadia National Park, in the north parking lot of Jordan Pond. I walked around the pond with Norway. We enjoyed beautiful scenery. sunshine, and a cool breeze. Meanwhile, my sister and mom went in different directions.

Jordan Pond, Acadia National Park

We regrouped and headed for a tasty lunch at Stewman's Lobster Pound in downtown Bar Harbor. On their patio, we sat at a picnic table with a gentle cross breeze. Norway climbed onto the bench next to me to get a closer look at the meal in the pot.

"Does he like it?" my mom asked.

"Oh, I'm sure he does." I handed Norway pieces of steamed lobster.

Norway at Stewman's lobster

After a delicious meal, we toured the town lined with gift shops, galleries, and snack places, including an establishment called Bark Harbor that offered dog goodies. We stopped at an ice cream parlor to pick up a snack. Norway double-dipped, getting samples from me and my mom's cup of ice cream.

Down the main street, we made another stop at Pink Pastry Shop, a bakery with whoopie pies displayed in the window. Maine is considered the "unofficial capital of whoopie pies." One legend says they were created by Maine farmers' wives, who used leftover batter for portable treats. They appeared in New England bakeries in the 1920s. They are a sweet cross of a French macaron and the old Hostess Suzy Q's. I picked out two whoopie pies: one chocolate chip and one chocolate. Phenomenal. The fluffy confections were tasty, and, more importantly, the icing filling was terrific.

After browsing, strolling, and eating around town, we drove back to Orono. Due to brutal afternoon traffic, the return drive took forty-five minutes longer. We wound down the nice summer day with a snack at The Family Dog near the hotel. The front had an open outdoor seating area suitable for dogs. Also, their hot dogs looked pretty good.

ORONO, MAINE, to MILFORD, MASSACHUSETTS

BEFORE SATURDAY MORNING'S departure, Norway carried Baxter the Bear while I hauled everything else to the car. Norway and I continued our trip through Maine.

After traveling ninety minutes south on I-95, we stopped in Gardiner to check directions and walk around the town. We went along the Kennebec River, where Oscar and I had traveled three years earlier. Then, we followed Water Street through the town, passing a variety of shops. The downtown had a classic New England feel with brick sidewalks and older architecture.

The town was founded in 1754 by Dr. Sylvester Gardiner, who took advantage of the Cobbosseecontee Stream's flow into the river to generate power. Ship-building and paper mills carried the economy through the mid-1800s, and other industries did well until the 1920s. Since the 1960s, the mills have declined and closed, leaving the community of six thousand with mostly retail and service businesses.

We paused at Frosty's donut shop to pick up a snack for breakfast. During the second part of our walk, we encountered several local Norway fans, especially two women stepping outside their gift shop to greet the husky visitor. Along the way I read the information and history boards. One recounted the history of the Kennebec River floods in 1896, 1936, and 1987, including devastating images of downtown Gardiner. Yet, the town has endured.

We left Gardiner and detoured south on Maine-27 to Red's Eats in Wiscasset. The lobster shack is my all-time favorite lunch spot. After parking and a brief walk, Norway and I stepped into the long line and chatted with others. I didn't mind the long wait because my sister and mom had not yet arrived. Luckily, they showed up ten minutes before we reached the front of the line.

"Perfect timing," I told them.

"How long have you been here?"

"About an hour," I said, looking at the long line behind us.

"Geez," my sister remarked.

"I know," I said. "But, it's always like this, and it's worth it."

"Sorry we couldn't wait with you," my mom said.

"That's OK. No reason for all of us to wait. Plus, Norway and I are fine. We've been talking with others. It is all part of the experience." Then, I suggested, "How 'bout you order while we look around for a place to sit?"

They took our space in line while I scouted locations with Norway. We found an empty table in a pleasant spot by the river. Moments later, they joined us with the trays of food. Lunch was tremendous! Red's Eats truly has the best lobster roll with chunks of lobster overflowing from the bun. Plus, the local homemade butter was outstanding. Add the fried zucchini and nice view of the water, and it adds up to a great lunch!

Lunch by the Sheepscot River

We enjoyed the meal, sharing lobster chunks with Norway. I soaked in the pleasant surroundings and enjoyed the moment with family.

After the delicious meal, we said our good-byes and parted ways. Norway and I left Wiscasset, taking US-1 South into I-95 South. Entering Massachusetts, we changed to I-495. Two hours later, I stopped for gas and to confirm driving directions. The gas station attendant happily offered information.

I have been asked, "Why don't you use Google Maps or GPS?" Well, I like being detached from the electronics. Using tech can be myopic—following directions without understanding your surroundings. And sometimes Google is wrong. Using a printed map, looking over the entire area, offers a better understanding of a neighborhood. That is what road trips and exploring are all about. Mostly, I prefer road signs to a GPS screen.

Thirty minutes later, we reached the Milford exit. The surroundings looked familiar, specifically the corner gas station where Oscar and I had waited for a tire repair. While searching, I opened my laptop and checked the address and an old map from 2014. I made a navigation change and found the La Quinta Inn, noting the construction across the street, slightly different from what I remembered.

After checking into the room, I trotted next door to Burger King for a chicken sandwich to mix with Norway's dinner. While he ate and lounged on the bed, I took care of laundry and watched TV. We fell asleep around eleven thirty. *Damn, I forgot to set the ocean sounds on the TV!*

MILFORD, MASSACHUSETTS, to CLIFTON, NEW JERSEY

WHEN I OPENED my eyes at 3:45 a.m., Norway was sitting up. *Better take him outside.* He roamed, took a leak, and fully relieved himself. *Ugh, I did not bring any waste bags.* I staggered back up to the room to pick up two bags. Back down the elevator and outside to pick up the load. Back up the elevator to the room. Back to sleep after turning on the television's soothing ocean sounds.

We got up at 8:15 for breakfast. Then, a quick email check, using La Quinta's super-fast internet connection. At checkout, the receptionist gave Norway a nice farewell with a pat on the head and a small biscuit.

Outside, Norway scouted the area and found his spot. Beside the wall, with his paw, he began digging out a few rocks, then some dirt. He carefully placed the biscuit in the crater. Then, with his muzzle, he started sweeping dirt onto the biscuit. Next, he added a few of the rocks. In between sweeping, he carefully pressed the dirt with his nose. It was nice and buried.

"Good job, buddy," I said to the satisfied pup. "Unfortunately, we're not coming back to get it!" (In the backyard, I have seen him dig up old treats he had saved.)

He skipped along with me to the car. I handed him another treat to work on while sitting in the backseat.

The Massachusetts roads were rough, but there was little traffic. We crossed into Connecticut, where the roads were newly paved. *Nice.* Then, we started hitting a slight bit of traffic.

At a stop in Hartford, Norway and I walked along a riverside path with statues and sights. The sculpture walk was Lincoln Financial–sponsored, which may have explained the numerous Abe Lincoln–themed plaques.

We ended in the downtown area and enjoyed a weekend fair with food carts and fireworks. We picked up a drink and a sandwich. The festive environment offered a bonus: coming from a nearby anime convention, lots of people were walking around in costumes. Besides the interesting character watching, Superhusky and I blended in well.

The afternoon drive was chaos. *Traffic congestion everywhere on a Saturday?* We endured the endless driving through Connecticut, New York, and New Jersey until we arrived at our destination at six p.m.

Just off the NJ State Route 3, La Quinta Inn was good as expected. Our suite by the elevator was quite spacious, which was appealing in the New York-New Jersey metro area.

When Norway began barking and seemed restless, we went outside to scout potential dinner spots. We ended up at Red Robin next to the La Quinta. It was easy, and the young Asian woman at the entry was super nice. She took our order, greeted the dog, and went inside. Ten minutes later, she returned with our chicken salad. The meal was suitable. Norway loved his chicken, but I was saving my appetite for pizza tomorrow in NYC!

NEW YORK CITY, NEW YORK

I COULDN'T BLAME Norway for waking at six a.m. I had left the curtain open, and it was sunshine bright. After a walk, we went for breakfast and ran into the sweet baby white pit bull mix. The owner seemed nice but a bit inexperienced. Yesterday, we met them when the dog was not leashed. We encountered them a second time at the elevator. Then, a third time near the breakfast room, where she walked into the dining area carrying the dog.

Since I couldn't leave Norway and risk a run-in, we took a fifteen-minute lap outside. When we returned, the breakfast entrance had cleared. I set Norway beside a sturdy chair. An Indian couple came in and glared at us. This was the third time an Indian family had outwardly reacted. Either they feared the dog, avoided him, or outright detested the animal. Undeterred, I went into the big breakfast area and grabbed a banana, an orange, and eggs for us. Then, I collected Norway, and we went up the elevator to our room.

The ten a.m. drive to New York City was an easy, direct path east on NJ-3 to NJ-495 and the Lincoln Tunnel. After paying to enter New York, we emerged near 34th Street on the west side. We traveled north on 9th Avenue into Columbus Avenue in the Upper

West Side. Most streets had open Sunday parking, and we found a spot rather easily.

The sunny, beautiful day was filled with dogs, people, runners, bikers, and horse-drawn carriages. All appealed to Norway, for better or worse! The interactions with Norway varied. One lady let her little foo-foo dog go to Norway. I tried to avoid them and guide Norway to the side, but she allowed and encouraged her dog to approach. *Why?* When I finally yanked Norway away, the happy husky had three long strips of foo-foo hair in his mouth!

Norway did get along with some dogs. And he mingled with the people, including several who took photos with him. Norway became a Central Park attraction.

Along the way, we snacked on spicy good falafel from a cart. Then, we stopped by a favorite pizza slice spot at 70th and Broadway. Two cheese slices and a twenty-ounce soda for $5.50. Great deal!

Norway eyes a slice

After finding a shady spot beside an apartment building, we enjoyed the snack. A bite for me. A piece for Norway. A bite for me. A piece for Norway. He licked the sauce off his chin. *Another fan of New York slices!*

We walked along Central Park, from 72nd to 42nd. On the way back, I tried to find the debt clock at 44th street and 7th. It wasn't there. *Construction? Or, did the gigantic numbers blow the thing up?* We returned to the car and drove to the Tribeca area. While waiting for my cousin Jim to finish work, Norway and I went along the pretty Hudson River waterfront.

Norway on the waterfront

When I found out Jim could not meet us, we got in the car at 6ᵗʰ Avenue and Dominick. Darted up 6ᵗʰ, cut over to 8ᵗʰ, up to 34ᵗʰ Street. Missed the turn but caught it going around again. There was no toll to go into New Jersey. With modest congestion in the tunnel, we emerged on NJ-3. We drove past Giants Stadium and a Ferris wheel set up for the state fair on our way to Clifton.

On the north side of the road, we pulled into a shopping center to try the new ramen noodle place. Pretty good soup and noodles for me; chicken skewers for Norway. Clifton proved to be a fine location, giving us decent access to New York City without having to pay the city's hotel rates.

CLIFTON, NEW JERSEY, to CLEARFIELD, PENNSYLVANIA

AT THE ELEVATOR, Norway and I encountered a young Indian guy. I hesitated as he approached us.

"Cute Dog," he said. "I love dogs. What is his name?"

"This is Norway," I said.

The kind young man crouched to pet the dog and chat for a moment.

See, not all Indian folks are averse to dogs.

We headed to the car, and Norway enthusiastically jumped in.

As we traveled west on I-80 and left New Jersey, the traffic thinned out. In Pennsylvania, the I-80 tollway road became smoother, and the speed limit increased from 55 mph to 65 mph to 70 mph. Roughly halfway into today's drive, we stopped in Bloomsburg, PA, where I noticed a visitor center. Inside, I asked for a dog-friendly restaurant suggestion. The woman immediately pointed to Marley's.

Along Columbia Blvd, I spotted the Marley's Brewery and Grille sign with a logo sketch of a dog. There was outdoor seating, with shade and an appealing menu. The theme, Marley the dog, came from an owner who had two dogs himself. The listed beers and ale specials all had canine names. I ordered a veggie burger with sides and chicken breasts for Norway. We enjoyed the break, relaxing and having a casual lunch. The food was terrific, and we had plenty of leftovers, which we carried out in Marley's doggie bags.

We drove thirty minutes to Milton to see the Chef Boyardee statue at the Con Agra location. Hector Boiardi started the brand in 1928. And production of the canned and box meals has been ongoing in Milton since 1938. Although unable to spot the statue, we did find a few neat areas with colorful murals and the spacious Veterans Memorial Park.

In the afternoon, we arrived in Clearfield. The Super 8 hotel was easy to find and park at. Inside, the giant suite had a full fridge, a microwave, a TV with HBO, and tremendous internet. There was a couch and lots of walking space in the main room. Outside, a small grass area fronted a view of gas stations, McDonald's, and Dutch Pantry.

Before dinner, we took a thirty-minute walk around downtown Clearfield—enough for Norway to burn off some energy. As we returned to the car, it started sprinkling. I gave a halfhearted search for Denny's Beer Barrel, home of the "Largest Hamburger Challenges." But we ended at Dutch Pantry, across the street from the hotel.

Inside, the restaurant was an old-school Amish-looking place. The menu highlighted turkey and gravy, burgers, and substantial comfort food. And the gift shop was full of licorice, candles, and other local items. Norway would enjoy the turkey, gravy, and some corn mixed with his dry food.

CLEARFIELD, PENNSYLVANIA, to PERRYSBURG, OHIO

LAST NIGHT, THERE was an unexpected problem: rabbits. Norway wanted to chase all of them—at two a.m. I tugged and coerced Norway back inside the hotel.

At 6:45, it went better without the nocturnal rabbits. I picked up fruit for breakfast and gave Norway leftover turkey. It was semi-frozen from the fridge, but the microwave solved that. Norway ate a bit, until he turned his attention to an empty plastic bag. He spent thirty minutes chewing up that thing. Meanwhile, I scanned email, checked the markets, and did the daily cryptic crossword puzzle.

While loading the car, we passed housekeepers taking a break.

"Cute dog," one said.

"Well, on his behalf, thank you." They smiled.

"What's his name?"

"Norway."

"Great name. Have you been to Norway?"

"Actually, I did spend a couple of weeks there. It is a wonderful place."

I mentioned I had visited Norwegian towns and fjords and had enjoyed some excursions, especially hiking with huskies.

"That's amazing."

Norway sensed more friends and began leaning against them, leaving a few white hairs on their uniform pants.

"Sorry about the shedding."

"He's such a sweetheart," they said. "How old is he?"

"About two or three years old," I guessed. "I got him in January. The people at the shelter said he was two."

"Shelter? Who could abandon him? He is so beautiful."

"I know." I shrugged. "Probably couldn't handle him; got more than they bargained for. He has tons of energy and has torn up my house."

"Really?" The woman turned to Norway. "Did you do all that?" He looked up and grinned.

"Oh god, yes. Tore up my clothes, CDs, remote control." I shared a couple of stories. "It's still worth it." I watched Norway smiling and enjoying the attention. "I met a lady who raises huskies. She told me he will mellow out in about five years!" I continued, "Five years? That is a lot of damage." I laughed.

"He is so sweet," they said.

We returned to the room to finish packing. I left the housekeeper a tip and a thank-you note. After double-checking the room condition, we departed.

We made three planned stops off the I-80 West. First, we checked out a big cow in Siglo, just south of Clarion. Interesting. Better was the scenery of the farms and town. Unfortunately, as we were walking around and taking photos, two guys drove up. "You're on our property," they calmly told us. Most of the area seemed abandoned. I guess we looked like intimidating intruders.

Norway and I returned to the highway and drove along until a pit stop at Sheetz for gas and snacks. I remembered they had bargain milkshakes:$2.25 for a nice-sized chocolate caramel brownie freeze.

Next, we visited the Avenue of 444 Flags in Hermitage, PA. The 444 Banners of Freedom represented one flag for each day the Americans were held hostage in Iran. In the middle stood twelve steel-and-glass panels, the War on Terror Memorial. A cemetery surrounded the area, along with a pet cemetery and dog park next door.

444 Flags entrance

Finally, we made a detour to the Dave Grohl Alley in Warren, OH, hometown of the drummer for Nirvana and founder of the Foo Fighters. It was a lengthy drive, but we enjoyed the downtown and murals along the alley. In addition to the dedication to Grohl, the alley featured the "world's largest set of drum sticks"—each about 23 feet long.

We finished driving off I-80 onto I-75, flowing into Perrysburg. In the La Quinta Inn parking lot, Norway recognized the hotel and led me to the entrance. After we checked into room 323, he immediately started sniffing around the furniture.

"Is it familiar, buddy?"

Norway climbed onto the bed. I flipped on the TV and threw my drink inside the fridge under the microwave. I recharged my electric devices in the outlets while checking online messages.

For dinner, we tried Cocina de Carlos Mexican restaurant, located in a shopping center beside a grocery store. A few metal dining tables were out front, but it was too hot and near passing people and cars. Instead, I ordered takeout: vegan tacos. And chicken tacos on the side for Norway.

I went outside to wait and noticed two women looking at Norway through the window.

"Don't worry! It's like sixty-five degrees in the car."

"We know. We hear the car running. Your dog seemed excited to see us."

I rolled down the window and let Norway peek out to greet them.

Ten minutes later, I picked up the order. It was fast service and a five-minute drive back to La Quinta.

Norway watches me prepare the final feast

The tasty beans, rice, salsa, and guacamole added to the delicious tacos. Norway cleaned his bowl and gladly helped me with some of the chips and dip. We saved room for our last road trip snack.

We returned to O'Deer Diner for ice cream. It ought to be called "Oh Dear!" for the serving sizes. I ordered a medium for $2.70, and the enormous cup contained a towering marshmallow and hot fudge sundae. I ate half of it, giving Norway a few vanilla licks, and had to toss the rest. *I will never learn.* The small size is good enough at O'Deer.

PERRYSBURG, OHIO, to HOME

AT TWO A.M., I woke to the ocean video on the TV. I like those sleeping sounds. The waves evoke the sense of lying on a beach. As we walked down the hall, we saw one of the rooms open with housekeeping inside. The woman greeted us. *Was she working?* That is a tough job, cleaning extra rooms at night. *Or was she just watching TV instead of going home?*

When we returned to our room, I switched the TV channel to rural, nature sounds and scenery. I slept soundly until Norway got us up at six thirty for a quick walk in the rain. We needed to get through Chicago before rush-hour traffic. *Maybe Norway's wake-up call was doing us a favor.* The one-hour time zone gain would be helpful. Two hundred and fifty miles to go!

I picked out a few clothes from my big duffel bag. I realized that I never wore two pairs of jeans, an extra swimsuit, a shirt, and shorts. I had worn the same small batch of clothes for three weeks—a mix of traveling light and personal lack of style. Meanwhile, Norway was playing with the toilet paper roll from the bathroom. *Another cheap source of entertainment.*

The ride back started great. The Ohio and Indiana Turnpike I-80/90 cruised. And the tolls were reasonable. We had a nice stop at Sunoco for gas. A banner promoted the "Official Fuel of NASCAR" across from a cool racing car in the lot.

The final lap of our road rally

We raced down the road, going 75 mph all the way to the Indiana border. There, I saw dark storm clouds. *Welcome to Illinois.* We were greeted with the pricey toll for the skyway, a storm with torrential rain, and crummy roads. Plus, we hit traffic at eleven a.m. in Chicago.

Eventually, we got home. I looked at the trip meter: 4,501 total miles in roughly three weeks. I turned around to see the back seat of the car was filled with white puffy filler pulled out from the ripped pillows!

"Looks like you've been busy back there, having fun!"
Norway smiled.
"We're home."
The first trip with Norway was a success.

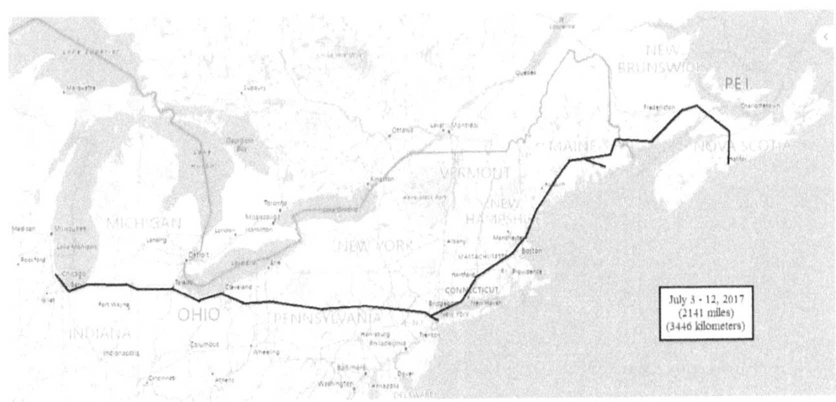

PART II

FARTHER EAST

"IS THERE A road?"

While skimming over online maps of Eastern Canada, I enlarged various areas, tracing the major highways. *Do they connect?* In articles about traveling through remote parts of Canada, I read there was road access by car on extensive miles of dirt and gravel to the Labrador border.

I had been to nine of the ten Provinces in Canada. The remaining one, Newfoundland and Labrador, was hundreds of miles northeast of Quebec. That was our mission for the next summer trip.

EVANSTON, ILLINOIS, to GREEN BAY, WISCONSIN

THERE ARE TWO general ways to the Northeast: under the Great Lakes and through the Eastern United States or over the Great Lakes and through Canada. To see as much as possible, the plan was to go up and east. Then, on the way back, go down and west.

In the morning, Norway and I headed north on I-94 to Wisconsin. It was a beautiful, sunny July day. We enjoyed our first stop in Milwaukee, walking along the riverfront and stopping for a photo at *The Bronze Fonz*. A standard trademark in downtown Milwaukee since 2008, this statue was a terrific place for a picture and view of the riverwalk.

A cool shot with the Fonz. Happy Days!

Afterward, we went over to the Brewery district, full of outdoor sites, local bars, and breweries. We visited the statue of Gambrinus, the king of beer. Then stopped near the large Pabst Brewery entrance for a photo. Adjacent was a block with etched sidewalks describing the history of the brewery. While I read the historic information, Norway took a cool rest under the shady trees.

We returned to the car, switched to I-43, and traveled north along Lake Michigan. An hour later, we entered Sheboygan to check out the tallest flagpole. The "world's tallest symbol of freedom" was rather easy to find, towering high in the distance. Located on the Acuity Insurance Company property, the 400-foot-tall flagpole carried a giant 70-by-140-foot flag. It was quite an engineering feat!

Dedicated in 2014, it included a symbolic teardrop paved base—a memorial to fallen soldiers from the Sheboygan area. We stretched our legs and read information about the site, and I tried my best to get a photo with Norway in front of the memorial. *This thing is tall!*

A canine patriot

We ate lunch at Qdoba, taking advantage of their outdoor seating. In a shady spot, Norway waited beside his white bowls while I ordered lunch for us. I returned with the bags of food, pulled the chicken chunks out of my burrito, and placed them in Norway's bowl with his dog food.

"Pretty good day so far."

Norway wagged his tail and happily gobbled up lunch. Meanwhile, I enjoyed resting in the shade and looking forward to our journey.

Following the break, we drove to the Microtel hotel in Green Bay. Conveniently located, with a direct route on Oneida Street to Lambeau Field, navigation would be rather easy. From Lambeau, we could go east toward downtown and the Fox Riverfront. Otherwise, I-41 North connected to highways that led to other parts of Wisconsin. Inside the room, I mapped out an itinerary for the next couple of days.

After the hotel break, we visited Lambeau Field. The stadium and Titletown made for a fine afternoon walk. We passed the Coach Lombardi statue, an enormous championship trophy, and other Packers history, finishing at the Lambeau Leap bronze statue.

Two faces in the football crowd!

Afterward, we visited the "world's largest hex nut" outside the headquarters of Packer Fastener, an industrial supply company. Although not as famous as Lambeau Field, the nut piqued my curiosity. The attraction was ten feet tall, made of stainless steel, and weighed over three tons. And it made the humorous claim, "biggest nuts in town."

After a full day, we hunted for dinner, settling for a sandwich spot next to the hotel.

TIMMS HILL, WISCONSIN

COLIN O'BRADY IS one of the great outdoor adventurers, having crossed Antarctica solo, completed the Explorers Grand Slam in record time, and rowed across the Drake Passage. This summer, he was on a quest to summit the highest peak in each state. I kept track of his scheduled path across the United States. Today, he would be ascending the highest peak in Wisconsin.

Colin and I have met several times, most recently at a hiking challenge in Vermont. This was a chance to catch up with him again. Norway and I were up at five a.m. The online Garmin tracker showed Colin in Rhinelander at midnight. He was spending the night forty-five minutes from Timms Hill. *Will he hike early in the morning and depart quickly? Or will he rest, get breakfast, and plan a later start?*

Unsure when Colin would start the hike, Norway and I promptly hit the road. It was better to be early than miss him. We drove 160 miles, arriving at Timms Hill by seven thirty. Nobody was there, and no names were written in the visitors' "mailbox" ledger.

At eight o'clock, we encountered a few people who had come to meet Colin. I learned they were highpointing enthusiasts from highpointers clubs that climb the highest natural elevation point in each state. Colin climbing all fifty in one month was very appealing to them. Also, I saw a sponsor and family wearing "High Points 50" T-shirts.

"Colin is due to arrive at 8:45," a follower informed me.

While waiting, Norway and I went up and down the hill path three more times. Norway was enjoying the trail scents and critters running by.

Atop the highest point in Wisconsin

Two large vehicles arrived carrying a small entourage, support staff, and Colin. He chatted with the crowd, and we had a brief chance to catch up since our last conversation. Also, I got to meet his fiancée, Jenna, who was traveling with him.

It didn't take long for the group to hike up the small hill to the highest point in Wisconsin. Colin took photos and handed out "50HP" bright green buffs to everyone. I placed one around Norway's neck. *Very sporty.*

Three adventurers conquer 1,951 feet

We briskly descended back down the path. Then, Colin left with the crew and raced to the highest spot in the next state. He would reach all fifty peaks in a record-shattering twenty-one days. *Quite a feat!*

After the gathering, Norway and I went to Hill of Beans, a charming restaurant with outdoor seating and a lovely view of a pond. The waitress asked the other diners if we could sit in the patio. All agreed, and the dog-friendly crowd asked about the husky.

The breakfast was good and massive. I was served eggs, a cinnamon scone, French toast, and sausage patties for Norway. This was plenty. Then, a huge wagon-wheel pancake came out.

The breakfast feast

"Looks like your puppy is eyeing those pancakes!"
"I'm sure he is," I answered. "I'll give him a few pieces."
"He's sitting nicely, waiting," the woman observed.
"Yeah," I commented, "or waiting to make his move!"
Norway can be smooth and sneaky. One time at home, I placed two slices of cheese on a plate, waiting for the bread to be toasted. In the next room, I checked the TV for a second to see what program was on. When I returned, I took out the toasted bread and put the slice of cheese on top. *Wait… Didn't I have two slices? Am I losing my mind?* Norway was sitting beside the counter. He gave a quick move of his tongue over his lips. He had swiped one of those slices!

After a casual ninety minutes, I wrapped the eggs and sausage for a Norway evening snack. We drove back to Green Bay. The trip to Timms Hill and the two-and-a-half-hour drive back was a success!

Afternoon break in the hotel room

Following a ninety-minute siesta in our room, we ventured out for part two of our Green Bay tour. Enjoying beautiful weather and sparse afternoon traffic, we visited the "Lighted Fish Tunnel," a 110-foot tunnel rigged with motion sensors. As we walked through, the fish sculptures on the wall pulsed with light. I think the attraction would have been better if we had visited at night. Nevertheless, the tunnel path led to more Packers sites and a nifty riverfront boardwalk with brewery, music, and boats.

We continued to explore Packers Heritage Trail and the surrounding area, until I spotted a Donald Driver statue, honoring the Green Bay Packer receiver. Next to it, on Donald Driver Way, was Titletown Brewery Company with outdoor seating. Norway and I sat in the bar area, eating poutine with Wisconsin cheese and watching customers taking in the summer day.

GREEN BAY, WISCONSIN, to SAULT SAINTE MARIE, MICHIGAN

WE HEADED UP US Highway 41, along the coast of Green Bay, which fed into Lake Michigan. Much of the drive had a pleasant view of the water to our right. Norway made himself comfortable in the back seat, either playing with his stuffed animals, snacking, or napping. Occasionally, he would drape his paws over the armrest and join me.

Norway riding shotgun over the armrest

We followed the map, taking US-41 to Michigan-35 to US-2. We paused for a snack and slushy at Jo to Go coffee shop in Escanaba. An hour later, we stopped in Manistique, at a section with a lighthouse, boardwalk, and nature path. This proved to be a good place for a walk along the lakefront sand and coastal rocks. Norway enjoyed the scents, Lake Michigan breeze, and wading in the cool water. He drank the water, splashed in the ripples, and played with the incoming waves.

Norway leading the way

In the afternoon, we arrived at Sault Ste. Marie. Check-in at the Super 8 went smoothly. The woman at Reception was polite, representing the mural behind her: a blown-up postcard attraction with bold letters, *Welcome to Sault Ste. Marie, Michigan.* She handed me two key cards. *I guess one key is for Norway!*

The room was directly down the hall, among extensive construction in the area. Inside, it resembled a studio apartment, with a massive bathroom, designed for a handicapped person. I filled Norway's bowl with sink water, but he drank out of the toilet instead. After his afternoon cocktail, he picked a spot for a nap.

Power nap

I looked up from the laptop. Norway was resting peacefully. His paws began twitching and galloping. He let out a few muffled ruffs. Then a playful whimper. His body moved around as he continued making sounds. He was having a pleasant dream. *Who is he running around with?* Hopefully, he was playing with his friends. I went back to writing until he finished his nap.

An hour later, we took a short drive to the riverfront. Norway and I walked around Portage Avenue and Water Street, browsing through the snack and souvenir shops, restaurants, and historical sites. Along the Soo Locks, in the distance, I could see the bridge to Canada.

The Soo Locks were impressive and notable. In the 1840s, after discovering iron and copper in the Upper West peninsula, producers needed to transport the minerals down to Detroit and Cleveland. However, there was a twenty-one-foot elevation difference between Lake Superior and Lake Huron, which created rapids along the connecting St. Marys River. A decade later, the Soo Locks were built to bypass the rapids. Using a series of gates and chambers, boats were raised or lowered between the differing water levels of the lakes. As the boats got larger, additional, bigger locks have been built. I could see two giant commercial vessels on the nine-hour transition path. It is a marvelous and integral waterway system.

Norway and I walked along the locks and the riverfront shops. After buying a box of fudge from Fudge du Locke, we landed at a restaurant with outdoor seating. The wooden patio beside Karl's Cuisine was the deck of a boat in a pond. The empty area worked for us, providing a sunny view of the bridge to Canada. Also, a lighthouse statue standing out from a mini-golf section added atmosphere. The food was terrific, and the college waitress was sweet, giving Norway lots of attention—and chicken strips!

SAULT SAINTE MARIE, MICHIGAN, to NORTH BAY, ONTARIO, CANADA

AT SIX A.M., I opened my eyes. A hind paw dangled against my head. Norway was resting comfortably on three-fourths of the bed. I rolled a few inches over and went back to sleep.

Two hours later, I rose to check out the hotel breakfast. From mediocre offerings, I picked out two ripe apples and free packaged blueberry muffins for later. The shower had lots of space, but there was nowhere in the bathroom to place clothes or toiletries. Plus, there was a strange smell in the bathroom. *At least it wasn't from Norway.*

In the lobby, I took advantage of the business computer to print out maps. Meanwhile, Norway made friends with a guest staying at the hotel. The gentleman had a husky at home, and we shared stories about the behavioral similarities.

"Mine is lots of fun and smart."

"Smart," I agreed. "But, more mischievous. Is yours sneaky? I put a muffin and water on the table. In the next room, I grabbed my work materials, came back to pick up my car keys and water, and headed for the door. *I'm missing something.* Where was Norway?"

"He snatched it, didn't he?"

"Yep. I looked through the window. Norway was gnawing at a plastic bag. He had swiped my muffin! I took my eye off for one second. He is a magician."

"Sleight of paw."

"Yeah, we're talking about you!" I said to Norway, who enjoyed the attention.

After checking out, we drove over the I-75 international bridge into Sault Ste. Marie, Ontario, Canada. We stopped at a few odd statues listed in *RoadsideAmerica*: three crazy cartoon cows, a moose holding up a hunter, and a giant baseball. The mini-scavenger hunt around town was a mild test of my map navigation skills as well as a trip to a few humorous sights.

After the morning drive, we took a break at a Tim Hortons parking lot. While walking around and stretching, Norway was greeted by a couple who had a husky at home. *Norway must have a lot of relatives in this area.* I went inside to pick up a chocolate freeze, a Tim Hortons favorite.

We drove on Ontario Highway 17 around Lake George and alongside the North Channel. By afternoon, we reached Sudbury to see the "Giant Nickel." The visit became a long treasure hunt, until I spotted a sign to the attraction. We followed a succession of directional signs that wound us through the entire city. Eventually, we reached the worthwhile detour.

Completed in 1964, the thirty-foot-high Canadian nickel was composed of steel. Located at the Dynamic Earth Science Museum in Sudbury—"the nickel capital of the world"—it proved to be a nifty photo op. The area was a good spot to stretch and walk, including panels with a bilingual history of the giant nickel. Interestingly, the famous big nickel—or, *Le celebre* big nickel—weighed 13,000 kg and was roughly 64 million times the size of the actual coin.

Norway and the Giant Nickel

We finished today's driving and checked into the Ramada Clarion Resort. Beside a golf course, the rooms opened to a small swimming pool. The room was spacious with a fridge and microwave, as well as a table and chairs. The cable TV fare was becoming more like Quebec, carrying extra French channels. There was limited news, a few random shows, and Showcase, a Canadian entertainment channel. In the afternoon, I watched a rerun of *Private Eyes*, an entertaining show filmed in Canada. The Canadian internet got me to Canadian AOL to check email. Otherwise, the connection was so-so, likely due to the surrounding trees and lake.

After a long day in the car, this was a fitting time to use the abundant space surrounding the resort. Also, the hotel had a restaurant at the golf club. Julie, the check-in woman, recommended it, claiming she ate there most nights. We gave it a try, enjoying the comfortable outside seating beside the golf course. Unfortunately, there was limited food selection, plus, the young chef mixed in bacon bits and messed up part of the order. Nevertheless, Norway had no complaints, finishing his portion of the meal.

NORTH BAY, ONTARIO, to OTTAWA, ONTARIO

I OPENED MY eyes and saw Norway roaming. I put on an extra shirt and shoes. Then, I picked up the leash and—*What the?!*

"Norway," I sighed. On the carpeting was a chewed key card. "Is this what you do in the middle of the night?"

Norway wagged his tail.

Fortunately, he had not started on the second key. *Now, I know why they give me two keys!*

We headed out for a morning stroll.

* * *

We left North Bay, traveling east on Ontario-17, which went along the Ottawa River. After ninety minutes, we stopped in Pembroke for a driving break. At Riverside Park, we walked by campgrounds, soccer fields, playgrounds, and even horseshoe pits. For lunch, we tried Loggers Cookhouse, which was part snack bar, café, and food truck. The fries and chicken fingers were a good snack.

We finished the second half of the drive. Following an early check-in at the Ramada, we had time to explore Ottawa. Having visited many Canadian cities, I was curious to check out the capital of Canada. We parked in the Shaw Centre, suggested by the hotel front desk clerk. He said it would be more expensive but a good location. The cost was $6 CAD, which was dirt cheap compared to what I would pay in Chicago.

Norway and I walked around for a couple of hours. We saw the Parliament, the eight locks leading to the Rideau Canal, and centennial tributes to the 1918 World War I victory.

Near the Parliament, we viewed the Terry Fox memorial statue. In 1980, Fox began his Marathon of Hope, running across Canada to raise money for cancer research. After 143 days, his bone cancer returned and forced him to stop at Thunder Bay. He passed away in 1981 but still inspires people today.

While the sidewalk path was busy with residents and tourists, few were in the spacious Parliament area. It seemed a noteworthy place for a photo. Across the street, we approached a police officer and asked him to take the picture. He was quite polite and walked over with Norway and me to the center of the massive building. Hopefully, we were not pulling him away from his post!

The Parliament

Norway and I retraced our steps through Ottawa, to the Rideau Canal Locks and past the National War Memorial in Confederation Square, and back to the car. Our tour of Ottawa provided a positive first impression. Despite traffic, including bicyclists cruising by and crowds, the capital of Canada had impressive architecture, outdoor eateries, and cool parks along the Rideau Canal. Someday, we must return to explore Ottawa further.

We drove along the river, leaving downtown toward our hotel. We stopped at a pizza place off Prince of Wales Drive, two miles north of the Ramada. The meal could've been better. The garden salad was a tasty mix of fresh lettuce, tomato, and crisp peppers, but they forgot to include dressing. The meatballs for Norway smelled good, and he gobbled them up, but they were very small servings. And the pizza ingredients were fine, but the slices came from under a heat lamp. Fresh pizza would have been tastier. Nevertheless, it was suitable takeout.

The Ramada was conveniently located on Prince of Wales Drive, a main road. The Ottawa airport, as well as the canal, provided good landmarks. It was easy to reorient myself if I got lost in the city. The hotel was next door to another Tim Hortons. *I should look at the company's stock price.* It was a better, less expensive version of Starbucks.

We had a large, comfortable room with preferred wood floors. A sliding door led outside to a patio and chairs, and an easy walk for Norway. The room was just off the river. The hotel even offered paddle boat rentals. *Norway on a paddle boat would be a funny sight!*

On the bed, I sat beside Norway and found a suitable show on the TV. As I watched, I petted Norway on his face and back. Then he rolled over and invited me to rub his belly.

"Nice hint," I said and scratched his belly.

He closed his eyes and soaked in the massage.

OTTAWA, ONTARIO, to QUEBEC CITY, QUEBEC

IN THE BATHROOM, I found Norway resting in the cool bathtub. He had a strange love-hate with the shower and bathtub. He didn't mind peeking inside while I was showering. And he didn't mind napping in the cool bathtub. But when it was time to get a bath, he did not like it!

At home, I have a large sink in the basement. Oscar fit perfectly and would sit reluctantly inside as I gave him his bath, but Norway was not so cooperative. He would fidget, and although it was four feet off the ground, the husky would try to jump to make a getaway. As I poured water and shampoo, I would hang onto him and do my best.

I tried alternative methods. In the summer, I bathed him with the hose in the backyard. In the snowy winter, I tried the bathtub. As I shampooed and sprayed him with the water stream, he tried to escape. Once, he leaped over my shoulder, scampered out the bathroom door—leaving a trail of water in the hallway—and to his getaway through the doggie door to the backyard. *Ugh.*

Using another approach, I would drag or trick him into the shower bath, close the doors, and, wearing a swimsuit, I'd battle and bathe him. Funny thing, it was mostly useless. As soon as we finished and I towel-dried him—which he liked!—Norway would happily trot away. Once outside, he'd roll in the grass. Then, find a comfortable spot in the dirt.

In the empty tub

Norway and I walked across the Ramada grounds by the pool, near the river, and around the buildings. It was a sunny, low 70s morning, and the bugs and mosquitoes were not out yet.

Inside the hotel, we paused at the breakfast area. The woman at the front desk offered to entertain Norway while I picked out a delicious apple and warm chocolate muffin that looked like it had been delivered by Tim Hortons. The orange juice was a concentrate, but, overall, this Ramada was a good spot.

We resumed our journey across Canada, entering Quebec Province. Two hours later, in Montreal, we made a brief lunch stop at the "big orange ball"—Gibeau Orange Julep. At the shaded picnic tables, I had lunch while Norway enjoyed his dry dog food, chicken tenders, and my fries.

We continued east on Quebec-40 for ninety minutes, pausing at Port Trois Rivieres for a driving break. Founded in 1634, it is one of the oldest settlements in Canada. Named for the three channels at the mouth of the Saint-Maurice River, it has developed into a major port.

At Parc Portuaire, we took a beautiful walk along the St. Lawrence River. At the time, they were setting up an extreme sports event coming in a few days. There was a pool beside a ramp, set up for a wakeboard competition. We must return to Trois Rivieres someday.

Our hotel arrival in Quebec was delayed by traffic. The last three miles took over thirty minutes. When we entered Le Dauphin, the reception area offered complimentary drinks. *I appreciate the extras.* Our modern room provided nice amenities, including dog bowls with treats and a dog blanket (though Norway would likely jump into the bed). I set down my laptop to check messages. One year later, the laptop computer recalled the hotel Wi-Fi signal. I used the fast internet to review local streets and shops.

We took a ride to the pet store. I found a French/Quebec version of simple solution pet cleaner for any accidents. Meanwhile, Norway was amused by a squeaky toy another customer was squeezing, so I added one to the bag.

Just down the street and around the corner, we found Thai Express in a little food court by another hotel. The chain restaurant offered fresh and good-sized portions. I ordered extra dishes to try different things, to have chicken for Norway, and to keep leftovers during our two-day stay. The chicken soup was terrific, and the pad see ew was pretty good too. Norway cleaned his dinner bowl. Twice.

QUEBEC CITY, QUEBEC
(day 2)

THE HOTEL LAUNDRY room was fifteen feet from our room. After a few checks, a washer became available at seven thirty a.m. I threw in a load of clothes and picked up breakfast. La Dauphin provided a ton of choices. I collected a bowl of fruit: a combo of canned fruit mixed with sliced fresh fruit. Also, I scooped a serving of scrambled eggs for Norway. And grabbed a cup of hot chocolate. I hurried back in case Norway decided to redecorate the room.

After gathering the clean clothes from the laundry room, we headed out and drove fifteen minutes to Montmorency Falls. I remembered the directions, where to park, and the pathway to the hiking trail. It was a gorgeous sunny day, with a cool breeze. Hopefully, it would last through our time in Quebec.

Norway and I marched up the dirt trail through the greenery. Eventually, we emerged at the top of the steep hill. We followed a path behind the falls to the scenic overlook. Unlike last year, our view was clear to the city. While I admired the panorama, Norway enjoyed the surrounding folks and meeting a six-month-old puppy at the park.

Montmorency Falls

Following our morning hike, we went back to the hotel. In the room, I ate the leftover pad see ew for lunch. Norway gobbled the chicken—refueling from his workout this morning.

In the afternoon, we headed to Old Quebec. From the D'Youville parking structure, we walked straight through town toward the funicular and Dufferin Terrace. There was a large crowd, due to the Friday music festival. Norway dragged me along as we weaved through the people. Meanwhile, I navigated us away from horses and dogs that would trigger the happy husky.

We met two couples from Nashville. They came up to us, one couple mentioning their husky was at home. Minutes later, we crossed paths again. They sparked another conversation, showing an interest in the logistics of dog travel. I happily recounted the modern ease and opportunities of traveling with a dog.

Norway and I deliberately walked to Quartier Petit Champlain in search of "Umbrella Alley." We passed the shops and cafes to Rue du Cul-de-Sac. At the picturesque display of colorful overhead umbrellas, I took multiple photos of Norway beneath them. Then we sat in the shade, enjoying our time watching each passerby. A gentleman wearing medieval purple French garb was walking around, chatting with tourists and taking photos. The Samuel de Champlain character gave us a friendly greeting.

In the background, I spotted the Nashville couples for the third time, having lunch nearby. One of them saw Norway and me, came over, and offered to take our photo.

Under the umbrellas

Twenty minutes later, it occurred to me: *I should give them my card.* My math website had photos of my travels with the dogs. When they noticed I was a math tutor, we had a thirty-minute conversation about tutoring and teaching. They were all involved in math, statistics, and English as a second language, both in the classroom and one-to-one. In between the petting and attention, Norway had an eye on their lunches.

"Can I give your dog a piece?" One of the women pulled some meat out of her sandwich.

"Sure, of course. He would like that."

She handed him the piece, and Norway gently took it. Then, he waited for a follow-up.

"He'll shake your hand, if you want," I said to them.

She held out her hand, and Norway eagerly lifted his paw. *I haven't done much training, but Norway knows how to respond for a treat!* She handed him the reward.

"He's a gentle dog," they said. "And he likes the sandwich."

"Oh, yes," I said. "Norway will try any type of people food. I came home one evening and found my entire kitchen counter swept clean of the groceries."

"No way!" they reacted.

"It's true. Huskies will do that. I had placed some groceries on the kitchen counter. But it wasn't high enough. Everything was gone." I continued, "I went in the backyard and found Norway sitting among the sweet potatoes and apples that he had meticulously carried through the doggie door outside—some in the bags and others one by one. Quite a shopping spree!"

I showed them a photo.

Cleanup in aisle five!

"That is funny," they said.

"I know. The items had little bites in them. He seemed proud of himself. I was impressed."

We finished our conversation about teaching, traveling, and Norway. Perhaps I would be in touch with them another time.

Norway and I continued walking around the cobblestone paths of Old Quebec. Then we started back up the hills and stairs to the Royal Battery and Dufferin Terrace. We appreciated the super-wide, spacious part with views of the St. Lawrence River. After a stop for ice cream at our spot from last year, we wound our way toward the entrance.

"Husky." I heard a child's voice. I turned to see a young girl around six years old pointing at Norway. The mother agreed with her daughter. "Yes, it's a husky."

"You have a gorgeous dog," she called out to me.

"Yes, he's a good one!"

"It's a husky, right?"

"Yep, he is a husky. Brown eyes. But, a husky—and part wolf," I joked.

After the girl gave Norway a light pat on the back, we continued down the road to the entrance. The locals and tourists were watching Norway as we walked by. We had a couple of incidents where Norway barked playfully, startling nearby people. But, overall, most complimented him. On the drive out, the cashier gave me two dixie cups with cold water for Norway. *Everyone loves the dog!*

Back in the hotel room, I tried the TV. The Quebec channel options became few and far between. Half were in French, a bunch of sports I never watch, and the news channels (English and French) were overtly political. Since each room had a DVD player, I checked out the movie selection at the front desk. They offered about thirty choices, but nothing appealed to me. I had either seen it or was not interested in paying five dollars to watch.

After catching the end of Tom Hank's *Philadelphia*, I watched *S1MONE*, starring Al Pacino on the one movie channel. Not bad. Afterwards, I caught a one-hour documentary about the recent Thailand cave rescue. The Discovery Channel had put together a news segment about last week's rescue. Harrowing. Norway and I went to sleep around ten o'clock, following a terrific—and tiring—day in Quebec.

QUEBEC CITY, QUEBEC, to BAIE-COMEAU, QUEBEC

"THERE'S A GAP."

There's a notable line in the movie *Speed* with Keanu Reeves and Sandra Bullock. Reeves's character, Jack, suddenly learns there's a gap in the highway, which leads to the classic scene where the bus jumps over the missing portion.

"There's a gap," I mumbled to myself. While double-checking tomorrow's travel time and route from Quebec City to Baie-Comeau, I noticed the road abruptly stopped at a waterway. *Was there a road detour?*

I enlarged the online map and realized the waterway required a ferry. *Rookie mistake.* This naïve US traveler had no idea. Mildly concerned, I mentally ran through the worst-case scenarios. If necessary, how far would I have to circumvent the waterway, adding miles and time to the route?

Fortunately, I learned of regular ferries that carried vehicles and accommodated pets on leash. According to the website, it was free of charge. *Free!* I noted the route: QC-138 to Baie-Sainte-Catherine, then a ferry to Tadoussac across the channel. And resume on QC-138. Excellent, the Nissan would not have to jump this gap!

* * *

At six a.m., Norway was ready to go. For the first time in a week, there was rain. While not thrilled about driving in this, I was grateful it occurred today rather than yesterday, while hiking at Montmorency and walking around Old Quebec.

The drive was fine, as mini-towns were scattered along the way. It is always comforting to know, that if stranded, we could walk to get help. QC-138 was a pretty road along the St. Lawrence River. We paused at La Malbaie, one of many spots to pull over for a view.

At Baie-Sainte-Catherine, we pulled in line with the other cars. A couple in the next car smiled at Norway sitting in the passenger side. We chatted for a few minutes while waiting to proceed. After greeting the conductor, we drove onto the ferry. *Very efficient.* During the thirty-minute ride across the Saguenay fjord-St. Lawrence River connection, Norway and I got out to stretch and take in the views of the marina and surroundings. It was a pleasant ride.

We departed the ferry on the other side and continued along Route 138, keeping an eye out for lunch spots. Thirty minutes later, we settled in Les Escoumins. Norway and I took a quick hike around nearby trails at Sentier du Moulin. Then, I ordered takeout from Pecherie Manicouagan restaurant, a nice *poissonnerie*. Luckily, the rain had stopped. So, at a nearby picnic table, we had a crab sandwich, fries, and dry dog food.

Two hours later, we arrived at the Hotel Le Manoir in Baie-Comeau. It was a charming, vintage place with ornate decorations and rooms. At check-in, there was a hitch: the hotel did not realize I had a pet with me. I double-checked my email receipt. It specifically noted they had arranged a pet-friendly room at the hotel. Expedia had messed up the reservation. Nevertheless, the young man at the front desk found a room for Norway and me.

Norway checking out the view

Inside the beautiful room, we had a magnificent view of the bay. The TV options were good, with several channel choices. Wi-Fi was rather slow, possibly due to the weather, location, or too many people on the network. At least it worked.

After 250 miles and several hours of driving, Norway had accumulated tons of energy, especially since the weather was drizzly and cool. Now the husky was running around the room. Before deciding on dinner, we took a few moments to check out the surroundings. I picked up an MP3 player and grabbed my favorite sweatshirt with two husky holes in the sleeve.

A few months earlier, I had come home and found Norway in the backyard, hoarding a pair of blue jeans and three T-shirts. He was resting his head on my sweatshirt. I collected my clothes and put them back in the dresser drawers. The next day, I came home and found the drawers open and my clothes in the backyard again! *How does he do that?* A week later, I watched him paw at a drawer until it slid open. *Latest Norway rule: no new clothes can be placed in the lower drawers.* I did supply a few old, stained shirts in the bottom to give Norway something to steal.

Norway and I walked down the hallway, past some very nice artwork, and through the furnished lobby. Outside, we did a lap around the nearby spacious park. It offered a pleasant view of the bay, workout equipment, and playground. The bay had an incredible summer chill where I could see my breath. *Husky weather and sweatshirt (with holes) temperatures.*

We ordered takeout dinner from Marco Pizzeria. The French-Canadian woman was very nice, patiently taking my order. (The extent of my French vocabulary was *merci, bonjour,* and *papillon.*) The salad was tasty and fresh, with chicken for Norway. And the pizza was quite *bon.* A reviewer had written that the sauce was too sweet, but I liked it a lot. Following our picnic in the room, we watched movies and relaxed.

BAIE-COMEAU, QUEBEC, to LABRADOR CITY, NEWFOUNDLAND and LABRADOR

AT FIVE A.M., Norway stood up and walked across me. Then, for good measure, he turned and walked back across me again.

"OK, OK, I get the message," I said. "I'm up." I pushed aside the paws that were digging into me and got up. Norway was smiling and ready to go.

After cleaning up, I took Norway for a walk into nearby Pioneers Parc. Around the corner from the hotel, we could see birds flying across the overcast bay. The weather had improved from yesterday, but no people were around. I noticed more landmarks and a garden at the front of the park. Instead of flowers, they had planted vegetables! Clever and productive. We passed the outdoor gym, a large stage, and a cycling path along the St. Lawrence River.

Norway and I finished at the bronze monument of Colonel Robert Rutherford McCormick in a canoe. McCormick was the founder of Baie-Comeau in 1937 and owner of the *Chicago Tribune.* He visited the region and eventually opened a pulp-and-paper mill. The statue of him rowing faced his paper mill and offered a view of the town's heritage district.

Back at Le Manoir, I took advantage of their business center. Using one of the internet-linked computers, I printed documents related to Trans-Labrador Highway 389 and the upcoming hotel in Labrador City-Wabush. Then I emailed my mom, reminding her to check later. *If you don't hear from us, then we're stranded in the middle of nowhere.* It was nothing to worry about. But it was important to have someone keep track of us during this part of the trip.

At checkout, I asked if we could return on July 18. I appreciated the location and comfort of this hotel. Unfortunately, I learned the hotel was booked next week.

As we left, an older woman looked at Norway and greeted us. I realized what all the French speakers had been saying to Norway: *"Beau chien."* It means beautiful dog! *Bon* is good. *Beau* is beautiful. Norway is both.

With a full meal, good night's sleep, and morning walk, we were ready for the marathon journey ahead. Highway 389 all the way to Labrador. I noted some of the highlights and low points during the lengthy 350-mile (580-km) drive.

KM 0 – 214 was a mix of road conditions. Some parts were nicely paved; others consisted of gravel, potholes, or bumps. The steady travel included scenic winding roads through the wilderness and mountains. We passed a power grid at KM 95, and reached Manic 5 at KM 214.

Located on Highway 389, Manic 5 power station was the feature of the day, demonstrating epic Quebec engineering. Beside it was the Daniel-Johnson Dam on the Manicouagan River, the highest multiple-arch dam in the world. I had seen the Hoover Dam in Nevada. This one was as impressive and picturesque. One of the fun facts was that if you made a sidewalk with all the concrete used to construct the dam, it would extend from the North Pole to the South Pole. We got a nice view from a patio at the welcoming area.

Manic 5 generating station ("Dam, that's a great photo!")

We continued up the road past the massive dam, getting a closer look. The Manicouagan Valley and Reservoir (supposedly created by an asteroid 214 million years ago) behind the dam were magnificent.

Just beyond this site, the inevitable unpaved access road began.

KM 214 – 317 consisted of a dirt-and-gravel road. It took over two hours to grind through it. We stopped along the way. We weren't hungry; we just needed a break from tough driving. I walked around the open space with Norway while trying to avoid the bugs.

At the 317 KM stop, we ran into the young couple from the ferry yesterday! They had already driven to Labrador City and were heading back. They mentioned that KM 317 - 480 would be paved. But the last section is winding, slow, and awful. "The worst," they warned. They advised me to avoid the trucks because the kicked-up gravel can chip your window. Also, they emphasized going slowly over the railroad tracks or any sharp gravel turns. I appreciated their insightful advice.

Halfway between Baie-Comeau and Labrador, I topped off the gas tank at $1.77 CAD per liter. *Yikes.* Gas was $1.31 CAD per liter in the cities. I wasn't sure of the exact conversion rates, but filling up the Nissan seemed expensive. Regardless, the next stop was 250 km away. I did not want to chance it.

At KM marker 320, I saw a moose! Unfortunately, I was unable to slow down in time to get a photo. The graceful, big creature faded off the road into the woods. I would not see another animal, except a dead moose lying on the side at marker 330.

On the smooth road, we cruised all the way to KM 480.

Then, **the KM480 – 550** path was awful, coarse gravel, and winding. The few stops were brief, as we were swarmed with bugs.

After a ten-plus-hour journey, we reached the provincial border!

We found Newfoundland

We connected to the Trans-Labrador Highway Route 500 and drove into Labrador City. Along the town's main road, I noticed Tim Hortons and Scores, two familiar, convenient options. And we could try local fare during the next two days. Five miles past Labrador City was Wabush. Thankfully, it was easy to find the hotel and park. The check-in took less than three minutes. I smelled BBQ from the hotel restaurant. It looked tasty, but it was a buffet only and did not offer takeout.

Inside the Wabush Hotel, or the Sir Wilfred Grenfell Hotel, we had a small, simple room. But it provided cable TV, fridge, bed, chair, desk, and air conditioning if needed. I was delighted to have anyplace open to me and Norway! We were in a remote part of Canada with few options.

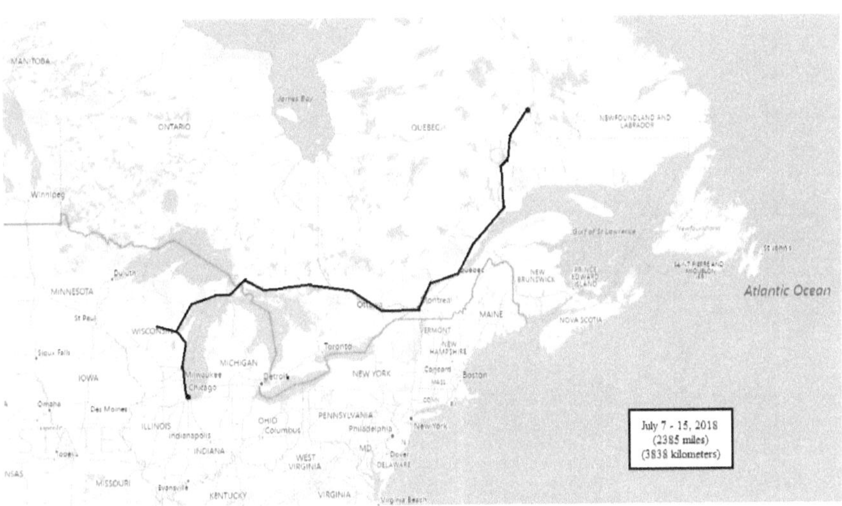

The hotel Wi-Fi was solid, even faster than the Wi-Fi at the more luxurious Baie-Comeau hotel last night. Sometimes the cheaper places perform better. First task was to email Mom. I sent a proof-of-life photo at the Newfoundland/Labrador welcome sign.

Made it. Almost 2,400 miles. The 10th Canadian Province!

After a break, we went up the road to pick up dinner at Scores. It was a score! Norway devoured his chicken breast mixed with dog food, mixed with the Scores KFC-flavored gravy. The salad and poutine worked for me. We settled in our room to watch TV and sleep. I looked at the clock and learned we lost an hour due to a time-zone change. We were in Atlantic Daylight Time.

LABRADOR CITY (day 2)

I WAS THRILLED to have plenty of time—with minimal driving—to explore Labrador. Although only seven thousand people lived here, the area provided plenty of activities. We found the Barking Lot, a large dog park with an enclosed fence and view of Wabush Lake. Despite little grass, it was fine. Norway walked around, sniffed, and played with an old ball he found. Nobody was in sight except landscapers taking care of the neighboring softball fields.

Afterward, we tried the Labrador City welcome center. Two nice women offered advice about visiting the town, which was basically a few blocks of restaurants and the mall. The rest was mostly residential, near open hiking trails. The woman from Wabush mentioned a walking path along Jean Lake just past the hotel off Grenfell Drive. Looking at a map, I noted two places to try for dinner: CJ's and Jordan's. Labrador City demonstrated the pros and cons of small places: while there are few choices, you get to try all of them!

The town was easy to navigate: lake, airport, main strips, and residential streets. It used to be a thriving area, supported by the iron mines. Once the mines closed, bars and restaurants followed, and residents left for more populated places.

We visited the Labrador City Mall. Inside Walmart, I picked up a birthday card for my nephew. Conveniently, next door was a post office, which offered a free postcard to send with Aidan's birthday card. The Labrador City postcard illustrated a train carrying iron ore. He was a big train fan.

On the way out, I grabbed a chocolate iced drink from Tim Hortons. Several truck drivers formed a line around the mall parking lot for the drive-thru. Inside, it was empty, and I had my drink in two minutes. I noticed the language change. Where Quebec was French, Newfoundland/Labrador was a "Fargo-style" northern Canadian English. So, Jean (pronounced "Zzhan" in Quebec) became Jean ("Gene" in N/L).

In the afternoon, we walked the path—a mix of dirt and wood planks—around Jean Lake. After I applied powerful mosquito repellent, the bugs finally stayed away. The outing provided good exercise and fresh air for Norway and me. The 3.1 miles were lengthy but enjoyable, and we encountered no one else on the path. We had an undisturbed, isolated view of the lake and trees. Occasionally, I reminded myself that no one knew where we were. *Stay on the path. Do not get hurt.*

Hiking alone at Jean Lake

After a few hours of internet stuff (me) and napping (Norway), we tried CJ's Pub for dinner. The menu mostly consisted of chicken fingers, beef sandwiches, and such. No salads. Instead, we returned to Pizza Delight/Scores and picked up chicken breast and gravy to pile in Norway's bowl. For me: a side salad, small pizza, Coke, and chocolate dessert. The expensive feast was understandable in this remote mining town.

LABRADOR CITY (day 3)

AFTER WATCHING *AMERICA Ninja Warrior*, I fell asleep at eleven wearing a sweatshirt and hood to avoid new mosquito bites. I still had itchy spots around my head, shoulders, and neck. Hopefully, they would go away in a day or so. With it drizzling overnight, I had slept well.

Today, we intended to try another hiking path: Tanya Lake—a bit shorter and different than Jean Lake. Maybe go back to the dog park? It depended on the weather. Otherwise, just rest, fill up with gas, repack, and reset. Tomorrow would be another rugged marathon day of driving.

I explored the TV programs. CBS, ABC, NBC, Canadian, and New England US affiliates offered morning shows. I turned off the junk, checked email, and mapped plans for today. When the rain dwindled and the sun began peeking through, I lathered on the mosquito repellent and we took off.

I was unable to find the lake walking path. Suddenly we were on Tamarack Blvd, which led back to the dog park and softball fields. While I listened to music, Norway fetched the ball and happily ran around for thirty minutes. When we got back into the car, Norway was satisfied … and the car interior was decorated with mud.

We stopped at a convenience store near the hotel. From the lean supplies on the shelves, I picked out a tangy Sunny D drink and a packaged apple/raspberry flaky pastry. Then we returned to the room to enjoy breakfast.

* * *

In the afternoon, we drove fifteen minutes over the border to Fermont, Quebec. Meaning "Iron Mountain," Fermont was founded in the early 1970s to serve the iron ore mine at Mont Wright. Decades later, the mining town has a current population of about 2,500. At the entrance, I noticed a welcome sign and billboard promoting the local businesses.

Up the road, we saw a park area with a giant Caterpillar dump truck. The machine was honored for over 100,000 hours of service spanning seventeen years at the mine. A board explained its significance and work accomplishments, but I couldn't translate the French writing. Still, it was a fitting symbol of the mining town.

Norway playing with a purple ball he found

Behind was a view of the walled city. It had a military fortress appearance due to its housing structure. Built in 1974, "the wall" (*le mur ecran*) was constructed around the settlement to counter the harsh environment. Located in northeastern Quebec, the latitude is above the 52nd parallel, the same latitude as Siberia. Fermont's windscreen wall structure, 1.3 km long and 50 meters high, was designed to address the strong northerly winds and to create a warmer microclimate inside for the residents. Although the architecture was functional, plain, and bold-looking, it was interesting.

The structure contained the city hall amid residential, commercial, and educational facilities. I went inside for a few minutes to tour the mall, which had a post office, co-op, groceries, restaurant, hotel, and specific stores. Afterward, Norway and I walked around outside before succumbing to the mosquitoes. On the way out, we stopped briefly atop a hill to get a little better view. Fermont was a worthwhile excursion.

We returned to our Labrador hotel room for a siesta. After lounging around for a few hours, we rallied to grab dinner. Still raining, we drove ten minutes into town. I spotted a Subway and picked up a sandwich, meatballs and chicken patty for Norway, chips, and cookies.

In the room, we enjoyed dinner, watched reruns of the comedy *Tosh.O*, and prepared to get up as early as possible to head back.

LABRADOR CITY, NEWFOUNDLAND and LABRADOR, to BAIE-COMEAU, QUEBEC

DESPITE THE AIR conditioning unit running continually, our room remained warm. At 3:15 a.m., I noticed Norway lying near the door. We went outside to a refreshing chilly breeze, and he relieved himself twice. *Good dog*.

Back inside, Norway popped up onto the queen bed and took up 90 percent of the space. I squeezed in and went back to sleep, wearing the sweatshirt and hooded mosquito armor.

In the morning, we prepared for the return trip. While packing the car, I noticed a dead bird stuck in the grill of the Nissan. *Yuck.* Simultaneously, Norway eyed the roadkill and tried to grab its head. *Gross!* I plucked it out in time.

The drive back to Baie-Comeau was easier, with pleasantly cool and overcast weather. We kept the windows open the entire way, and retraced our route, bypassing sights seen a few days ago. The drive went ninety minutes faster, taking eight and a half hours. Benefiting from the time zone change, we arrived in Baie-Comeau by two thirty EDT.

We went through the familiar town, stopping at Parc des Pionniers to get Norway some exercise and take advantage of a pretty day along the water.

Afterward, we headed over to the La Caravelle hotel to check in. As we walked toward the entrance, a guy said dogs were not allowed anymore. *Hmmm?*

I went inside and saw a note: "*Non Chiens.*" I knew what that meant.

The receptionist mentioned that BringFido had called the hotel to confirm a pet-friendly room. The request was denied.

"I knew one of my hotels was cancelled," I explained. "I thought it was the Quebec City one."

"Sorry, this hotel does not have a reservation for you," the woman politely told me.

Now, I had to scramble at four o'clock to find a hotel. First, I needed internet. I drove to Le Manoir, where we had stayed four days ago. No last-minute vacancies, but my internet Wi-Fi access still worked. I checked my email. BringFido had cancelled my Quebec City hotel. But they didn't contact me regarding the Baie-Comeau hotel until today—at noon, while on the road. *Why didn't they contact me two days ago?*

In the parking lot of Le Manoir, I looked up hotels that took dogs, available today. I found two prospects. The other three required phone calls. I had no phone service in Canada. I drove to the first place, Hotel Le Comte. It did not exist. At the address, there was a steak place with the same name. But no hotel.

Next, I drove ten minutes on Route 138 to Blvd. Lafleche. Recognizing these places from four days ago, I found the Comfort Inn rather easily. They did have a room available, for $160 CAD plus a $25 CAD pet fee. Without other options, I booked it. Our six-year road trip record remained perfect—we've never had to spend a night in the car.

We were given a room on the second floor. Unfortunately, Norway did not like these stairs. They were concrete, with gaps between steps. I had to drag him up. The room appeared fine, the internet was fast, breakfast was included, and the location was good. We were on the western part of Baie-Comeau, fifteen minutes closer to Quebec City.

Among the restaurants and ice cream places, we tried a Greek restaurant for dinner. Takeout included chicken kabobs, spanakopita, salad, rice, and bread. A bit pricey, but everything in Quebec had seemed pricey. We filled up on the terrific meal but left room for ice cream. On the way back, we stopped at Le Pignon Glace. Beside a giant chair in the front, the shop served a pretty good rainbow soft-serve ice cream.

At last, we settled into the Comfort Inn. The air conditioner did not go on, and I couldn't find a thermostat. Then, suddenly the Wi-Fi didn't work. *OK, where is the comfort?* Overall, it was better than staying in the car. But I was looking forward to moving on to Quebec City and, eventually, back into the United States.

BAIE-COMEAU, QUEBEC, to QUEBEC CITY, QUEBEC

AT 6:15 A.M., I sat in bed and turned on the TV. *Private Eyes*, the appealing detective show with Jason Priestley and Cindy Sampson, had a new episode on Showcase. Meanwhile, Norway woke up and continued playing with the tennis ball he found in the parking lot yesterday. *Top-notch road-trip entertainment.*

We escaped the hotel on Route 138 West. Then, we retraced the succession of towns along the St. Lawrence River to Tadoussac. We boarded the ferry and crossed to Baie-Sainte-Catherine.

Norway on the ferry

We continued along 138 west to La Malbaie. Then detoured onto *"Route Du Fleuve"* Highway 362. The leisurely, scenic drive along the St. Lawrence River reminded me of driving on the Pacific Coast Highway 1 in California or the Maine coastal highways in the US. At the same time, there were no easy places to eat with a dog in the cafes. We skipped lunch and snacked on energy bars and treats.

At Baie St. Paul, we reconnected to route 138. There were more cafes and restaurants along the road, but each had many visitors. Rather than fight crowds with Norway and struggle to park, we bypassed and found a large open field for sports, biking, and activities. After forty-five minutes of exercise in the open area, we drove the last hour into Quebec City.

The Howard Johnson hotel was near the airport. *Where are the planes?* Somewhere around Parc Montmorency I missed the turn-off and was on Route 40 West. *I needed to stay on 138 West.* Afraid of hitting traffic, I got off and started zigzagging in a westwardly direction, hoping to find the 138.

Eventually, I pulled over to ask a random woman in a parking lot. She pointed me back to 40 West. "It will turn, and you'll see Wilfred Hamel."

"Wilfred!" I told her. "That's what I want." Wilfred Hamel Blvd. is Route 138.

The hotel was in a decent location, among other hotels, with the usual easy dining places, dessert, and extra options. Mostly, I knew where Autoroute 540 was, so I knew I should be able to get out of here tomorrow without getting lost.

HoJo was visibly a bit old, and there were restrictions. But those were positives for us:

1) Visitors must park next to their room. *Great! I had a reserved spot.*
2) Guests must use the sliding door to take dogs in or out. They cannot go into the hotel. *Great! We had easy access to outside.*
3) Hotel rooms were floor without carpet. *Great! Less likely to cause damage.*

We tried the nearby Chinese restaurant, General Tao. It was about twenty-five bucks for two egg rolls, rice, and chicken with vegetables. While it seemed Quebec pricey, the ingredients were fresh, so, a good meal for Norway and me.

I tried the television. The evening shows were either garbage or in French. The cable menu did list several entertainment options, except they were locked out. *Perhaps I have to pay extra for these sta-tions?* I picked up a candy bar from the vending machine, passing several young people standing near the laundry. By nine o'clock, Norway was sleeping on the bed, and I was exhausted.

QUEBEC CITY, QUEBEC, CANADA, to STRATTON, VERMONT, UNITED STATES

AT FIVE A.M., the air conditioner was cranking, so the hotel room was comfortably cool. I checked the laundry space two doors down from our room. The washer and dryer were completely empty. Convenient opportunity, without leaving Norway alone for long.

While waiting for laundry, I tried the TV again. Only infomercials, French shows, or CNN. I did not fit their target audience. It would have been nice to relax with some entertainment before the drive.

After collecting the laundry from the dryer, I took a quick shower. Norway jumped in the tub, then jumped out. Then joyfully jumped on the bed, leaving damp paw prints on the sheets. *Well, I guess that was some entertainment.*

The hotel breakfast was weak. The apples were no good, and the "fresh fruit" came from a can. I picked two wrapped muffins for the road. Since there were no eggs, Norway was out of luck.

When we loaded into the car, I handed him a treat to chew on. He retreated to the back seat to enjoy his breakfast.

We got on the 540 Sud/South, which led to the 73 Sud/South, which led to the 20 Ouest/West toward Montreal. Near the 200 km marker on Route 20, we stopped at an odd sight: dinosaurs near McDonald's, Esso Gas, and St. Hubert's Chicken. It appeared to be a tourist draw, with numerous cars in the parking lot—including ours. The fast-food joints and gas must have benefitted from the dinosaur displays. The giant figures lingered around picnic tables and walking spaces.

Norwaysaurus Rex taking a break

We resumed the drive, and at QC-55 turned south toward Vermont. Heading for the border, I gathered my Canadian cash and pile of Canadian change collected in the car. I purchased gas and another chocolate ice at Tim Hortons.

We joined one of the long car lines waiting to cross into the United States. In the passenger seat, Norway watched the action. At the border window, I had a nice conversation with the official. He had a female husky at home! We spent a few minutes chatting about the dogs. I felt bad about slowing down the line, but I did enjoy talking to a fellow husky owner.

We crossed into Vermont and traveled to Dog Mountain—a must for dog-lovers. Home of the Stephen Huneck Gallery, the canine nonprofit sits on top of 150 acres of scenic space in St. Johnsbury, VT. I remember going a few years ago with Oscar. Now I was returning with Norway. We took photos, walked around the grounds, and visited the gallery full of dog art. We went next door to the Dog Chapel, where I said a prayer, honoring all the past dogs, including Oscar.

On top of Dog Mountain

Afterward, we drove down the winding side road back to the highway. At the corner, I saw Riley's Fish Shack. This seemed like a perfect spot for lunch with a shaded outdoor seating area. Plus, orders could be accepted at a takeout window.

I tried the lobster roll, fries, and soda. While waiting, I collected Norway, his water, bowls, and food from the trunk. Then we set ourselves in a comfortable spot.

A few moments later, lunch was ready! We relaxed and ate, and I was pleased that we had made it back to the States. Our trek to Labrador was a success. After lunch, I eyed a dessert sign promoting the apple caramel crisp sundae. *Gotta try that!* Plus, they had a puppy sundae: ice cream and dog biscuits. *Yes, we have time for this.*

After a delicious dessert, we continued along the Vermont roads to Quechee Gorge. It had been mentioned by one of my students' parents. Their family had a summer place in Vermont and often went to the gorge to hike around.

At five o'clock, we arrived, just as most of the crowds were leaving. We passed the welcome center, then went up and down the trails and into the gorge. Above was a historic bridge where Route 4 crosses the gorge. The steel bridge, built in 1911, was over 160 feet high and offered a terrific view of the gorge and Ottauquechee River. In addition to great photo ops, boards describing the history of the area were placed along the trail. It was a nice, scenic afternoon hike.

Quechee Gorgeous

We finished today's drive at Stratton, VT. I found the town rather easily, remembering the path from last October. I picked out Black Bear Lodge, having stayed there last fall. It offered a good complimentary breakfast and welcomed pets.

Our room was spacious, even larger than I had remembered. The cable TV package included the Hallmark channel, news channels, and American entertainment. It was getting late, and I was tired. Instead of walking to the village for dinner, we tried the hotel restaurant, where I ordered a kale salad with meat on the side, plus an order of chicken fingers to ensure Norway got enough food. The meal from Table 43.1 was good. Norway's beef side was a nice filet. And my salad was hearty. Mostly, it was convenient: a guy delivered it to the room. Without a call, he just showed up!

STRATTON, VERMONT
(day 2)

THE APPROXIMATE ELEVATION of Mt. Everest is 29,029 feet. And, 29029 is an *Everesting* challenge, organized in places around the US and Canada. The 2017 inaugural event was in Stratton. The challenge is a simple idea: start at the bottom of a ski mountain and hike up. Then, at the top, take the gondola down. Repeat. After seventeen times, you will have ascended 29,029 vertical feet— matching the elevation of Mt. Everest.

Last October, I participated in the first event with approximately 175 people. During the weekend, there was a base camp with numerous tents beside the lodge. The hiking, food, and music began on a crisp, colorful fall day. The extended weekend included a mix of pleasant weather, as well as chilly nights with bits of frost. Now, I was back with Norway in July.

I carved out this part of the road trip to see Stratton in the summer. I thought it would be fun to climb the mountain—only once—with Norway. We reserved a room at Black Bear Lodge, the same place I had stayed overnight before the 29029 Everesting event. I knew it was near the mountain as well as the quaint ski town with shops and restaurants.

After an early morning snack, I packed for the hike: Norway's water bottle, water for me, energy bars, and dog treats. With camera and leash in hand, I was excited for today. With wonderful weather, I eagerly anticipated the hike, a lunch in town, and a lobster dinner.

Norway was fired up this morning, enjoying the cooler temperatures and smells around the Stratton hotel. The extremely nice staff provided lots of attention to the husky and offered tourist recommendations.

We left Black Bear Lodge and walked up the road to Stratton Village. We passed through the town to the bottom of the ski hill. After taking a souvenir photo, we started upward. Norway began racing and dragging me. "Pace yourself!" I called out. I knew the mountain would get steeper, and it would take more than forty-five minutes, mostly uphill.

Trailblazers

Norway settled in and began walking just ahead of me. The climb was familiar, although I was not nearly as in shape as I was last year. We methodically went up the mountain.

The hike was fun and nostalgic, as we ascended the same path. Funny, an old 29029-event sign remained on one of the gondola foundations. It read "6 more to go," indicating the number of gondola columns to the summit.

It was a seventy-degree, clear, comfortable day. Knowing I was ascending only once made the one-hour climb easier. Also, in spurts, Norway went into husky mode and pulled me up the hill! I appreciated the boost. Along the way, we stopped for breaks and took photos, and Norway did some sniffing.

At the top, it was noticeably cooler with a pretty view. During our water break, we ran into a couple from Massachusetts traveling with their brown-eyed husky. The dog, Gretchen, looked like a fifty-pound version of Norway! It was interesting to observe their similar behaviors, although Gretchen seemed a bit easier with other dogs. She and Norway started growling and getting fired up. The dogs looked like siblings!

Gretchen and Norway

We walked around the top of the mountain area, passing a large group of hikers. Next, we encountered a group of morning yoga people. After resting, snacking, and talking to hikers, we followed the path to the Fire Tower. A half-mile through wooded trees we reached the tower but did not go any higher. Since the tower could only hold four at a time, a dozen people stood waiting their turn. And dogs were not permitted. During the way back, a guy showed me the video he had taken from the top of the tower. It provided a nice view above the tree line, reminding me of the view from Timm's Hill in Wisconsin last week.

Norway and I trotted back to the gondola. Halfway through the twelve-minute ride down, Norway fell asleep. He was never into scenic views.

Gondola nap

At the bottom, we got off the gondola and went a few hundred yards to Stratton Deli. In the middle of the village, it was a fine place for lunch. The caprese sandwich, BBQ chips, Dr.Pepper, and chocolate chip cookie hit the spot! Meanwhile, I fed Norway slices of Boar's Head salami. We enjoyed a table in the shade and a good view of the plaza as people walked by.

After the pleasant lunch, we went back to the room and relaxed. I downloaded, cropped, and deleted photos. Then, I checked email and talked to a friend on the phone. After a three-hour siesta, I got up and took Norway for a walk. The sun slowly set behind the mountains, leaving the air clear and cool. We encountered dog lovers and owners, particularly an old guy who had an eleven-year-old husky at home.

After a lap around the village, I ordered dinner from Mulligan's. Saturday was lobster night, featuring their single steamed-lobster special. I ordered two single lobsters with two Caesar salads to go. The lobsters were a bit lean in the meat, but still a good deal. And the meaty parts dipped in the melted butter were fantastic! *No complaints from Norway.*

I was very pleased with this day. The hike went as planned, helped by beautiful weather. We met some nice folks and had great food. Norway the mountaineer went out like a light.

STRATTON, VERMONT, to MILFORD, CONNECTICUT

WE LUCKED OUT. After a beautiful, sunny day—perfect for hiking and an outdoor lunch—it cooled down noticeably last night. By seven a.m. this morning, it was dreary and raining. Thankfully, we were not hiking today!

We departed Vermont and drove into Massachusetts, stopping at a few places listed in *RoadsideAmerica*. In Greenfield, the ATM inside a tree seemed worth a look. The figure was at a shopping plaza off Route 2. Up close, I realized the twenty-five-foot-tall tree stump was made of fiberglass. It had a creepy H. R. Pufnstuf, cartoonish look. There were a few engraved hidden animals as well. *I guess money can grow in trees.*

We drove another ten minutes on Route 2 to the "flower bridge" in Shelburne Falls. Built in 1908, the trolley bridge over Deerfield River connected the towns of Shelburne Falls and Buckland. Twenty years later, the trolley service stopped, and the bridge became dilapidated and covered with weeds. Fortunately, the town eventually purchased the bridge, and volunteers transformed it into the bridge of flowers. People began to donate soil and decorate flowers, rejuvenating the four-hundred-foot-long, five-arch bridge.

Although pets were not allowed on it, Norway and I got a good view of the flower bridge. Then, we walked around Shelburne Falls. The Great River Hydro at the end of the road included interesting plaques describing the power-generating Deerfield River.

After passing through Massachusetts, we made an extended stop in Hartford, the capital of Connecticut. We stopped at the capitol, a suitable, spacious area to walk and stretch out. The capitol building was impressive and ornate, surrounded by several statues of historical figures. Across the massive lawn area was a weekend jazz festival with live music and food carts.

In the afternoon, we ended at the Red Roof Inn PLUS+. Located just off I-95, at mile marker 35, I could see the towering Red Roof sign. After easy parking, the check-in was quick, although the woman at the desk was not very friendly or positive. She had a baby in the office with her and seemed unhappy about working at the hotel on a Sunday.

"The suite is sweet!" I said to Norway. I had paid an extra twenty bucks to upgrade, and it was spacious with two rooms. The bedroom had a TV and bath. The living room contained another TV, a couch, a chair, and a workspace. Plus, it had a microwave and a fridge. All carpetless floors, so Norway could stay cool, although, he mostly hopped onto the pleather couch in one room or a bed in the other.

We had two fantastic nearby dinner options: thin pizza or lobster rolls. Unfortunately, both were closed on Sunday.

"We're out of luck, Norway."

We drove to Lasse's, a half mile away. I intended to try the eggplant and cheese, plus chicken parm for Norway and me. But it closed at four because of a one-time electrical upgrade.

"Geez," I said. "Tough town to get a meal in."

Rather than search for another restaurant, we went to the next-door Subway. The teenager was super-nice when I ordered a twelve-inch veggie, a side of meatballs, an extra chicken patty for Norway, and three cookies. I added popcorn chips from my car and soda from the vending machine. The extravagant meal cost $12 plus a generous tip for the inspiring teenager at Subway.

After dinner, Norway enjoyed the room. He snagged a tennis ball from the car and played in the living space of our suite. I enjoyed watching him amuse himself while hoping he wouldn't knock something over.

MILFORD, CONNECTICUT, to HARRISBURG, PENNSYLVANIA

AT CHECKOUT, THE Monday morning guy was much nicer and cheerier than the check-in woman last night. We left after nine o'clock, hoping to avoid traffic. We started in Stamford, CT, to see a newly-placed giant Marilyn Monroe statue of her famous pose over the windy NYC subway grate. I had the address *271 Bedford* written down and used *the force* to find the location. I knew it was the north side of downtown. I exited I-95 at the second Stamford exit. It seemed close to downtown, so I went toward some tall buildings. I took State Street—since "State" or "Main" generally run through downtowns—and followed the road until I noticed a sign pointing to downtown. We zigzagged a bit, until suddenly merging into Bedford Street! The buildings were numbered 112, 120, 140... We proceeded to the 200s and picked out a parking spot with a meter.

I turned off the engine, looked out the passenger side, and saw two massive legs! I had parked right next to the statue. The controversial twenty-six-foot-tall piece was detailed and risqué. You could see Marilyn's sculpted underwear, and her rear was facing the building behind her—a church! I watched several people walk through the park to get a photo. The provocative attraction seemed to lure tourists. It certainly brought us to downtown Stamford.

After a few photos, I observed other smaller statues on display. Apparently, there was a summer exhibition, titled *Timeless*, featuring other sculptures by Seward Johnson, the Marilyn Monroe artist. We walked past many of the thirty-six pieces placed around town, which included a man lying on a bench, two kids playing, a gentleman reading a newspaper with his dog beside him (Norway liked that one!), and a sculpture of a photographer (I took a picture of that one.).Ironically, they placed a life-sized hot dog vendor at a street corner—just ten feet from a vegetarian restaurant. *Coincidence?*

Norway and I walked through the appealing downtown with lots of places to eat and hang out: pizza, vegetarian, outdoor patios, and cafes. Unfortunately, it was too early for lunch. On the way back to the car, I met Lorraine, a Colombian woman in her sixties who loved the dog. After chatting for fifteen minutes, she offered her phone number, inviting us to call if we returned. Also, she reminded me to make sure I put money in the meter. "The officers around here do check."

Suddenly, I realized our walk around town was longer than expected. We raced back to the car, and two minutes later I caught a Stamford cop about to give me a ticket.

"Sorry, sir," I called out. "I lost track of time. I paid for an hour. It just expired."

I never imagined spending so much time, but we enjoyed walking around the statues and exploring Stamford. Sympathetic to my explanation, the officer withdrew the ticket.

We returned to I-95 and headed south. The turnpike sections were a bit pricey, but they reduced driving time significantly with smoother roads and higher speed limits. Regardless, traffic speeds varied from cruising to a dead stop. And getting past NYC and through parts of Philadelphia would be excruciating.

I had been to Philly a few times. This would be the first time we visited the Rocky statue. Traffic or no traffic, we would get there. After winding down the streets, finding parking, and tracking the address, we found the Museum of Art building. Before us were the seventy-two steps that Sylvester Stallone ran up. Norway and I did our best.

Flying high

We looked around for the Rocky Balboa statue. Constructed in 1980 for *Rocky III*, Stallone donated it to the city, which added a cool, popular attraction. Off to the side, at the bottom of the steps, a crowd of people stood in line, waiting to take a photo with the larger-than-life bronze statue.

We joined the line of fans. As we neared the front, I asked the folks behind us to take our picture. At last, it was our turn. I went to the statue, bringing Norway along. He was not facing the camera— and the crowd of people were waiting and watching us—so I swiftly swept up the husky. He yelped. *Ugh—scaredy cat.* I was not hurting him, but he whined anyway. Finally, we got the photo.

The Italian Stallion

When I set Norway down, he smiled and wagged his tail. After taking back the camera and thanking everyone, the champ and I were off.

On the way back to the car, we encountered a young woman with two dogs in the park. As she threw a ball, the dogs chased it, and Norway went crazy. I walked over to her, and we talked for fifteen minutes. She was from Philadelphia but had attended UCSD.

Instead of returning to California, she accepted a job offer at home. Her young dogs were friendly and well-behaved. Norway got a few sniffs, but I didn't release him. While it would be fun to watch him run with his new friends, I was afraid I wouldn't be able to catch him if he changed his mind.

Old East Coast cities tend to have congestion, winding roads, and one-way streets. I got stuck in "one-way hell" trying to get out of Philadelphia; the roads had me going east, east, east, and I needed to get on I-76 West. Still, I was thrilled with our stop, and eventually we were back on the highway.

We arrived at today's destination after crossing through five states in one day: Connecticut, New York, New Jersey, Delaware, and Pennsylvania. Not bad! Inside our La Quinta Inn room, greeting cards and licorice whips were set on the beds. I grabbed them before Norway could. I explored the cable channels and started thinking about dinner. After sorting through local restaurant recommendations, determining easy takeout, the right type of food, closest location, I decided to drive around the area and pick something.

We ended at the Eisenhower Pizza Shop, a half mile from the La Quinta on Eisenhower Blvd. Inside, it looked a bit ominous— just a lone guy with a scarf, talking on the phone. *Was he working alone? Employee? Owner?* A lady came in to pick up an order. Then she left. *Customer? Delivery lady?* I took a chance and ordered a twelve-inch cheese pizza. And I added a chicken salad. The guy said there would be the equivalent of a chicken breast in the salad, enough for Norway.

"Should I come back? Or, is it easier to deliver?"

He claimed, "It should take ten or fifteen minutes."

Perfect. I walked Norway around the lot and listened to talk radio in the car.

When I returned fifteen minutes later, there were two cooks inside. And my order was ready.

We got back to La Quinta by eight thirty p.m. I grabbed Norway's bowls and dog food. Then, I bought a Dr. Pepper at the front desk. The pizza was good. The salad was plentiful. Plus, they wrote a personal thank-you note on the pizza box. "Thank you.

Chris" with a sketched smiley face. *Nice touch.* Below it was written, "Enjoy!"
        We did!

Friendly pizza dinner

HARRISBURG, PENNSYLVANIA, to GETTYSBURG, PENNSYLVANIA

AFTER YESTERDAY'S LONG travel day, we planned to minimize today's driving. We would proceed through York to Gettysburg; approximately sixty miles. We were moving, but with a bit of a break.

Since the rain had paused, Norway and I started with a walk on a nice pathway in historic midtown next to Front Street and the Susquehanna River. Along the trail were sculptures and info boards. A Holocaust memorial, fireman memorial, and Harrisburg History Project meaningfully accented the river area. On the drive out, we stopped to glance at the impressive capitol building.

We made a brief detour into Hershey to see the candy-themed banners lining the street. Then, we passed by the sweet amusement park on the way to view the "house within a house" in Derry Township. Remarkably, the wooden Session house, built in 1732, was sealed in a glass outer house in 1929 by M.S. Hershey. It was a quirky piece of architecture in the parking lot of Derry Church, near an old cemetery.

We backtracked toward Harrisburg, then, headed south on I-83 to York to check out the USA Weightlifting Hall of Fame. There were York barbells next to the museum. Norway waited while I did a quick tour of the museum. Inside were a variety of exhibits, including photos and statistics of power lifters, old lifting materials and weights, and tributes to people who developed and popularized the sport. The facility was impressive, comprehensive, and well-maintained.

Norway and barbells

We stopped at Maple Donuts for a snack. I sampled a tasty apple fritter and a maple twist. Next month, Maple Donuts was having a day where you "pay your age for a donut." I was sorry we would miss it.

We followed US-30 to Gettysburg. Our hotel, the 1863 Inn of Gettysburg, was centrally located with convenient parking. The comfortable room cost $100, which included breakfast and a $20 pet fee. A terrific rate, so I added two nights, allowing extra time to relax and explore and give us a driving break before the last stretch. Mostly, if it continued raining, we could delay our sightseeing. There was so much to see in Gettysburg.

When the rain stopped, we walked out of the hotel and started up Baltimore Avenue. Immediately, I saw all kinds of Civil War–era displays, buildings, and statues. I listened to music, exercised Norway, and learned bits of interesting history.

Norway and Mr. Lincoln

Gettysburg remains one of my favorite places. In the historic center, we walked up and down the streets, passing shops, historic markers, and buildings from the 1860s. I saw a candy shop with a variety of sodas in the window. *I could get a few treats and set them in the refrigerator for later.*

As I looked for a spot to set Norway, a young woman came outside.

"He can come in."

"Really?"

"Yes, dogs are welcome!"

This proved to be good marketing. Inside, I spent more time—and bought much more candy—than I would have alone. With Norway enjoying the air conditioning in the shop, watching the customers, and lunging for candy, we stayed for a while.

Mouth-watering candy and a sweet dog

Sweet! The candy store was a good stop. In addition to two sodas, I left with tasty taffy, a Big Hunk bar, and random classic candy types.

Gettysburg seemed to receive lots of dogs because most shops either promoted accepting dogs or they prohibited them, which was understandable for antiques and restaurants. When we returned to the inn, I asked the woman at the desk for restaurant recommendations.

"What are you in the mood for?"

"Pretty much anything. Good food and pet friendly. Outdoor seating."

"O'Rorke's," she mentioned. "It's down the street."

That was good enough for a try. Since it was humid, we weighed taking the food to go. Moments later, it began drizzling outside. Rather than eat on O'Rorke's patio, I called their number and ordered takeout. Besides, it was easier to eat in the room and watch TV in the air conditioning.

I joined Norway, and we went downstairs, through the lobby, and out the front door. We headed toward Steinwehr Avenue and discovered the O'Rorke's sign. The entrance to its patio was conveniently across the street from the1863 Inn. Also, near a custard/ Italian ice place to sample later.

While Norway stayed in a covered spot out front, I went inside and waited for a server. Occasionally, I peeked out the window and watched each passerby say hi to Norway, side-step him, or look with curiosity. A waiter directed me to the bar, where the woman retrieved my order. I paid and headed out.

Back at the room, I realized I had made a rookie mistake. I didn't check the bag, and they hadn't included utensils or ketchup. Luckily, I kept extra utensils in the car, and since I'd ordered sweet potato fries, ketchup wasn't necessary.

We enjoyed the three-course meal. First, the chicken salad was solid with good dressing; the chicken strips on top went into Norway's bowl. Second, the sweet potato fries and angel hair pasta with marinara—the chicken on the pasta went into Norway's bowl. Third, a sweet white chocolate donut for dessert. I handed Norway a piece without the chocolate. Big fan of Maple Donuts.

GETTYSBURG, PENNSYLVANIA (day 2)

I SLIPPED OUT of the room and went downstairs to check the complimentary breakfast. Beside the lobby were dining tables, coffee, and amenities. A doorway led into the main breakfast area. At that point, posted signs indicated no pets allowed. *Maybe Norway could join me by the outer tables in the lobby area?*

The breakfast seemed OK, offering waffles, eggs, breads, muffins, and bananas (very ripe—likely due to the humidity). A machine served concentrated juices. I scooped a cupful of scrambled eggs for Norway. Still full from dinner, I skipped the other food.

I passed folks watching *Fox and Friends,* went upstairs, and returned to the room—just in time. Norway had his hind legs on the chair and his front paws on the desk next to the laptop. His nose was next to the candy! And the TV remote.

"Sneaky," I said to him. "But too slow."

I guided him off the table.

"Try this instead." I handed him the scrambled eggs. Norway was not interested.

"Sorry, that's the best I've got right now."

I checked messages, sipped hot chocolate, and relaxed. We had two full days ahead!

A few years earlier, I had been to Gettysburg with Oscar. It was a brief visit, on a rainy day. Today, I was back with Norway, with extra time. I made a list of places to visit:

1) *Friend-to-Friend monument; Statue of Gravedigger; Lincoln Train Museum*
2) *Visitors Center (sit with Lincoln)*
3) *National Military Park Entrance*
4) *High Watermark of Rebellion*
5) *Pennsylvania Memorial*
6) *Virginia Memorial (Confederate Avenue)*
7) *Longstreet Monument*
8) *Devil's Den*
9) *Round Top*

There was a knock on the door. A polite housekeeper asked when she could service the room.

"No problem," I said. "We can step out right now."

Norway and I went for a ninety-minute walk. We started at the top of the list and scouted around the area. Gettysburg is full of monuments and history, mixed with shops, pubs, and attractions. At eleven o'clock, the streets were rather quiet. *Because it's a weekday? Or the overcast weather?*

We proceeded through town, across the battlefields, and alongside the cemeteries, bypassing any pet-restricted areas. I was reminded how pleasant Gettysburg is with clean streets, maintained walkways, and no graffiti. Perhaps it was due to the historical importance of the area and the respectful visitors to this town. The area was like an outdoor museum—and kept that way.

We returned to the hotel lobby and went to get change for the laundry. While greeted by tourists and a few of the housekeepers, Norway soaked up the attention! At the room, the husky immediately plopped down on the cool bathroom floor. I gathered my dirty clothes, and just as I headed out, Norway popped up and came over. I gave him snacks and stepped out.

* * *

In the afternoon, a rested Norway and I headed to the car. The Nissan's trunk was open! Damn, the electronic mechanism popped the trunk. *How long was it open this morning?* Fortunately, nothing was missing. Either the area was full of honest people, or nobody wanted dog items and junk from my trunk.

I shut the trunk and led Norway to the front seat. He jumped in, ready for an auto excursion.

The Gettysburg landscape is amazing. There are monuments and memorials scattered around the actual battlefields. The military names—Lee, Longstreet, Meade—and historic places were all there. We drove and walked through much of it today. Excellent.

The weather was humid and overcast with on-and-off rain. *I can't imagine being a young Civil War soldier, living in those damp, unsanitary conditions.*

A few hours later, we returned to the room. After uploading photos, I scanned a local online map for dinner options. I picked out Appalachian Brewery Company (ABC), a Pennsylvania pub just a brief walk from the inn. I looked at the menu online beforehand to make ordering quick.

While Norway waited outside ABC, I went inside the full restaurant, up to the bar, and ordered. When I came outside, several patrons and ABC staff were excited to meet the husky visitor.

After ten minutes, the food was ready! I paid and made sure I had utensils and ketchup packets. Due to the damp weather, instead of on the ABC patio, we dined in the hotel room. Exhausted from walking around all day, it was a treat to sit in the air-conditioned room and watch TV.

The black bean burger was fantastic, having a unique flavor with corn and other ingredients mixed in. Plus, it was substantial. I gave one-third of it to Norway, leaving more than enough for me. The salad was good. The house honey mustard had a flavorful kick.

For dessert, we tried Rita's Italian ice and frozen custard. The delightful place was just outside the back lot of the inn. They gave Norway a vanilla cup. I got their gelati with layers of vanilla custard and cherry-flavored ice. Tasty. And I sampled their chocolate gelati, which did not mix as well. I'll know better for next time. Norway was pleased. The delicious dessert was well worth a trip back.

GETTYSBURG, PENNSYLVANIA (Day 3)

WE CONTINUED CHECKING items off our Civil War list.

Norway relaxing in front of the monuments

To burn off some energy, I followed Norway a half mile toward a dog park. At the recreation area, we walked around the football, baseball, and soccer fields, as well as a running path with work-out exercises. Eventually, we stumbled onto the dog park near the southwest corner. *Nice!* The massive clean enclosure contained plenty of running space among trees and grass.

Since there was a black shepherd mutt in the big dogs' area, we did not go inside. Instead, Norway ran along the fencing with him. Then we wandered over to the smaller dogs' area. A little pup came up to the fence and happily ran with Norway!

Aware of the warming temperatures, it was time to walk back. During the return, I could see the top of the 1863 Inn in the distance, so we took side paths straight through. Then I recognized Hunt's restaurant, the back of Rita's and O'Rorke's, and eventually the 1863 Inn entrance. Back into the air conditioning!

Although it was a hot day, better suited for the pool, we drove to check out more battlefield sites. With few cars, it was easy to drive around. Occasionally, we stepped out to get a closer look at the sites. The blazing heat and humidity were constant reminders of how miserable the Civil War was.

We met several folks, including a Florida family who approached Norway. They remarked that they didn't see huskies where they lived. We found Devil's Den and could see Round Top in the distance to finish off the list of sights to see.

After recharging for a few hours, I got Norway up, and we went to check out old-time Victorian Photo Studio. We walked up the stairs and entered. A young guy wearing a Metallica T-shirt appeared, as a family with a dog came down. This got Norway very excited.

The guy worked with the other family to pick photos and finish the order. He didn't say anything to us. The family liked Norway. After five minutes, it was best to leave. I realized Norway might be tough to work with—especially wearing an 1860s costume. He is not always fond of accessories. Then we would have to get him to sit still for a photo. *Working with fifteen-year-old Oscar in Branson was easy. I'm not sure about three-year-old Norway in Gettysburg.*

As we went past Hunt's Battlefield Fries & Café, I saw the "Sorry" sign. Further along, I realized the sign read "Sorry, we're drinking." They were open! A man sitting in front went inside and brought out the young waitress. I ordered a cheesesteak, fries, salad, and freshly squeezed lemonade.

Waiting for the Battlefield Fries

Sitting out front, we snacked and watched the folks go by. Although enjoyable, I wanted to feed Norway in the room. So I collected most of the sandwich and some of the fries to go.

We finished the day at Rita's. Now, an experienced, two-time customer, I knew what to get: another layered vanilla custard, gelato, and frozen cherry slush mix. Norway savored his vanilla cup. A cool way to end the day.

GETTYSBURG, PENNSYLVANIA, to ZANESVILLE, OHIO

AFTER A SOUND sleep and a pleasant shower with ample water pressure, I packed up both suitcases. We checked out of the inn and resumed our drive on Lincoln Highway 30. The stretch offered a casual pace with no traffic, and most side roads were limited to forty mph.

We made a nice stop at a fruit stand. Originally, we paused to get a picture of the old Franklin County apple truck on display. The ten-foot-tall, one-and-a-half-ton metal sculpture symbolized the numerous fruit stands along the early days of the Lincoln Highway. While looking over the giant replica truck, I thought, *Why not have some fruit for breakfast?* Across from the display was Shatzers fruit market. After sampling a peach and an apricot, I picked out a few more, plus some kettle corn. Delicious and cheap.

We continued driving west on US-30, taking a break at the "giant coffeepot" in Bedford. The point of interest was an homage to places built along the Lincoln Highway, the first coast-to-coast highway. Constructed in 1927, this eighteen-foot-tall coffeepot was a gimmick to attract motorists to the gas station and café. Years later, the coffeepot became a bar with a hotel behind it. Decades later, the coffeepot was returned to its original spot and restored to a roadside attraction.

After passing through Schellsburg, PA, and its main street with banners honoring local war heroes, we arrived at the impressive Flight 93 National Memorial in Shanksville. Although dogs were not allowed in some areas, there was plenty of open space for us. From a distance we could see the large white marble Wall of Names, honoring the forty passengers and crew who died in the hijacked plane on 9/11.

After walking around the countryside, we went to the visitor and educational center. Outside, we were able to listen to a park ranger talk about the park, while showing us the metal scaled map of the area. Also, we got a terrific view of Memorial Plaza.

View of Memorial Plaza

Wandering the grounds gave a somber sense of the crash site and events of 9/11. There were panels with information, as well as views of the surrounding rural areas. Near the entrance, in the distance, stood the ninety-three-foot-tall Tower of Voices, due to be finished and dedicated later in the year. Forty chimes would be hung after that, for the courageous voices that were lost. Overall, this was a worthy detour in the countryside of southwest Pennsylvania.

We resumed driving west on I-70, spent a brief ten minutes in West Virginia between Pennsylvania and Ohio, and a couple of hours later, we arrived in Zanesville.

I noticed the "Y" bridge as I went to the info center in Zanesville. We drove over the bridge, then stopped nearby. It has been noted as "the only bridge you can cross and still be on the same side of the river." Norway and I took a walk onto parts of the Y bridge. Eventually, we drove up to Putnam Hill Park to get a bird's eye view of the design.

The Y bridge in Zanesville

In the area, we hunted down the "circle of vases," a pottery exhibit in the grass beside the road. Then, looking at the map, I found the war helmets monument. The pile of 297 helmets was a powerful sculpture. The dedication honors the 297 men from Muskingum County who lost their lives in World War II and the Korean War. We passed the "Amish car dealership," which displayed a horse and buggy on its roof. *Did they sell buggies as well as cars? Come to think of it, where is there an Amish buggy seller?* On the way out, we passed some appealing local murals, particularly an Amish buggy scene and a train along a river.

We arrived at the Super 8 around seven thirty. Following a long day of driving, Norway was excited to go up the stairs, down the hall, and into the room. Before I could set out his bowls, he was drinking out of the toilet.

The room was basic, without shampoo in the bathroom—just soap and lotion. I always have extras. The room was a little musty, but the air conditioner would take care of it. The Wi-Fi was mediocre, but the cable TV had some good choices. We were next to a Subway, gas station, and a McDonald's. The whole area had a truck-stop vibe, but at least I could see the car from my room window. In the end, it served its purpose.

ZANESVILLE, OHIO, to HOME

WE HAD GOOD luck with traffic today. Every road bottleneck was going the other direction. To finish the trip, we made some pleasant stops.

In Dayton, OH, the waterfront offered boardwalk areas with flowers, shops, and sculptures. Along the Inventors River Walk was a giant ice cube tray, recognizing Arthur Frei, who worked at Frigidaire in 1933. He patented a method to release the frozen ice from the tray.

At the end of the street, we spotted the Five Rivers Fountain of Lights that went off each hour. The nice attraction ran along the RiverScape MetroPark. Five fountains jetted water between two hundred and four hundred feet in the air above the meeting of the Great Miami River and the Mad River. It was appealing and an interesting bit of water engineering.

Watching the Dayton fountain

Several tents were set up for the weekend markets. Behind them was an eye-catching Wright Brothers display. The 1905 Wright Flyer monument was a giant tribute located across from Van Cleve Park riverscape. It reminded me that the fathers of aviation, Orville and Wilbur Wright, innovated at their bike shops in Dayton. They went to Kitty Hawk, North Carolina, to take advantage of strong wind conditions. It occurred to me that the Dayton University sports teams were the Flyers.

An hour after leaving Dayton, we paused in Richmond, Indiana. There were colorful murals and a small town in which to walk around and stretch our legs. Then, on I-70, we passed New Castle, home of the Indiana basketball hall of fame. In Indianapolis, we turned onto I-65 and headed north. Crown Point, IN, provided our final spot for an afternoon walk.

An enduring kiss and Norway

A twenty-five-foot statue called *Embracing Peace*, by American artist Seward Johnson, replicated the 1945 *Time* magazine photo, "Kissing the War Goodbye." This giant depiction of a sailor and woman celebrating in Times Square was displayed temporarily in a large park among the sportsplex in Crown Point.

We crossed into Illinois and hit traffic in downtown Chicago. Eventually, we made it!

The successful five-thousand-mile summer trip covered a dozen states and three Canadian provinces.

Bring Norway

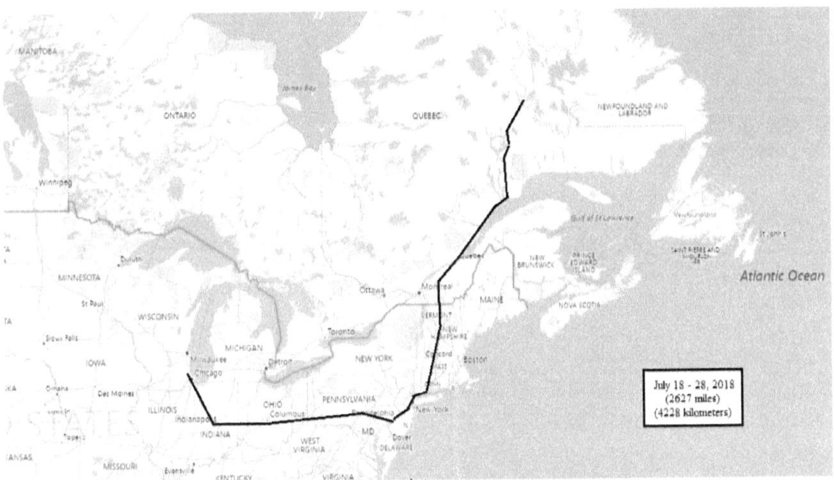

PART III

SOUTH

NORWAY HAD PROVEN to be a terrific young traveling companion. As spring break approached, I was excited for another road trip. A ten-day school break allowed enough time for a substantial adventure. The plan was to drive a multistate loop south of Illinois. A few years earlier, Oscar and I had done a similar route. Norway and I would retrace some of the trail.

The day before departure, I cleaned the kitchen, packed two bags, and collected travel items.

Norway accompanied me around the house, sensing something was going on.

"Going on a road trip tomorrow!"

As I gathered Norway's items, he eagerly watched and followed.

EVANSTON, ILLINOIS, to LINCOLN, ILLINOIS

RATHER THAN DRIVE to St. Louis today, I decided to leisurely head partway. *Good call.* The congestion at ten a.m. through Chicago was awful, eating up a lot of time. Once out of the city, traffic on I-55 flowed. And, past Joliet, cars and trucks were flying over seventy-five mph.

As lunchtime approached, we stopped in Pontiac. After adding gas, we parked in the historic downtown, five years after my first visit with Oscar. It was sunny and fifty degrees. We greeted the Abe Lincoln statue next to the Livingston County Courthouse. The nifty life-size figure honored young Lincoln, who had tried cases in Pontiac.

Meeting the Lincoln lawyer

The painted mini-cars from five years ago were gone. But the Route 66 and retro-murals remained, providing sharp, colorful decor. Since Mario Pizza was closed, we tried Fontana Cafe. We took a place in the outdoor patio, which had not been used in months. It was perfect for the husky. The caprese sandwich, fries, and soda were a nice alfresco lunch.

Beside the Route 66 mural

After another lap around town, we drove out. While we cruised on I-55, Norway slept in the back. It was a pleasant surprise to see Norway quietly snoozing as I drove. Energetic and raring to go when we stepped outside the car but mellow and set during long stretches of driving. Meanwhile, I had plenty of time to think and listen to XM Satellite Radio.

We passed through Normal, the town decorated with Illinois State memorabilia. After a brief stop at Carl's ice cream, where a giant statue of a friendly fellow holding a burger and ice cream stands in front, we returned to the highway.

In the afternoon, we arrived in Lincoln. I was glad we didn't have two more hours of rushing to St. Louis. Instead, we eased through town and found the Best Western Lincoln Inn, next to a giant Abe Lincoln lawyer sitting aboard a twenty-five-foot-tall covered wagon. The plaque explained that this Lincoln was the only town named after the president while he was still alive. And the enormous Railsplitter wagon in the open grass area claimed to be the world's largest covered wagon. While I took photos, Norway chased the critters in the grass.

Norway facing Lincoln in Lincoln

Inside, no one was at the reception desk. No problem. While waiting and unwinding, an older couple from Iowa greeted Norway. They had raised several huskies over the years.

As the woman petted Norway, the husky leaned against her and soaked it up.

"He is so gentle. You have trained him well."

"It wasn't me," I admitted. "I'm terrible at training. But I am good at consistency. Plus, I've become patient. Can't change a husky."

"They do have a mind of their own," she said.

Moments later, a young woman came to the desk and promptly checked us in.

The room was at the other end of the hotel. Not surprised. Pet rooms are often placed at one end of a hotel. Sometimes very close; other times, not. Inside our room, I checked email, flipped on the TV, and searched for any items Norway might snatch. Meanwhile, Norway sampled the flushed toilet water, then he climbed onto the bed to nap. *Chasing little creatures is hard work!*

Before dinner, we took a tour of the town. After a bit of misdirection, I turned a five-minute ride into a twenty-five-minute one to find downtown. We walked around for an hour and sought out a few attractions. First, I spotted the phone booth on top of City Hall and the Fire Department. Believe it or not, a phone booth was high above us. It seemed like a launching spot for Superman. It was placed up there in the 1960s for a spotter to issue weather warnings. The phone line went to a desk below in the building.

Nearby, we found the Lincoln Courthouse, tiny church, and visitor center. For a small slice of history, a watermelon statue commemorated the day in 1853 when Lincoln the lawyer honored this new town by slicing a watermelon and ceremoniously pouring its juice onto the ground. Lincoln had provided legal services to the town's planners. And someone suggested they name the place after him. In place of alcohol, watermelon juice was used to christen the new location. Lincoln would return in 1860 as president-elect and in the funeral train in 1865.

On the way back, I picked up Chinese food from Chi Family Restaurant. The outside was a dilapidated strip mall, but inside lots of people were eating and picking up takeout. *You can't always judge a restaurant by its cover.* They offered tasty dishes and generous portions.

Back in the room, in front of the TV, we enjoyed a feast of Mu Shu veggie, chicken and veggies, and an egg roll with homemade sweet sauce. Afterward, I gave Norway a treat in place of his fortune cookie.

LINCOLN, ILLINOIS, to ST. LOUIS, MISSOURI

AT SEVEN A.M., Norway was looking at me.

"You got some *schmukis* in your eyes," I said to him. I removed the black gunk from his eyes with my thumbs. He seemed to appreciate it. "Much better, handsome." He smiled at the tone of my comment.

I got up, checked email, and grabbed some of the breakfast offerings: a couple of mini muffins, a banana, lemonade, and eggs for Norway. I wrote down a few spots listed on *RoadsideAmerica* for the trip today. After a final lap around the giant Lincoln wagon, we were off.

During the morning drive, it was cold and drizzling. But, fortunately, as we pulled into Springfield, the rain petered out. We walked around the state capitol, pausing at the Lincoln mural—Michael Mayorsky's 2013 colorful portrait of Lincoln when he was a surveyor. Over two thousand square feet, it filled the side of a building at 5th and Jefferson. Up close, you could see it was a pixilation (or, pointillism) made of 650,000 little squares. Mayorsky explained that each square represented the life of one soldier who died in the Civil War.

Lincoln and Norway surveying the area

Down the street, we strolled through the park area, passing statues, historic information boards, and other tributes. The capitol was a commendable stop. As we finished the hour break and climbed into the car, it started to rain again.

We headed south to Alton, IL in search of the nine-foot-tall man. It was a thirty-minute detour but worth learning about the cool story of Robert Wadlow, the tallest man. Born in Alton, Wadlow was known as a friendly, gentle giant. He grew to almost nine feet tall before passing away in 1940 at the age of 22.

Tallest man in the world

Beside the life-size statue was a replica of Wadlow's giant living room chair and a display with his story. A few fans of Norway willingly took photos of us, fitting Mr. Wadlow in the picture view.

We weaved our way out of Alton, down Highway 3, and into St. Louis. Sunday parking was free, and we found a spot. It was sixty degrees, and the sun broke out between the clouds. *Finally, a warm spring day!*

We walked around the Arch area, where I remembered my last visit with Oscar around the Drury hotel, Angelo's restaurant, the Dred Scott monument beside the old courthouse, and the amazing Gateway Arch.

Enjoying St. Louis

I followed the map and found our Airbnb. Instead of settling inside, I entered the Wi-Fi code and searched the internet for a snack. I selected a Mexican place located three blocks from a Ted Drewes.

Palacios restaurant was a bizarre establishment. Inside the dimly lit bar, some Mexican guys were shooting pool. Still, the family-owned place seemed to be nice enough. And the burrito was tasty. Unfortunately, the nearby Ted Drewes frozen custard was closed until spring.

We retraced our way back, stopping at Tower Park, a terrific, spacious public space filled with dogs walking around, squirrels everywhere, people biking, and the atmosphere of a pleasant spring day. This was an ideal spot for our burrito picnic.

When we returned to the car, I opened the door and reached in to grab a towel. *Too late.* Norway snuck through and climbed into the passenger seat, leaving paw prints on the driver's seat. I wiped them away and sat. As I turned on the car's engine, Norway gave a quick shake and splattered excess water from his coat.

"Nice."

He happily stared out the front window, tongue hanging out, and watched the park action.

We found our way back to the Airbnb. After opening with the code, I climbed up the steep stairs to scout our spot. It was a sharp place, with living room, bedroom, and kitchen. It felt strange being in someone's home instead of a hotel, and I was paranoid that Norway would destroy something. He already stepped in mud thirty minutes earlier. I hoped he would not stain any of the furniture or shed his white fur.

I led Norway from the car to the entrance. After two minutes, Norway finally took up the challenge and climbed the stairs. While he investigated the new surroundings, I fiddled around with the remote control. I found the movie *Baywatch* on Hulu. It was suitable. I heard thunder, and it started to rain outside. Twenty minutes later, the sun was shining. *Welcome to St. Louis.*

The movie ended at seven o'clock. Although it was turning dark outside, I wanted to get Norway out. Plus, it was early. So, I followed the map, and fifteen minutes later we were at another Ted Drewes. *Holy smoke.* Sunday evening, the parking lot was filled. We parked on a nearby neighborhood street and wandered over to the crowd.

Ted Drewes frozen custard is legendary. It began in St. Louis around the 1930s. A friend told me years ago it was a must-visit in St. Louis. Since then, I try to fit a "concrete"—their thick custard shake—into every visit.

That evening, the ten lines moved quickly. *So many flavors and mixes.* I ordered a mini cherry and a mini M&M concrete. Then, the young girl serving me offered a cup for Norway!

The crowd was very supportive, helping me with the order and making room for the husky. As was custom, the server presented my concretes upside-down. I walked away carrying three small cups, with Norway eagerly trailing me. I found a bench to sit and enjoy the custard snack. Norway plowed through his vanilla cup. Then he shared the cherry one with me.

During the drive back, I recognized the landmarks: the park, the Vietnamese restaurant, and the names of the main streets. As I drove back, lightning came out of the sky. By the time we got back, it was pouring rain. *Just a normal spring day in St. Louis.*

We parked directly in front of the apartment, just twenty feet from the doorway. Still pouring rain, we waited in the car and listened to the radio. Since the Airbnb Wi-Fi signal reached to the car, I checked for weather updates on the laptop. When the rain eventually slowed, we darted inside.

In the living room, I searched for something to watch on Hulu or Netflix. I seldom have great success with Netflix. Whenever I stay with a friend, I skim through the Netflix menu. Mostly, I find movies I have seen or unappealing shows. No interest. But, this time, there was a new movie I did want to see: *The Dirt*, a docudrama about Motley Crue, the '80s hair band.

The Dirt was a good flick. The book was better at telling the story. However, the movie offered Motley Crue music, something you can't hear in a book.

I hoped Norway wouldn't get any rockstar ideas about trashing hotel rooms.

ST. LOUIS, MISSOURI, to MEMPHIS, TENNESSEE

EARLY THE NEXT morning, I heard birds chirping. *The rain must have stopped.* I put on shorts and a sweatshirt with three holes in the sleeves, courtesy of Norway. We walked down the steep steps. Norway led the way, then he waited for me at the bottom of the stairs.

Outside, Norway dropped a huge load, which was a relief because he had not gone in a day. And, after several long whizzes to relieve his bladder, he was reset. We walked around the Tower Grove East neighborhood near the Airbnb. Old, classic row walk-up houses stood beside Fox Park, a spacious area that included a locked dog park. Norway enjoyed the exercise, chilly weather, and scents.

"No murdering!" I called out to Norway as he eyed a squirrel enjoying a nut. Norway loved to chase the critters. On occasion he would catch one, but, then, he didn't know what to do with it! Sometimes he would play with it. Other times, the stunned creature would get loose and run off.

Back at the Airbnb, the shower was nice, having overhead spouts that feel like a waterfall. After dressing and packing, I turned out the lights, stripped linens off the bed, and inspected the apartment. It looked good. *Norway's a well-behaved rock star.*

We departed at eight thirty, hoping to avoid Monday morning traffic. Two hours later, we arrived in Cape Girardeau, MO. This was a nice spot to walk, take some photos, and add to our mileage count.

We were attempting the "year in miles" athletic challenge. For runners, the aim is to log 2,019 miles in the 2019 calendar year. For years, I've walked Norway and Oscar twice a day. Using a rough estimate, I'm sure we went over two thousand miles in many twelve-month spans. This year, I decided to accurately keep track with Norway. In addition to walking five to six miles per day, every day, I took photos and kept a spreadsheet to document the one-year challenge.

In Cape Girardeau, a long stretch of illustrations decorated the wall that banks the Mississippi River. The Wall of Fame mural contained famous Missouri folks from Mark Twain to Vincent Price to George Brett. This would be a good place for photos, highlighting our 2,019-mile walk challenge.

I set the camera on a ledge that faced the main mural shot. Then, I set the ten-second timer, grabbed Norway, and snapped a photo. Not bad, but Norway was squirming and facing the wrong way. Second attempt. I reset the timer.

"Ready!" Norway excitedly trotted with me to our spot. We turned and faced the camera just in time. I looked at the image. Not bad. Then, I got an idea to take one of us walking. After three tries, I captured a photo of us walking one of our 2,019 miles.

Mile 480 of the year

The Missouri Wall of Fame mural was remarkable. Although several years old, the colors and detail were terrific, displaying countless famous Missourians. As we walked, I noted the variety of people that included Dred Scott, Rush Limbaugh, Dale Carnegie, and Betty Grable. Continuing along the wall, an extensive timeline showed the Missouri area from the 1200s to modern time: floods, the Civil War, President Taft's visit, commerce, and development. It was an appealing way to get a perspective of history. Plus, I could see the extent of engineering used to keep the Mississippi from flooding the area and the significance of it during the Civil War—holding the Mississippi River and the elevated area nearby was a vital strategy.

Cape Girardeau was our only planned stop today. Norway and I continued through the quiet commercial main street and climbed the overlooking hill where the courthouse stood. We could see the river and the Bill Emerson Memorial Bridge. Back down at the car, I grabbed an energy bar, handed Norway a big dog treat, and we took off.

Back seat leg room

Following a rest and a Norway water stop on the Arkansas border, we finished our drive to Memphis. At three thirty, the traffic flow was good. *No rush hour in Memphis?*

The Econo Lodge was just off the I-40, affording a direct path into downtown Memphis tomorrow. Our suite had two beds, a couch, and a lounge chair. Without carpet on the floors, no dog worries. Smoke was starting to seep in. Some moron who couldn't read the No Smoking sign must have been next door.

I handed Norway a complimentary biscuit from the front desk. He tried to bury it in the couch! *Must be saving it for later.* Then, he hopped on the bed to take a nap.

We stepped out at five o'clock to get Norway's miles in, and I hoped to pick up dinner on the way. The woman at check-in offered a suggestion—Playita de Mexicana—as an alternative to nearby Cracker Barrel and Wendy's. We passed through cigarette butts and random trash, the next-door hotel, and the gas station at the corner of a busy street. We trotted across and continued to

Playita Mexicana. *Perfect.* There was a spot for Norway to wait beside the glass entrance to the restaurant.

I ordered chicken fajitas, a chicken taco side, and a beef taco side. While waiting, we walked around the plaza. At Pizza Hut, I went inside to get a soft drink. Then, we returned to pick up dinner. It was a feast for fifteen dollars. Plus, the employee threw in extra chips and salsa. In the room, the fridge and microwave could store and reheat the chicken and beef if Norway wanted a late-night snack. Or, he could retrieve his biscuit from the couch.

MEMPHIS, TENNESSEE
(day 2)

AT 3:40 A.M., Norway was pacing the room. In the chilly outside, we did a five-minute walk. He sniffed around and did some business, so it wasn't a total waste of time. Since we had a full non-travel day in Memphis, there was extra time to sleep in.

When we got up, I outlined places to visit, including potential dog-friendly restaurants in the city. Meanwhile, I got a waft of smoke from someone next door breaking the rules. I jumped in the shower. The smoke smell went away, and the water pressure was like a fire hose!

After leaving a message for Beth, a friend in Memphis, we drove onto the I-40, then I-240, and turned off at Walnut Grove Road, straight to Shelby Farms Park. *What a place!* The entire park is over four thousand acres, making this Memphis spot one of the largest urban parks in the country. There were forty miles of trails for hiking, biking, running, and walking.

Norway and I chose a paved path around Hyde Lake, passing buffalo, ducks, and other enticing excitable creatures for Norway. It was sunny and high fifties, and others were enjoying the spacious, scenic area with their dogs.

Toward the end of our walk, Beth joined us. Afterward, we followed my friend back to her nice neighborhood. Beth parked her car in the driveway. When she got in my car, Norway plopped onto her lap! Beth turned to me with a surprised smile.

"Sorry about that," I said to her. "Norway, you gotta hop in the back," I said while guiding and persuading him into the backseat.

We headed to downtown Memphis. We spotted the Elvis statue, strolled by the shops and cafes, and toured the main strip of Beale Street. At the end of the block, we learned that Beale Street did not permit dogs when a cop politely approached us. *Oh, well. Time for lunch.*

A hound dog in Memphis with Elvis

On Main Street, we found Aldo's Pizza, which offered seating for Norway. It was chilly outside, but I had an extra jacket to share, so we enjoyed pizza, salad, and drinks on the patio. Norway chomped on pizza bits, which distracted him from passing horses, the tram, and an occasional dog. Although Beth's birthday was in two days, she insisted on treating her visitors to lunch.

Norway picking pizza over picture

There were plenty of leftovers to box up. I was unsure if we would eat it later or just throw it out, but I hate wasting food. In the end, neither happened. We gave the extra slices to two homeless guys sitting in the park.

Norway, Beth, and I drove to the other end of downtown to check out Mud Island River Park. After walking across a bridge, we headed to the island in the Mississippi River. Besides the nice water view, there was an enormous model re-creation of the Mississippi River and all the riverfront towns, including buildings and streets! The concrete attraction offered geography, history, and interesting design ingenuity, making it a fascinating and enjoyable display.

Norway enjoyed sniffing and checking out the plants and smells. Meanwhile, I was amazed by the display's detail. The thousand-mile Mississippi River was scaled to one-half mile. And, all the main cities and communities along the river were embedded in the map design. It was fun to trace St. Louis, Cape Girardeau, Memphis, and other towns we had visited. This was a cool place, especially when considering the materials and planning needed for construction. Best of all, the model is laid out in front of the actual river!

I think Beth liked it; although being a Memphis native, she may not appreciate this site as much as my touristy self! After an hour, we returned to the car and headed back. At Beth's home, she kindly offered cookies, popcorn, and snacks for our trip.

The thirty-minute ride back to the hotel was fine, considering the rush-hour traffic. In the hotel room, I uploaded photos. Then, I managed to check email and eventually send some messages through the crummy Wi-Fi. For dinner, we reheated leftover chicken fajitas, one tortilla, and hot sauce. Norway had chicken and run-off juice, and I had onions, peppers, beans, and rice with the tortilla and sauce. *Bueno.*

MEMPHIS, TENNESSEE, to NASHVILLE, TENNESSEE

I COLLECTED TWO cinnamon roll packages as we checked out of the Econo Lodge. Ten minutes later, we returned to Shelby Farms Park and walked around another section of Hyde Lake. Clear and crisp outside, we found another great spot to explore. We saw birds and wildlife, including a few roaming buffalo in the distance. At one point, Norway took a moment to give them a good stare.

After the three-mile morning walk, we hopped onto I-40 and headed east. In Jackson, TN, we stopped for gas and tried the film and movie auto museum, but it was closed. The building had dark-tinted windows, so I couldn't peek inside to see what we were missing. We drove off, and two hundred miles from Memphis, we arrived in Nashville. We ran into a bit of traffic at two o'clock but eventually got onto I-65 and ten minutes later parked at the Red Roof Inn.

The suite contained a king bed, TV, open workspace, and wood floors. Nice. *I should be able to sweep up Norway's shedding*, I hoped.

We took it easy for a moment. I checked out notes and maps from a previous Nashville trip with Oscar. Norway rested by the door. Sunny outside, I became motivated to check out Franklin. About fifteen minutes away, it offered a historic downtown to get some walking miles in.

The downtown Franklin area had convenient, free parking. The town welcomed canines with complimentary dog bowls stationed around the streets. Norway sampled the water bowls and made a few more human friends. We got in a bit of scenery, exercise, and Civil War history.

We settled on dinner at the Mellow Mushroom. The pizza place offered spacious outdoor seating in the shade, facing the Confederate monument in the downtown square. Built in 1899, the statue *Keeper of the Square* has an unknown soldier towering thirty-seven feet over the plaza. Despite attempts to erase the history, this piece still stands.

The Mellow Mushroom's patio was a perfect place to relax and watch people go by. The pizza was very good, and, the crust was chewy and tasty. Occasionally, a dog came close, but the patio barrier restrained Norway. Or, perhaps he was tired from a long day. I wrapped half of the pizza and Norway's meatball sandwich. We could reheat them later in the room. We were pleased with the Franklin excursion.

At 8:45 p.m., I received a message from my friend Erich. We got in the car and drove ten minutes to his house. Since Norway was shedding, and his wife would not be happy with a messed-up home, we sat around his table near the front door. After a few minutes of trying to jump onto Erich's lap, Norway mellowed and eventually lay on the floor while we talked. In addition to catching up, he offered sightseeing suggestions.

"Radnor Park is near you," he said. "Great place for a dog."

NASHVILLE, TENNESSEE (day 2)

I WAS DELIGHTED Norway did not wake me for a midnight stroll. At 6:45 a.m., we went three steps from our room to a door leading outside. Norway got excited, even trying to leap above the second-floor wall to get closer. We turned the corner toward the stairs, and coming up was another husky!

"Wow, how did you know there was another dog so close by?" I said to Norway as he eagerly tugged me along.

The two dogs had a cordial one-minute greeting, while I chatted with the other husky's owner. I learned he and the eight-year-old pup were from Boston, traveling to New Mexico.

We tried Radnor Lake State Park, just a few miles from the hotel. Although we couldn't use the dirt trails, dogs were allowed on the paved Otter Creek Road. Wooded views and nature smells lined both sides of this road closed to cars. With lots of room to roam, Radnor Park was perfect for our morning walk.

Right behind you!

We encountered walkers, joggers, and dogs along the way. Norway happily walked fifteen feet ahead of me.

"Oh my gosh," a startled older woman said. "He scared me. I thought it was a loose wolf!"

When Norway rounded the bend, from her vantage point, looking into the sun, he looked like a wolf.

"Then, I saw the leash, and you turned the corner."

"Sorry about that," I said. "He likes to lead the way."

The woman stopped pushing a buggy holding two little dogs. While exchanging stories, I learned she had driven all over the country for the past twenty years.

Further along, we met a vacationing couple from Gurnee, IL. Then met a guy from Wilmette, five minutes from my home. Meanwhile, Norway met plenty of dogs and people, accompanied with plenty of compliments. Also, we saw turtles, birds, and nature. It was a terrific outing.

We headed to downtown Nashville for lunch. There were lots of places to eat in the Hillsboro area near Vanderbilt. During a pleasant sixty-five-degree sunny day, the patios were open. We passed BBQ, bagels, and burgers. Because of crowds or menu options, we ended at Fido Cafe. While I snacked on a burger and sweet potato fries, Norway napped or accepted greetings from a passerby.

After lunch, we walked to nearby Fannie Mae Dees Park, known locally as Dragon Park. The centerpiece was a colorful pair of mosaic sea serpents. The 150-foot-long playground creatures were covered in fun painted mosaic tiles. Created in 1981 by artist Pedro Silva, the recently renovated figures were eye-catching and a fantastic playground item for kids.

Norway and I drove down Music Row and crowded Honky Tonk, eventually weaving our way to Two Rivers Dog Park. A modest crowd watched their dogs roam around the huge grassy field. Norway and I started outside the fence.

After a lap, we boldly wandered inside the enormous park, keeping our distance. Norway was great with people and children but unpredictable with other dogs. Sometimes he becomes overwhelmed with excitement. Two German shepherd puppies boldly—or naively—came over to Norway. There was a scrum, and the shepherds started yelping! They did not retreat; instead, they stood their ground and cried out. Norway wagged his tail, jumped around, and tugged on the leash. He wanted to play, but he was overexcited. Eventually, I cut our losses and we left.

In the evening, we met Erich at Tin Roof 2. A nice crowd filled the outdoor seating along the bar. Although packed for the Tennessee/Purdue NCAA basketball game, Erich had found a central table. Norway and I sat, snacked on bar food, had a drink, and reveled in sitting outside! It had been a while since I had enjoyed a seventy-degree day. Lots of people paused to say hi to Norway. And, with the use of chicken and shrimp bribes, he behaved, rested, and sat on the bench beside me.

NASHVILLE, TENNESSEE, to COLUMBUS, INDIANA

INSTEAD OF A five-hundred-mile, one-day trip directly home, I decided to break it up into two days of driving. From Nashville, we would pause in Indiana, about halfway back home.

When Norway got me up at seven, I arranged a list of sights and copied maps of Louisville, the Kentucky back roads to the "fork," and directions to the Jim Beam distillery.

At nine a.m., we embarked on I-65 and drove through Nashville, onward to the first stop: "Fork in the Road," located northeast of Franklin, Kentucky. Located off the beaten path, I needed the map.

Norway reaches a fork in the road

In the middle of a quiet rural intersection we encountered a very sleek and clever giant fork! *Who thinks up this stuff?*

During the worthwhile detour, we toured the backwoods of Kentucky, passing cows, scenery, and serene grassy farms. We encountered two local roadworkers, where I made sure my exit was correct. They pointed the way, and we headed along US-31W.

We returned to I-65 and continued north until exiting to visit the National Corvette Museum in Bowling Green. We parked in the visitors lot across from numerous pristine Corvettes. With plenty of area to walk, Norway darted and raced all over the place. We did a lap around the giant museum, viewing the outdoor banners of Corvette clubs and dedications to the notable brand.

Norway living the dream

Afterward, we wandered next door to Art's Corvette. We went inside for a brief look. Old Art was still there. I greeted him and paid five bucks to enter. After a brief tour of the classic cars, we left. Many more places to see.

We continued north until stopping at the Jim Beam Distillery in Clermont, KY. It was easy to find along Bourbon Road and well worth it! The informative attraction included an outdoor tour with exhibits and historical information. Instead of the popular formal tour, Norway and I explored the area ourselves. Photos, statues, and the smell of bourbon. Fascinating to realize this place had eight generations of whiskey history, starting in the 1790s. We went along the stillhouse, distillery, restaurant, and the life-size bronze statue of Jim Beam himself welcoming everyone.

This husky is top shelf

Nearby, we glanced at the Jim Beam house. In front was a bronze statue of Booker Noe, the sixth-generation grandson of Jim Beam, lounging in a chair beside his dog, overlooking the production facility. Norway and I enjoyed this stop. Ironically, neither one of us drinks whiskey!

We returned to I-65 and continued to Louisville. We made a brief detour, driving down US-150 along Broadway east to see the "Kentucky Rushmore" mural. The local piece contained illustrations of Muhammad Ali, Abe Lincoln, Colonel Sanders, and Secretariat (the racehorse). Sort of worth going out of the way.

We passed through the Louisville neighborhoods. While waiting at a stoplight, I observed one of many tattoo parlors. Suddenly, the car jolted forward. Unfortunately, some guy rear-ended the Nissan. He jumped out and admitted guilt. "Sorry, I was on my phone." *Geez.* He then offered to write a check for the damages. I inspected my bumper. Opened the car's hood. I didn't see any damage.

We took Broadway back to downtown Louisville. It was easy to find, and there was plenty of inexpensive street parking available. No problem, since I had plenty of quarters to load into the meter.

We walked up and down the main street checking out the sights. The tallest and easiest to see was the "world's largest bat" in front of the Louisville Slugger Museum and factory. The 120-foot-tall bat was made of steel, weighing 68,000 pounds. It was an exact scale replica of Babe Ruth's 34-inch Louisville Slugger bat.

Norway at bat

After a nifty photo, we wandered down the street, passing several bronze baseball bats and plaques commemorating famous baseball sluggers. This Louisville slugger Walk of Fame extended for several blocks.

We passed a giant five-story-tall whiskey bottle in the window of a distillery. Then we reached the Galt Hotel, which presented the "Gallop to Glory," which saluted the winning jockeys of the Kentucky Derby. An ornate golden horse and jockey statue stood among countless handprints captured in concrete of winning jockeys since 1936.

After the sampling of bourbon, bats, and betting, we built a nice appetite. Hungry and tired, I saw Gordon Birsch with outdoor seating! I went inside and found out that part of the patio was closed. However, I could take the food outside and eat there. *Perfect!*... until the bartender said no takeout tonight. So, GB was out.

On the way back to the car, we crossed a taqueria with plenty of outdoor seating. I loaded Norway into the car. Then we drove four blocks back to Taco Luchador Taqueria. Carrying Norway's bowls, we went to the patio. While Norway held our spot, I went inside and ordered tacos, chips, and guacamole. The food was terrific. Norway ate his fish and beef, then he went to sleep. After finishing dinner, we packed up and raced north.

We arrived in Columbus, Indiana, around seven o'clock. There was a time change, so we'd we lost an hour. It seemed strange, since we'd traveled directly north from Tennessee to Kentucky to Indiana.

The La Quinta Columbus-Edinburgh was just off I-65, with good signs and in view. The Friday evening check-in was quite busy, and, surprisingly, they only had one person behind the desk. She was competent, but they could have used another person. While waiting for the line to shorten, Norway and I stepped outside for a moment. Then, back inside, Norway was greeted by families and kids in the La Quinta lobby.

Eventually, we settled into a nice, spacious suite with a desk and a couch. Norway jumped on the couch, jumped on the bed, and drank out of the toilet. After touring the room, he passed out on the bed. Long day for Norway!

I checked my email and then decided to get dessert. We walked five minutes down the street to Freddy's—a burger and frozen custard place. This perked Norway up! The restaurant was an ideal setup with an open front door. I had a clear line of sight twenty-five feet to Norway while I waited in line. I ordered a regular concrete with M&M's and a mini concrete with cherry flavor to share with Norway.

Norway was a hit. I had set him to the side, leaving plenty of walking space, but everyone stepped over to pet him as they entered the restaurant. Norway the greeter loved it.

A female worker came out. "He is beautiful." Norway was smiling. "Can I get him a 'pup cup'?"

"Oh yes." I spoke for Norway. "He would love that."

Next, a cook offered to prepare a special burger patty for Norway. Everyone was so nice. I received the pup cup and patty. While waiting for my custard, Norway started calling out to me.

"One second," I said to the eager husky customer waiting for his snack!

The custard was a satisfying treat. And certainly no complaints from Norway. Mostly, the first-class treatment and husky extras were outstanding.

We returned to the hotel. As we approached the elevators, four people entered one. As we stepped aside to wait for the next one, they warmly invited us into the elevator. *Norway brings out the best in people.*

After the nap and late snack, Norway was alert. Plus, across the hallway was a room full of kids having fun. Norway was standing by the door. I think he wanted to play with them!

COLUMBUS, INDIANA, to HOME

ALTHOUGH DRIZZLING AND dreary outside, I mapped out a few sights to see within fifteen miles of Columbus. Then, a quick stop in Indy, then home. We had plenty of time, including a one-hour time zone gain. I went to shower and found Norway lying in the tub.

Chillin' in the bathtub

Instead of forcing him out, I went downstairs to check La Quinta's breakfast. I picked out a bagel, a muffin for later, and scrambled eggs for Norway. I trotted back to the room. When I entered, Norway was at the door waiting. Following the quick snack, I showered, dressed, and packed. Also, I picked up trails of white dog hair clumps scattered around the room. *Norway was decorating the room.*

We left the hotel on IN-46, drove five minutes east, across I-65 and the Driftwood River, into downtown Columbus. Beside the Bartholomew County Courthouse, we visited the Limestone Pillars Veterans' Memorial. The monument was impressive with names and dates etched on the twenty-five forty-foot-tall pillars. More interesting (and sad) were copies of letters and postcards sent home to families before the soldiers went MIA or were killed. It was a worthwhile detour.

We walked around the surrounding area for about thirty-five minutes, giving Norway a good mile-and-a-half walk. The small community with a few shops looked like a town trying to revitalize. I would have liked to check out the ice cream parlor that had been open since 1900, but the stores were still closed at nine thirty a.m.

We traveled north on Washington Street to US-31 North, driving fifteen minutes in the drizzle to Franklin. We saw the big rocking chair on the side of the road, in front of a furniture store. We continued east to the unique "grave in the road." A grave from over 150 years ago sits in the middle of a country road! Honoring her request in 1831, Nancy Burnett was buried on a scenic hill overlooking Sugar Creek. In the 1900s, the county wanted to build a road through the spot. But her grandson would not allow her remains to be moved. So, now the road splits at her grave, with one lane on each side!

We followed US-31 at Whiteland and found the "Garden of Gas Station Signs." There were a few dozen gas station signs mounted on eighteen-foot poles. The signs dated back to the 1930s to 1960s. The collection by Alan Ray Whitaker, displayed beside his business, was a colorful, nostalgic sight.

After the brief detours, we made one stop: the Fountain Square Historic District in the southeast part of Indianapolis. It seemed like a hip place with artists, trying to make a comeback. Many of the shops and buildings were in repair. Some cafes, a few cool painted murals, and historical markers showed lots of potential. For an hour, I took pictures, and Norway enjoyed the bit of exercise. On the way out, while looking for the I-65 North entrance, we passed Lucas Stadium. I saw a Peyton Manning statue, so I parked and got a few photos of the area. The stadium is cool-looking—a little bit of the Lambeau Field feel—except for Colts fans.

Once we left Indianapolis, the driving shit-show started. It seemed anything that could make it long and miserable happened. Pouring rain for an hour made the drive on I-65 annoying. We stopped for gas while the rain was pouring and the freezing wind was kicking up. At BP, I think we found the slowest gas pump on Earth.

We continued driving on I-65, and the pouring rain turned to wet snow. When the lousy weather eventually passed, the traffic emerged. An accident at the I-80/94 merge caused a massive delay.

We passed that and flew at seventy mph—for five minutes—until we hit the downtown Chicago traffic and endless construction.

At last, we passed downtown and cruised in the express lanes, until we reached the I-94. More traffic. *What is going on?* At three thirty on a Saturday afternoon, traffic was going every direction.

Eventually, we got home. *We covered 1,650 miles in eight days. A success!*

I woke Norway up, and he followed me out of the car. We entered the house, and he headed to a favorite spot in the backyard.

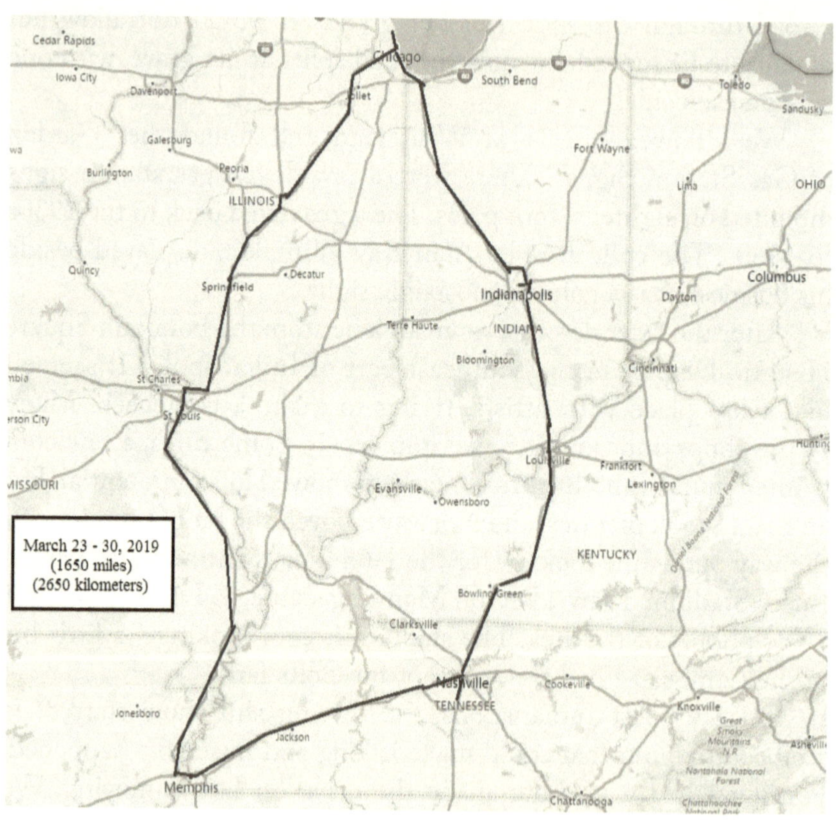

PART IV

LAKE MICHIGAN

IN THE SUMMER, I began considering road trip options. While I love the Black Hills area in the West, I was not motivated to drive that far. And we had gone to the East. *Where could we get to in a simple road trip?*

I tried to think of something different and not too expensive. *How about driving around Lake Michigan?* There were a few places I had never seen. It was a relatively easy route for us. Maybe the lake would moderate the summer heat?

A few days before departure, I finished the food in the refrigerator, paused the mail delivery, and gradually packed our items into the car. We were ready.

After Norway jumped in the car, I went to the other side and sat in the driver's seat. Just as I turned the ignition, Norway climbed onto my lap.

"How are we going on a road trip with you sitting on my lap?"

Norway sat contently while the car idled in the driveway. He licked my face.

"Thank you." Then, I encouraged him, "Gotta slide over."

He smiled, tongue hanging, and looked at me.

After I guided him to the passenger seat, we took off!

EVANSTON, ILLINOIS, to GREEN BAY, WISCONSIN

ALTHOUGH ONE HOUR away, I had never been to the Kenosha downtown or lakefront. Over the years, I had driven past Kenosha and even visited the outlet stores off I-94. This was the first time I exited the interstate and drove seven miles east to the Lake Michigan shore.

On the way to the water, we paused at a mural of Donkey Kong and Pacman. The classic characters were painted on the side of a building that housed a game room and bar. We continued one mile to the shore, starting at Veterans Memorial Park to view a tribute to the casualties of war. The park included a seven-foot-tall bronze Lone Soldier, a veterans' memorial fountain, and an eight-ton boulder from Okinawa. Next to the area was an open walkway and harbor out to Lake Michigan.

Leading the way in Kenosha

We discovered an impressive, clean area of concrete walking paths and grass. The walkers, bikers, and people with dogs were enjoying a clear, sunny day, with a pleasant summer lake breeze. We had an open view of Lake Michigan.

During our walk, we met a couple from central Missouri who had a few dogs and kids at home. The young guy wanted to meet Norway. When he opened his arms up, Norway plowed into him.

"Sorry about that," I half-apologized, half-laughed.

"No problem. He just wants to play!" The guy and his wife hugged and wrestled with Norway. He wagged his tail, enjoying the interaction with two new friends.

We continued north on I-94 to Milwaukee. We cruised around town past the Harley Davidson Museum and 3rd Street historic area. The bobblehead museum was appealing, but understandably, pets could not go inside. *Who knows how many heads Norway would try to snatch!*

We parked near the riverfront to stretch and visit the Bronze Fonz. A Mexican guy and his friends watched me aiming the camera. Since Norway was flopping around, I couldn't get a good shot. Norway is so handsome, but he seldom poses for an easy photo.

The onlookers walked over and offered to take our picture. The amiable guy insisted that we take as many shots as needed to get the desired photo.

Norway is too cool for a photo

The guy handed my camera back, and the others gathered to meet the husky. Four more friends for Norway.

After walking several blocks, we drove through the brewery section and around different road views of Milwaukee, then returned to the highway. Last year, we drove along Lake Michigan on I-43. This time, we connected to I-41 and headed northwest. On the way, I noted the local promotions: an inside gun range, fireworks, pro-life billboards, strip clubs, as well as anti-porn and anti-trafficking signs—along with many US flags.

While passing through Fond Du Lac and the southern part of Lake Winnebago, I scanned over the storefronts and restaurants.

"Great place to open a fondue restaurant!" I cracked. No response from Norway. He was enjoying the view and breeze from the window.

"Fond Du Lac fondue. A fondue name that's a lock." My weak humor didn't connect with the canine audience.

Regardless, I suspect plenty of terrific cheese dishes were in this part of Wisconsin.

When we reached Oshkosh, I drove off to find an "Atlas Shrugged" sculpture. In front of an architecture and construction management firm, the bronze figure was holding the world on his shoulders. The words *Fight to be Free* were etched at the base of the Greek god, perhaps a tribute to the Ayn Rand novel. Above it flew a big US flag and a medium-sized Israeli flag.

Twenty miles north, I learned Appleton, WI, was the hometown of Harry Houdini. Downtown, we found a bronze sculpture of the famous escape artist in a straitjacket. And I found a lion painted with Houdini history in front of the History Museum at the Castle.

Norway cooling off by Houdini

Our afternoon walk ended at Houdini Plaza. Nearby was a pub with outdoor seating. The Bazil's Pub patio was filled with fifteen women at various tables and no guys. *Is Lawrence University a female school? Was this coincidental?* While checking the menu, a few of the women approached to meet Norway.

We brought the veggie burger, fries, and chicken strips to a table fifty feet away across a grassy area. It was eighty-seven degrees with no breeze; Norway was tired out. While listening to the background sounds of conversation and music, we rested in the shade and enjoyed our summer meal.

At five thirty, we reached the Super 8 in Green Bay, located just off I-41. Looking at a map, I noted it was an easy route to Lambeau Field, with lots of places to eat along the way. Inside was a welcoming lobby with popcorn at the front desk. The comfortable room, with two beds and lots of cable channels, included a fridge, extra chair, and desk with open work space. Most importantly, there was quality air conditioning for Norway.

GREEN BAY, WISCONSIN, and STURGEON BAY, WISCONSIN

"OH, LORDY, YOUR breath is fierce."

Norway was awake and leaning into me. He had doggie breath mixed with a bit of dog biscuits.

"You know there are two beds here," I reminded him.

Seeing me wake up, Norway wagged his tail. Then, he stood up, leapt off the bed, and happily paced along the door.

"Alright." I climbed out of bed and grabbed the accessories and we headed down the hallway outside.

After the early morning walk, I showered, then darted up the hall to grab a small orange juice, a banana, two bagels, and some egg remnants for Norway. Following the morning routine, Norway and I began today's itinerary.

We drove down Oneida Street to Lambeau Field. At eight o'clock Sunday morning, in late July, the lot was almost empty. Big signs were set up for the start of football training camps, but for the most part there were few people.

We parked in front of the atrium with the Lambeau and Vince Lombardi towering statues. Norway led the way around the stadium. Then we wandered across the way to investigate Titletown.

I discovered an impressive community, with a gameday setup of bars and restaurants, an enormous kids' playground, and a youth football field. Raised above was Ariens Hill, where visitors could go upstairs and get a bird's-eye view of Lambeau Field. Further along, we approached an area with Ping-Pong tables, bocce ball, and a fifty-yard-dash field and clock.

I watched a few guys running up and down the stairs at Ariens Hill. Apparently, the lower part is filled with water to create an ice rink in winter. All of it was free and clean!

Norway and I finished our walk, passing several houses with decorative walls and Packers murals, viewing areas, and fan tributes. We ended at the *Lambeau Leap* statue, where we met a guy and his father from Mississippi. During our brief conversation, they were nice enough to photograph Norway and me landing in the Lambeau Leap Crowd.

Celebrating in Green Bay. "Touchdown!"

On the way back to the car, it occurred to me that those Mississippi natives were likely Packers fans because of Brett Favre. I had played fantasy football for twenty-five years, and fifteen of them included Favre as my quarterback. I remembered Favre was from Mississippi.

We hit the road, driving up Highway 57 to Door County. Fifteen miles beyond Sturgeon Bay was Whitefish Dunes State Park, which featured a trail leading to a beach area open to dogs. Super cold water and reduced beach due to high tides, but Norway did enjoy it! He dipped his face in the water and gulped it up. Then, he ran back and forth in the shoreline water and sand.

Cool down at the dunes

We hiked the other way to Cave Point County Park. It was a nice trail (aside from the mosquitoes) with a view of Lake Michigan and scenic rocks from the water.

Building an appetite, we returned to Sturgeon Bay for a late lunch at Sonny's Pizzeria. The hostess offered a table upstairs with a view of the bay and boat harbor. On the way, we made a notable entrance into the crowded upstairs area when Norway panicked at the top of the steps. He was scared and resistant to the spaces between the steps. It took some persuasion and encouragement from onlookers to lead him up.

We enjoyed the meal of fresh salad, Margherita pizza, and soda—with chicken strips for Norway.

Norway's lunch

After he polished off his bowl of food, Norway rested on the wood-plank patio. It was a nice afternoon, and everyone was polite to Norway, either petting him or walking around his sprawled body. Following the meal, I carried Norway down the three flights of spaced stairs. He happily trotted back to the car with me. We drove an hour back to Green Bay, where we recharged in the hotel room.

Our day ended with a snack from Smart Cow, a yogurt bar.

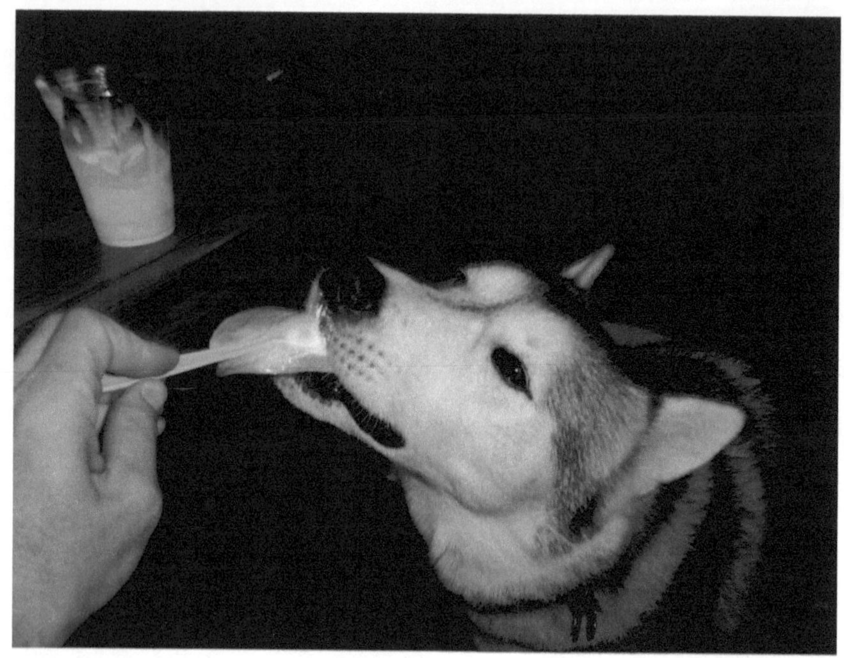

Norway's snack

Norway savored several spoonfuls of the vanilla treat. Meanwhile, I uploaded photos, made notes, and snacked on my ice cream. I turned and saw that Norway was waiting.

"Yes?" I showed him his empty ice cream cup. "You ate yours too fast!"

Norway stared at me, paused to bark, then said, "Aar-Rah-Rah-Raaah" in Husky talk.

"Aar-Rah-Rah-Raaah," I echoed back to him with the same pitch and tone.

"Rah-rah-rah," he came back.

"Rah-rah-rah," I said. He tipped his head with curiosity.

"You want a snackee?" I got up from the chair, pulled out a biscuit, and handed it to Norway.

He gladly snatched it from me, went over to a comfortable spot, and enjoyed his treat.

GREEN BAY, WISCONSIN, to ST. IGNACE, MICHIGAN

AT FIVE A.M., we were wide awake. It was wet outside, just as the weather forecaster predicted. I printed a screenshot of the map from Green Bay to Munising to St. Ignace and wrote down towns and route numbers to ensure no wrong turns. Regardless, Lake Michigan was to the east. How lost could we get?

Since the rain had stopped, I took Norway outside around the two neighboring hotels.

"It's gonna be a steamer today."

Although overcast, temperatures were in the high seventies. The parking lot was half empty, a big difference between Sunday morning and Monday morning—which likely explained the difference in daily hotel rates. After a ten-minute walk, we returned through the lobby. We passed the empty breakfast area. *Damn, we got up too early, before breakfast was available.*

In the room, I picked clothes from the small travel bag, and Norway hopped into the comfortable bed to lie down. I went into the bathroom to shower.

"Norway, are you sleepwalking again?" A bunch of paw prints were in the bathtub. *I wonder who did that?*

While I showered, the bathroom door popped open. Norway walked inside and sat on the floor towels until I finished.

We took advantage of the hotel's complimentary breakfast. And, following a good snack, we were out the door before eight a.m.

Our first stop was Peshtigo, WI, where a devastating fire occurred on October 8, 1871— the same day as the famous Chicago fire. Its fire museum with information boards stood alongside the Peshtigo Fire Cemetery, which included a memorial marker and mass grave for 350 fire victims who could not be identified. The area was full of interesting history and outdoor sights … and fiery mosquitoes.

Following written directions, we connected to US-41 until Marinette, then over the bridge and across the state border to M35 in Menominee, Michigan. Next, we followed that to Route M67, which connected to State Highway M94 leading to Munising.

After briefly stopping at a scenic spot overlooking the Munising Harbor, we parked downtown. Norway and I took a little walk, passing a few colorful murals and tourist shops. After one mile, I saw the edge of town and signs to Pictured Rocks, a notable attraction. We turned around and headed back toward the car.

We picked up a bag of northern Michigan sweet cherries from a guy with a makeshift stand beside his truck. At four bucks a pound, they weren't cheap. But I am lured by fresh produce, anticipating food from the source would taste better than purchased in a grocery store. Sometimes it did. Sometimes it did not. Nevertheless, I like to support the cause. Plus, the man had a one-year-old dog beside him.

Further along the main road, we stopped at a Hawaiian shaved ice spot. It had a tiki design, surfboard, and a Hawaiian-style hut. Five bucks for a massive grape and cherry shaved ice. A refreshing snack to help me cool down, a few hours before getting dinner. *Who knew you could get Hawaiian shaved ice in the middle of Wisconsin?* Interestingly, the shaved ice hut was just two buildings down from a Dairy Queen.

We walked through "Art in the Alley," passing some nifty paintings. When we returned to the car, the temps were back in the eighties. Time for some fierce auto air conditioning for Norway.

We drove down the road for a brief stop at Munising Falls. The short trail to the falls was dog acceptable, including a nice stretch in the shade.

After cruising through the town, I got on track to the Pictured Rocks. Unfortunately, the road directly to the Pictured Rocks shoreline was closed! I watched three cars go around the signs and onto the gravel road. *Would they get stopped?*

I asked an older couple for an alternative way. They weren't sure, aside from hiking five or six miles through trails. Also, they suggested a route up the road that led to a closer spot, requiring a couple of miles of hiking. *Seems possible.*

To make sure I understood the directions, we pulled over, and I went into a tourist gift shop. When I asked the woman, she showed me a map. If I circled around, there was another route that got me to Pictured Rocks! I appreciated her help, but I passed on the five-dollar map that provided only a small two-inch section of relevant area.

Aided by her directions and local detour signs, I followed the route and got to Miners Castle. It was an amazing, vast view of Lake Superior. On the sunny and clear day, the clean blue water shone. A few boats went by. If you leaned over, you could see portions of the carved-out colorful rocks. Apparently, the best views required a boat. Nevertheless, it was a terrific first impression of this area. Plus, it was not very crowded. Just a few nice travelers whose kids wanted to greet Norway.

Enjoying the view of Lake Superior

The afternoon was quickly fading, plus we'd lost an hour going from Wisconsin to Michigan. Time to head to Manistique and then to St. Ignace. On the way out, an older woman on the trail greeted us. She turned to Norway.

"He's a nice dog."

"Yeah, he's a good one," I added.

She reached down. "Enjoying the walk around here?" she said to Norway.

"Yes," I answered for him. "It's a bit hot. But he's doing well. Are you from around here?"

"I'm from Minnesota."

"Which part?" I asked.

"Near Duluth," she said. "I'm spending a week going around Lake Superior."

"Really?" I answered. "We're driving around Lake Michigan. We just made a detour to see the Pictured Rocks Coast and Munising."

While the woman followed her path, we continued walking to the car. Before leaving the park area, I took a photo of one of the maps on display. Then I asked the park ranger to confirm my chosen route. He did one better, handing me a Michigan map! This would be helpful for the other end of our road trip.

The driving distance was more than expected. However, the sixty-five mph speed limit and lack of traffic helped make up time. Plus, we got a nice view of Lake Michigan as we went from Manistique to St. Ignace. We pulled over at a scenic view of Mackinac Bridge. At the spot, a guy offered to take a photo of me and Norway. Norway squirmed a bit, but we got a decent shot.

A view of Mackinac Bridge

While I set Norway down, several people approached to meet and greet him. The guy handed the camera back to me.

"Thanks for the shot," I said.

"No problem. Glad to help," he said. "I have two boxers at home. I should have brought them."

"Maybe next time," I said. "He likes coming with me. Anywhere. It could be the gas station, a road trip, or around the block. Norway likes to participate."

As we neared St. Ignace, I spotted the tall wooden tower. I had read that it cost a buck to climb up for a view. I pulled into the lot, cranked up the air conditioning, and left the locked car running so that Norway could chill. Inside the Curio Fair souvenir shop, I paid one dollar and scampered up the hundred steps to the top. *This is not for people afraid of heights.* I had a clear view of the bridge and water. Then I skipped down the wooden tower past the graffiti, through the shop, and out the front to the car.

In town, we drove down the main road observing the shops, reminding me of last year's Sault Ste. Marie visit. Restaurants, souvenirs, fudge, pubs, and pasty shops. The ranger had explained pasties were pastries with meat inside. *Sort of like empanadas?*

We checked into a nice room with a towel folded up like a swan on the bed. Unfortunately, the Wi-Fi was terrible. We were at the tip of Michigan, so I guessed reception might be tough. I needed the connection to find a hotel for tomorrow.

What is that?

It proved difficult to find a place to eat with Norway. The few restaurants with patios did not accept dogs. Many of the places permitted service dogs, but I would never use the service dog scam to get in. Besides, who would believe my energetic husky was a well-trained service dog?

We adapted and went to Village Inn. I ordered a veggie burger, fries, and chicken breast for takeout. Then, we walked across the street to a park with picnic tables and view of the harbor and lighthouse. The veggie bean burger was tasty—especially the bun and cheddar cheese. Afterward, we had ice cream at Mackinac Double Decker next door. As we finished, it started to rain. Time to retreat to the room.

There was no Wi-Fi improvement in the room. Unable to use my laptop, at eleven p.m., I booked a hotel thru BringFido using my phone. Sight unseen, I picked a motel in Manistee. The hotels in Traverse City, Empire, and Ludington were a hundred dollars more expensive or unavailable. We would see what rat trap, or hidden gem, Norway and I booked for tomorrow.

SAINT IGNACE, MICHIGAN, to MANISTEE, MICHIGAN

DESPITE A LATE night, we were up at six thirty a.m. I grabbed juice, more eggs for Norway, and fresh fruit of honeydew, grapes, and cantaloupe, plus a donut. Then I cleaned up and got dressed. The hotel had my bathroom favorite: a high shower head that swamps you like standing under a waterfall.

The plan was a pleasant three-mile walk around town with Norway. The route along the water could add easy miles to our 2019 challenge total. We were at 1,206 miles for the year. With five months remaining and less than 800 miles to go, we were on pace to finish in December.

Norway was energized by the cooler sixty-one-degree temperature. We walked through the quiet St. Ignace downtown, passing a notable museum, memorial spots, shops, and a view of the harbor. On the way back, we walked along the wooden Huron boardwalk that extended beside the entire downtown waterway. Interpretive signs with history and lifestyles of the Straits of Mackinac, and parts of nineteenth-century ships on display, accented the route. It took about an hour, and we met our three-mile goal.

On the boardwalk

With two hours until checkout, we made a quick trip to Castle Rock. For one dollar, Norway and I darted up the stairs to the top, where we got an enormous clear view of the water and Mackinac Island. The platform on top of the rock was a little intimidating, especially for tall people. The side walls were low, so it seemed easy to fall over the side. *This is high up!* After a few photos, we scampered back down, stopping to chat with the owner, who took a liking to the husky visitor.

After checking out, we stopped at Lehto's to try a pasty. I learned these pastries were designed originally to be substantial meals for farmers and miners, or any remote worker who could not get to a midday food source. The best part, the owner explained, was they stayed warm for hours. I tried a veggie pasty, which looked like a calzone or huge empanada. And I added a big chocolate chip cookie.

During our departure, Norway and I stopped at a park just before the Mackinac Bridge. I appreciated the clear, beautiful view, and Norway liked the cool air. I took photos of the bridge, the waters that led to Lake Huron and Michigan, and the blooming flowers. Plus, I read about the history of the bridge. Completed in 1957, it is the fourth largest suspension bridge in the world. The entire bridge connects the upper and lower peninsulas of Michigan. Structures like this are impressive, considering the manpower, technology, and determination to build something that has lasted sixty years, withstanding temperatures and winds.

Enjoying the view of the Mackinac Bridge

I followed the foldout map I'd gotten from yesterday's park ranger. We drove onto I-75 and went over the Mackinac Bridge. The five-mile span crossed the Straits of Mackinac from the UP (Upper Peninsula) back to lower Michigan. On our left was Lake Huron; on the right was Lake Michigan. Ten minutes later, we turned southwest onto US-31 and spent time cruising the coastline. Between Charlevoix, Traverse City, and Manistee were lots of cherry and blueberry farms. Plus, smaller towns with a mix of harbors and lake views. Along the way, we made a few odd stops, including the site of the largest cherry pie in Traverse City.

Trotting by the largest cherry pie (pan)

In July of 1987, Chef Pierre Bakeries, with the help of hundreds of volunteers, baked and assembled the pie that weighed over 28,000 pounds. A local steel supply company constructed the eighteen-foot-wide and twenty-six-inch-deep pie pan. After setting a new world record, the pie served over 30,000 spectators. *Is there a world record for whipped cream?*

We took a lunch break at a park near Interlochen. Aside from a mother and a little girl, the place was completely empty. After a picnic in nature, in complete quiet, we finished the drive.

The Manistee motel was old-school—something you might have seen in a 1960s California beach town. Simple and dated. The woman was super-nice, coming out to greet us. While meeting Norway, she mentioned having three huskies at home, all of them rescues.

"That's a lot of energy," I commented.

"Yes, they keep me on my toes," she agreed.

The room's beds had metal frames and quilt blankets. I flipped on the old television that used a Roku device. The internet signal was lousy, which led to no TV reception. *Whatever happened to just turning on the television and getting a show?*

After trying to trouble-shoot, I returned to the woman at the desk for help. Curiously, when she walked in the room to show me how the Roku TV worked, it was on!

"Oh my god," I said to her. "I swear it did not work when I went to get you." And, Norway is not a TV repair dog.

"That's OK," she kindly understood. "It's working now."

It reminded me of bringing a troubled car to a mechanic. But when the mechanic checks the problem, it runs fine. Then, you go home and the car breaks down again.

Ten minutes later, the connectivity dropped and the TV shut off. *Ugh.* Meanwhile, I was not getting very far with my laptop Wi-Fi.

After a tedious ninety minutes, I managed to pull up the BringFido webpage and book a room for tomorrow night in Holland, MI. With limited internet, I was unable to search many options and simply took the first hotel that seemed OK.

At five thirty, Norway and I investigated downtown Manistee. The riverfront boardwalk was not open to pets, so we walked up and down the main street. It was mostly closed, with few people on the street and a lot of empty storefronts. It was interesting to contrast the lakefront towns. Some were vibrant and developed; others looked abandoned, dated, and dying.

We did interact with a few parents and kids who wanted to meet Norway. A father and daughter were across the street and waved us down—she really wanted to pet the dog!

As we approached them, he asked, "Is it OK if she pets your dog?"

"Of course," I said. "I think he'd like that."

As the daughter happily petted him, Norway turned his rear toward her. As she started to stroke his back, Norway leaned into her. She let out a surprise giggle.

"Looks like you have a new friend," I said to Norway. "Just don't knock her over."

Norway smiled and enjoyed the massage.

"He's a nice dog," the father said.

"Yeah, he's a good one. Terrific traveling companion."

I explained the towns we had visited. And asked, "Any places around here to eat with him?"

He mentioned the brewery.

"The lady at the motel suggested that place," I added.

The father pointed us in the right direction. After a final good-bye, Norway left his young friend and followed me to dinner. We found our way to North Channel Brewery. Although pets were not strictly allowed, they could sit just beyond the patio. They had water bowls set out for dogs, welcoming them as much as possible. I wondered if this was a Michigan regulation rather than the restaurant's choosing.

A family eating outside in the shaded patio offered to watch Norway while I ran inside to look at a menu and find a server. While I waited, through the window, I could see the family giving Norway playful attention. Eventually, I reached a waiter, and he handed me a menu. Immediately, I scanned and ordered a salad topped with chicken and the house apple cider vinaigrette. Then, quesadillas with salsa and chicken on top.

Overall, it was a terrific evening meal. As the sun was slowly passing, the temperature fell into the low sixties. They brought out an extra plate to pile the chicken onto. As I handed Norway chicken, I noticed the family next to us handing food to their three-year-old kid. After an hour—and lots of people greeting us as they passed the restaurant entrance—we paid the bill and headed back to the hotel.

We settled in the room. No cable, no internet. I returned to the front desk, and the nice woman was still there. I asked her to show me the remote-control features one more time. She walked with me back to the room. We entered, and Norway was lying on the second bed.

"Oh, no. Sorry," I cringed while Norway was relaxing in his comfortable spot.

She didn't mind at all. "My dogs always jump up."

The woman solved the Roku TV issue. Then showed that the cable must be hooked up to the antenna instead of the default cable setting. On the way out, she gave Norway a quick pet and offered to put a blanket on the floor. But, she admitted, "The bed does seem more comfortable for him!"

MANISTEE, MICHIGAN, to HOLLAND MICHIGAN

AT SEVEN THIRTY a.m., Norway was peacefully lying next to me on the double bed. We were up twice last night: 11:30 p.m. and 4:40 a.m. Otherwise, Norway snoozed on his bed—until he moved next to me on the small double bed. When Norway sleeps *next to me*, it usually means *on top of me* or *pressed against me*. He takes up as much space as he wishes.

Manistee Marina Motel got the job done. The walk-in shower had terrific water pressure and hot water. Places near water—lakes, harbors, and oceans—seem to have better free-flowing water. *Or, maybe that's just a coincidence?*

While packing items and luggage spread on the second bed, I tried the TV. It had the "cannot find connection" message. I clicked to the settings, moved it to "antenna," clicked "OK," and the TV turned on. *Got it!* Road trips can be educational.

We returned to Route 31 and headed south. At the Montague/Whitehall exit, we followed the 31 business route into the middle of the three-street Montague downtown to view the "World's

Largest Weathervane." It was impressive, standing forty-eight feet tall, with a twenty-six-foot wind arrow, and fourteen-foot replica of a schooner on top. There is a competing claim of "world's largest weathervane" in the Yukon. Standing with Oscar at Whitehorse International Airport, I viewed the Canadian DC-3 plane that spins on a pole when the wind changes direction. I think that airplane weathervane was bigger. But this one was certainly notable.

We walked around the sparse business district. I noted a nifty retro drive-up "Dogs n Suds," which served burgers and dogs. Also, the White River and the marina to White Lake provided some scenic shots. We got back in the car—or, rather, I dragged a bird-distracted Norway into the car—then crossed the White River, continued past Whitehall, and returned to Route 31.

Twenty miles south, we drove into downtown Muskegon, parking around the corner from the snowboarder sculpture. *The Turning Point* is a cool piece, sculpted in 2012 by artist Jason Dreweck. It honored Muskegon native Sherm Poppen's Snurfer and the birth of snowboarding. The metal sculpture has a ten-foot-high ribbon with one of Poppen's daughters riding the wave on a snurfer, the first mass-produced snowboard. At the base of the wave is a figure riding a modern snowboard. The trail represents the growth from humble beginning to Olympic sport.

Norway, in front of the snowboard sculpture,
eyeing the restaurant patio

Next to the statue was Dr. Rolf's Barbeque. A few people were eating on the patio, and their food looked good. With a dining area in the shade, around the corner from the car, this was a suitable spot. Norway and I retrieved his bowls from the car and took a break for lunch. I ordered delicious sweet potato quesadillas, with lots of BBQ sauces to choose from, and tater tots.

After lunch, I took a final look at the snowboarder sculpture. The mix of creative art, surfing, and skiing kept appealing to me. *Very cool!* We walked up and down Western Avenue, passing a Buster Keaton sculpture. The life-size statue was of Keaton, a Muskegon resident, standing behind a camera, filming the middle of the town's plaza.

In the area were murals, more statues, condos going up along the shoreline, and several restaurants. At the end was a strip of small shops. One had ice cream for me and Norway. The woman, who had five shelter dogs, donated proceeds to the local rescue.

Cool snacks for us in Muskegon

After the ice cream, we returned to investigate Matt's popcorn, a few doors down. The woman was showing the flavored popcorn to another visitor. "My husband makes it at home," she proudly emphasized. I love to support a local cause—plus, it's popcorn! I bought two huge bags, double caramel and kettle corn, which would last beyond the ride home.

We detoured inland on I-96 to Grand Rapids. Skipping the Meijer Gardens, because no pets were allowed, we tried other spots. It became the low point of the trip. There were signs indicating construction and the need to get off I-96.We exited and weaved through side streets and miraculously got to the Gerald Ford Museum and Library next to the Grand River in downtown.

What a mess. There were one-way streets, traffic, sparse parking, and congestion. We passed landmarks I had intended to check out. But it took a mile to reach open spaces. Instead of parking, I decided to drive to another spot. We ended at the bridge near 6th Street Park, the place we had entered before spending twenty-five minutes maneuvering through downtown. *Back to the start.* I put money in the meter, and we walked over the bridge and down Front Avenue to the "fish ladder" monument.

Like a lot of Grand Rapids, Fish Ladder Park was run-down, with graffiti and faded information signs. The exhibit was sort of cool, as I did see small fish trying to swim up the ladder. But, over-all, someone needed to upgrade the area.

We walked back across the bridge and to the car. I drove three blocks to the I-196 entrance. There was smooth sailing going east. But we had to go west, where the ramp was closed. We spent another thirty minutes trying to follow detours to the interstate.

"Not a fan of Grand Rapids," I mumbled, while Norway watched the spectacle from the passenger side. Eventually, we escaped and drove west to Holland.

Thirty miles later, we got off at the Holland/Zeeland exit. After ten minutes, I suspected I may have exited too early, so I turned around into more one-way streets, construction, and traffic. Back onto I-196. When we reached Saugatuck, I realized we had gone too far the other way. I used the opportunity to stop for gas, regroup, and turn around. Eventually, we drove into Holland, finally getting to the hotel.

In the end, the detour to Grand Rapids was a mistake. We never got to truly explore the town. And with the delays getting out of Grand Rapids, and passing Holland, it wasted over two hours that could have been better spent. By now, my blood was boiling from the frustrating driving conditions. Norway took it all in stride.

Our room was on the second floor, requiring longer trips to the car to pack and unpack. Although the room had few cable options, it did have one movie channel, which was showing *Crazy Rich Asians*, an entertaining film. Across from the fridge and microwave was a decent air conditioner. Norway was on the second bed, sleeping!

Throughout the movie, I checked the Wi-Fi. No connection. *Maybe there's something wrong with my laptop?* After an hour, I gave up. That summed up the day: just a lot of wasted time. Fortunately, there was no need to find another hotel. We were heading home tomorrow.

The hotel front desk provided free Holland maps. After a break in the room, we took another crack at Holland when traffic subsided. I woke up Norway and we went out. At seven o'clock, we had another two-plus hours of clear daylight. I drove back to 7th and Central, roughly where I had seen an interesting statue. A few blocks from there, we found free parking on the street.

Downtown Holland had a lot of nice shops and places to eat, with people sitting in patios on the sidewalks. Holland was a bit more upscale than Muskegon, and far more than Manistee. We found the statue of five people playing instruments. Then, I spotted Centennial Park, built in 1876. There was a big statue of the Dutch founder of this town. Plus, a cool flower creation of the *Wizard of Oz*. I met two guys in the park who mentioned that the man who wrote the *Wizard of Oz* used to vacation in the Holland area. As I looked at the display, Norway socialized with the two guys. They suggested going to the lakefront later. Specifically, Mount Pisgah Dunes and the overlook.

"If you climb to the top, you can see Lake Michigan on one side and the local Lake Macatawa on the other side." Two coasts!

After our walk around downtown, I followed the map to the shore. Among the line of cars in the area to view the sunset, I luckily found parking. However, I discovered the Pisgah Dunes boardwalk and trail did not allow dogs. Nix that plan.

All was not lost when we found Dune Dogz, an outdoor hot dog and ice cream joint. I ordered a chicken wrap and chips with lemonade for dinner. While waiting, a couple of kids came over to meet Norway. He rolled over and encouraged belly rubs … until the food came out. Our last evening was pleasant: seventy degrees and no bugs or mosquitoes. We finished with good soft-serve ice cream for dessert. Norway's vanilla cup came with two mini-dog treats on top.

As it grew dark, we walked back to the car. When we returned to the hotel at ten o'clock, the lot was relatively empty. *If the rooms aren't filling up, why not drop the rates?* This was the third hotel that was rather expensive, yet its parking lot was almost empty.

I grabbed my bag, two treats, and a water bowl for Norway. We settled in the room. Fifteen minutes later, Norway ate the biscuit and tried to bury the other snack in the bed. Having no luck at hiding his treat, he went to sleep instead.

HOLLAND, MICHIGAN, to HOME

NORWAY WOKE UP once at four a.m. I put on my shoes and got ready to take him out, but he didn't come to the door. Instead, he jumped into my bed. These middle-of-the-night escapades were killers—however, no accidents in the room. *I will take it!* I climbed back into bed, leaving my shoes on in case he changed his mind.

We got up at seven thirty. The weather had improved all week. It began with hot, humid temperatures in Green Bay. After a bit of rain on days two and three, the temps cooled down. And the last two days had been rather pleasant and sunny.

We left the Microtel parking lot and connected to Route 31 South. A Holland map found in the hotel's collection of tourist brochures proved to be quite helpful. We drove five miles south to Saugatuck to check out a "human-powered chain ferry." Just before we reached town, I noticed a turnoff for Saugatuck Dunes. This would be a great opportunity to see Lake Michigan Dunes and get some walking miles with Norway.

We found the dunes parking lot beside a path. We entered the dirt trail into the woods and started trotting along. Some of the dirt turned into sand. *Cool.* Then we walked. And walked. And walked. *How far do we have to go?* There were path markers along the way, so I didn't worry about finding our way back. Eventually, we spotted an opening in the woods. Suddenly, we were on sand and peering out at Lake Michigan!

Pressing his paws in the sand

In the distance, a couple appeared and walked along the water. Otherwise, it was isolated, empty coastline. Norway ran up and down the shoreline, drinking and cooling himself off. After fifteen minutes, we retraced our steps back to the car.

We drove to downtown Saugatuck and stopped near the "chain ferry." Active since 1838, it claimed to be the only chain-driven ferry in use, connecting Oval Beach to downtown Saugatuck. It was amusing to watch the conductor turn the crank that moved the ferry a few hundred feet across the Kalamazoo River. The process reminded me of riding in a paddle boat. Sort of leisurely and not as fast as a motorized transport, but it was pleasant, nostalgic, and did the trick. In the end, it beat driving around the entire waterway.

After watching the ferry come and go, I walked along the riverfront with Norway. Next to the ferry dock was a pretty green park area that featured a colorful mosaic painting on the bathroom building. Around the four sides of the restroom was a replica of George Seurat's famous painting *A Sunday on La Grande Jatte.*

We came back along another street, passing the nice shops and cafes. Again, I recalled the towns we had seen this week—some more developed; some nicer. Some had more notable sights to see, and others were more run-down or had less to offer.

After the Saugatuck visit, we cruised down Route 31 and I-196. Eventually, it merged into I-94. Next, we went to Union Pier, MI. My mom had fond recollections of her summers spent there in the 1950s. Now, it seemed to be one road with a pizza place, an ice cream shop, a bakery, swimming and recreational items, and a post office. Off the main strip were lake rentals and houses, plus private spots with private beach access. Ironically, a notable one was "Gordon Beach" (Gordon is my mother's family name).

After lunch at Mario's Pizza, we hit the road. Since we had seen the Saugatuck Dunes, I bypassed the Indiana Dunes turnoff. I was ready to go home. Mostly, I didn't want to chance running into rush-hour traffic in Chicago.

The last sixty miles took over two and a half hours due to construction, an accident, and just awful traffic. Eventually, we pounded our way through downtown and up to the north side of Chicago to home. We had finished our 1,323-mile lap around Lake Michigan.

Bring Norway

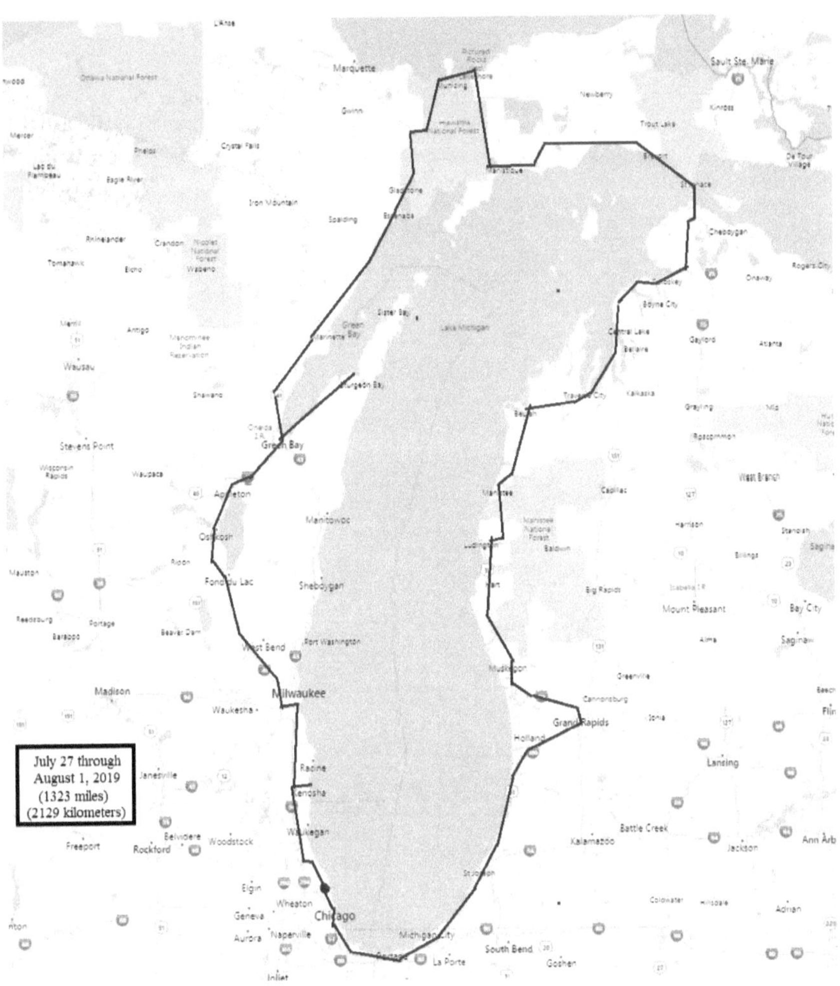

PART V

THE HEARTLAND

I'D HAD ENOUGH of the COVID mandates. After months in *Pritzker Prison*, I wanted to get out and taste pre-COVID freedom. On television, I watched stores opening, with people out and about in other states. However, it was still East Germany in Illinois.

I looked at the US map, checked the governors' mandates in other states, and plotted my path through Iowa and Nebraska to South Dakota. I was delighted with anticipation to see mask-free open businesses and happy people firsthand.

Ready to hit the road

EVANSTON, ILLINOIS, to DAVENPORT, IOWA

THE FIRST FIFTY miles went as expected. Midmorning traffic on the I-90/94 Expressway, construction on I-90 through Chicago, and industrial odor along I-55 just south of the city. Once the interstate met I-80 West, the road cleared, leaving big trucks and us. During the first hour, Norway was excited with anticipation. In the second hour, he comfortably slept in the back with his stuffed animal, blanket, and pillows.

We stopped in Ottawa, IL. Two years earlier, Norway and I had taken a weekend excursion to the Starved Rock area. After hiking in the afternoon, we explored the town, had dinner, and spent the night at a hotel in Ottawa. During today's midway driving break, we went to Washington Park to see the Lincoln vs. Douglas fountain and a mural commemorating the historic day. In the center of the park, two large bronze figures stood in the middle of a reflecting pool at the site of the first Lincoln-Douglas debate in 1858.

Norway at the Lincoln vs. Douglas fountain

We walked through town, passing several murals, and stopped to look at the "Radium Girl" figure. The bronze statue was unveiled in 2011, almost ninety years after the radium girls sued a dial company. They had spent years working at the company, putting bits of glowing paint on watch dials. To keep the strokes sharp, the women were encouraged to lick the tips of the paintbrushes. Unfortunately, the glow from the paint came from radium, which was toxic. Although the workers became ill, the company denied any effects, until a group of workers—the radium girls—went to the press and the courtrooms. Eventually, they won the lawsuit, and the practice stopped. The statue depicts a girl holding paintbrushes and a wilting tulip, representing the likely harm as a result.

We finished our walk at Tangled Roots Brewery and Lone Buffalo. The lunchtime waitress saw us through the window. She came outside and asked if we would like to sit at a table. The whole area seemed empty due to the damp weather or it being Tuesday. Or, COVID closures?

She brought out a bowl of water for Norway, saving me a trip back to the car. Then, I ordered a veggie burger, French fries, and a salad.

Although pricier than two years ago, the lunch was solid, and the conversation with the waitress was very pleasant; we mostly talked about Norway and her two dogs at home.

"Your puppy is so sweet."

"Norway is a good one. Actually, he is six."

"Really? He looks younger."

"He's got a young spirit. And still makes a mess." I pointed at her pants. "Sorry about that."

"It's OK. Mine shed on my black outfits before I go to work!" Norway's extra white fur was no bother.

After lunch, we did one more lap around town. A guy was leaving a shop with a little dog in his arms. Attracted to Norway, the little dog started yipping. I stepped to the side to prevent Norway from getting excited. But, as I was walking away, the guy asked, "Where are you from?"

"Just north of Chicago," I answered.

He told me he used to live in River North Chicago until moving to Ottawa. He was fifty-eight years old and "done with the nightlife. Too old to hit the bars," he went on. "Nice to get away from the city."

"So, you ended up down here?" Ottawa is a nice area near Starved Rock. But it was different from the city.

With a mask under his chin, he took a sip of his Starbucks latte. Then, he mentioned losing his theater production business due to COVID. Now, he was trying to figure out how to "reinvent himself" for the next few years until he could receive Social Security. He mentioned half-jokingly that "I should get a grift where I get money from dumb Trump people."

"What do you mean?"

"Look at all the money the dumb Trump voters give him," he said. Then, he grumbled about the vaccine, the Delta variant, and MAGA. *Awkward.* I doubt he realized I was the wrong audience. Although from Evanston, I was not a registered Democrat. I was a dumb Trump voter.

He took a drag from his vape and continued to opine and vent, assuming I shared his political views.

"He's been out of office for six months," I gently reminded him.

"Yeah, but he made a mess that Biden is fixing," Then he added, "If all the MAGA people would get the vaccine, things would be much better."

I looked down at Norway. *Well, at least you got your shots.* I waited for the disenchanted man to pause his rant, wished him luck, then we politely tiptoed away. That was too much negative energy for us.

Norway and I hit the road and cruised down I-80. Soon we reached Port Byron, a nice little spot for a driving break and walk. Along an open view of the flowing Mississippi River stood a thirty-foot-tall fiberglass bicyclist. Built in 2013, the old-timer on a penny-farthing high-wheel bicycle was given the friendly name Will B. Rolling.

Norway with Will B. Rolling

We followed Illinois Route 84 along the Mississippi on the Great River Trail. It winded into IL-92, down to Rock Island. Then, we crossed the bridge into Davenport, Iowa. I observed a lot of casinos, lotto ads, bars, and microbrews. *Was this the post-COVID world? Was it always this way along the Mississippi River? Or was this the new economy?*

In Davenport, we drove up Route 61/Brady Street, passing 34th Street, then 46th Street. When we went by 76th Street, I could see the Best Western off a utility road. We needed to turn around and drive back down Brady, south to 67th Street. Trying one of the crossroads, we found it.

The receptionist at the Best Western was a super-nice woman. Norway reached to have a look, placing his front paws on the high counter. The woman gave a kind smile and checked us in.

"How many keys do you want?" Hmm, most just give me two without asking.

I said, "One is all we need." Norway would just chew his anyway.

When I asked about the hotel restaurant, she said it was good. "Locals, not just travelers, actually go there to eat."

"How 'bout the Chinese takeout?"

"It's OK," she said. Not a good endorsement, but I was glad the receptionist was being candid. She mentioned several pizza places that delivered. Otherwise, most of the restaurants were a decent drive away.

"I think we'll give the next-door place a try." And take a driving break.

The Prairie Grille Restaurant was terrific. The guy on the phone was very polite and helpful, even delivering the order to us outside. As I signed for the tab and tip, we chatted about Norway and rescues. While he loved dogs, he worked too much to have one. Instead, he had adopted several cats.

I took a quick peek at the bags of dinner. Chicken nachos, a house salad, and chicken breast for Norway. We said good-bye and returned to the room.

Norway gobbled up the restaurant's chicken, leaving his dry dog food in the bowl. Then, he found a comfortable spot on the bed. Norway was worn out. I was tired and glad I had decided to drive two hundred miles to Davenport instead of two hundred seventy miles to Iowa City. *Slow and easy.*

At ten o'clock, I climbed into bed. Norway scooted over. Then, he jumped off the bed and lay on the carpet. Fifteen minutes later, he was breathing heavily and wide awake. So, I relented and did a lap around the Best Western with him.

On the way back to the lobby, the gentleman from the restaurant came outside. "Hey, how were the nachos?" he called out.

"They were great." I was pleased he remembered us. "Plus, he loved the chicken breast."

The gentleman and another guy leaned over to greet Norway. After a few minutes, he finished his shift and drove home. The other guy went back inside. Norway and I returned through the lobby, past the hotel pool, where a girl was swimming as her mom watched. *Swimming at ten thirty at night? Kids!*

Inside the room, Norway was back on the bed, relaxing.

DAVENPORT, IOWA, to CLIVE, IOWA

AFTER A SOUND sleep, we were ready to see what Iowa would bring. Following a quick shower, I took Norway for a lap around the hotel. The Best Western Plus Steeplegate provided lots of walking space to enjoy the seventies temperature and pleasant breeze, and Norway was on high alert, sensing the scents in the area.

By seven thirty a.m., the parking lot was mostly clear. With travelers in and out and the truckers long gone, the path through the breakfast area was easy. Next to a selection of "grab & go" items, I picked fruit, water, juice, and eggs in a Styrofoam cup for Norway. Back at the room, I found the receipt for the stay: *$130 for room. $30 for dinner. $15 for tax. $20 for pet fee. $196 total.* In Davenport, Iowa. On a Tuesday. The hotel parking lot was half empty. Were these Best Western prices or inflation in the entire hotel industry?

We went to nearby LeClaire to find its Freedom Rock. In 1999, Ray "Bubba" Sorensen first painted a giant boulder in Menlo, IA, to give recognition to military veterans. With the help of individual donations, he began painting rocks in each of the ninety-nine counties of Iowa. Every illustration is vibrant, with special paint used for the rock surfaces, producing a unique, meaningful attraction. During the winter, Bubba can be found painting indoor murals. The rest of the year, he travels around touching up Freedom Rocks around the state.

We viewed the Scott County Freedom Rock at a lovely spot off the Mississippi River. The impressive seven-and-a-half-ton painted boulder demonstrated Bubba's natural talent as well as skills polished while studying art in college. The colorful artwork, the symbolism, and the dedication plaza nicely accented the LeClaire riverfront.

Freedom Rock along the Mississippi River

Located opposite of Port Byron, IL, I could see the giant bicyclist in the distance across the river.

After admiring the Freedom Rock, we looked at a Wild Bill Hickok information board. Then we finished going down the main street. We met two older men seated and having coffee. The eighty-plus-year-old guy owned the coffee shop, and his friend was a local resident. They had a bowl of water, which Norway went after. Then, the gentle old man started petting Norway.

We had a forty-five-minute conversation about many topics, including LeClaire's history along the Mississippi River. During the 1800s, most riverboats needed a tug or river pilot to maneuver through the rocky fifteen-mile stretch of rapids. Otherwise, they risked damage from hitting a jagged rock. While the captains waited for available guides—or ship repairs—they stayed in the town. The rapids, rocks, and river-centric industries fueled LeClaire's early growth.

"How's the town doing?" I asked. "I see a bunch of construction."

"OK," they said. "Some of the shops adjusted during COVID. But we benefited from the Illinois people coming over here."

"I'll bet," I said. "Illinois is still locked down. The difference between here and over the border is noticeable."

"Yes," the guy said. "If you look above the road, it leads to nicer homes along the water. People are coming here, and many are building."

I looked up and down the main street, gauging if the tourism and locals could generate more commercial development. The location seemed a worthy alternative to Wisconsin and Michigan summer homes.

Norway and I left LeClaire and began our trek west across Iowa. In Walcott, we found a truck museum, where I could see old rigs from long ago. Nearby, a giant mural provided a solid I-80 photo opp. *Who knew the World's Largest Truck Stop would be a notable spot?* The scene was complete with rows of truckers parked at this Iowa fueling stop.

To get a photo of Norway and me, I scanned the area. A guy with a red "Make America Great Again" cap came up.

"Nice hat," I said.

He hesitated, then engaged in conversation. He and his family lived a hundred miles west of Chicago. "We have an old dog at home," his wife said while she and the grandkids petted Norway.

Norway and Lance hitting the road

Fifteen miles west, we pulled into Wilton to visit another Freedom Rock and a century-old candy store. Norway and I scouted around the one-street business district. I like classic small towns. There is always something to find and learn. Plus, in a small town, you have time to see everything!

We started at the Muscatine County Freedom Rock, which was dedicated on Labor Day 2020. Beside the railroad tracks and depot was a nice plaza with a pre–Civil War cannon, and a concrete star adorned with flowers—a tribute to the veterans. The centerpiece was the Freedom Rock containing painted scenes of Wilton military veterans and heroes.

As it started to pour rain, Norway and I found a spot under a storefront eave. A nice woman from the chamber of commerce office poked her head outside.

"You're welcome to come inside and wait out the rain," she offered.

"With him?" I asked.

"Yes, he can come in."

Since Norway was wet, I declined the kind offer. If we went inside, Norway would have given a big shake and sprayed water everywhere.

Around the corner, we visited the Candy Kitchen. Originally a confectionery constructed in 1860, the current shop opened in 1910. The nostalgic place had a candy store and classic soda fountain. The interior was very appealing, with a marble counter, walnut booths, and glass lamps. I appreciated how businesses like this carry through time. It had survived the Great Depression, World War II shortages, and decades of change. *Maybe they have a mail order and an internet market? Do they have enough local business to get by?* Hopefully, the Wilton population of three thousand and its visitors would provide enough support. Since the outside seating was not covered, I bought a few old-time candy bars and soda for later.

After much rain and time in Wilton, we cruised west on I-80. Since Norway was sleeping, we skipped the driving break and continued past the next Freedom Rock site and succession of small-town exits. Along I-80, I noted several Trump signs in the cornfields. So far, the sights in Iowa were a variety. Wide open fields with rows of ready-to-be-picked corn contrasted with unnatural wind farms of towering windmills.

After two hours, we reached Des Moines. It was bigger than I expected—a bustling city with mazes of highways, interstates, and expressways woven throughout. *I should have printed out more detailed maps.* Luckily, I guessed correctly and took I-80/I-35 instead of I-235. My piece of the Des Moines map, with a hunch, got us to the hotel.

At the Best Western Plus, the receptionist recognized the USAA credit card.

"Were you in the military?" he asked.

"I was not. My father briefly served. And, my brother had a long career in the army. Much of it overseas," I added. "How about you?"

He himself had been stationed in Germany from 1989 to 1991 before going to Iraq. *Much respect.* After the brief greeting, Norway and I went down the hall to our room. Inside, we found a couch and one bed. The air conditioner was rolling.

This Best Western was in a central location with lots of stores and other businesses. We stopped in at PetSmart to pick up a stain-and-odor removal spray. Forgot to pack it. While unlikely we would need it, we were prepared in case of an accident. The storefront had a COVID health notice but no restrictions. Inside, half the customers were wearing masks; the other half were not. I appreciated the freer atmosphere, and Norway enjoyed strolling up and down the aisles.

For dinner, we tried Tasty Tacos in West Des Moines. They had good prices and cranked out the takeout quickly. Chicken taco, chicken taco salad, and burrito. We returned to the hotel for our *fiesta*. We passed through the lobby of the hotel, where guests were watching Tucker Carlson on television. They nodded and smiled as Norway and I walked past. In the room, Norway gobbled the chicken. Then he offered to help me with my salad and burrito.

CLIVE, IOWA, to FREMONT, NEBRASKA

WE SKIPPED EXPLORING Des Moines. Its size and layout made sightseeing an extra effort, so I was content to move on to the next place. We started at Menlo, the site of Adair County's Freedom Rock. This one felt like part of a scavenger hunt. In the middle of open fields, off the side of Iowa Highway 25, was a metal shed with information, photos, and a pen with spiral notebook for visitors to sign. Then, we looked at the beautifully painted rock—the first one by "Bubba" Sorensen near his hometown of Greenfield, IA. This mural honored Pat Tillman and other historic armed service volunteers. On the other side was an illustration of a POW from the Greenfield/Menlo area. It was another special tribute to those who defend the country.

Admiring Pat Tillman and heroes on the Freedom Rock

Norway and I were alone looking at it. The rural area and pond provided a peaceful surrounding for the nice dedication. Occasionally a truck would go by on the gravel road. It seemed the spot did not get the traffic it deserved. *Maybe add an I-80 road-side sign?*

We took another detour off I-80 to see the Coon Rapids entry sign. The town entrance would be a good photo op of the corn and heart of Iowa. Unfortunately, thirty minutes later, we found out the sign was under construction! We had driven out of the way for nothing, although it gave us a chance to see the rural farmland.

As we circled around back toward the main interstate, I kept an eye out for other options. I decided to visit Audubon, population two thousand. The pleasant town center had a nice walking area, including a park and over two hundred bird mosaics. *Perhaps Audubon is related to the Audubon Society?* Down the street was a slick clock on a corner Victorian building. The stained-glass clock was twenty-one feet tall and featured John James Audubon with his dog, Zephyr, beside him. Audubon City and Audubon County, Iowa, were named after the naturalist, artist, and ornithologist.

Located a mile down the road was a feature attraction: Albert the Bull. At almost thirty feet tall and fifteen feet from horn to horn, it claimed to be the world's largest. While there was construction to update the fifty-year-old guy, at least it was visible.

Back on I-80, we made a brief stop to see "the beetle"—a black-painted Volkswagen beetle body suspended on eight giant black metal legs. Nifty piece of artwork. And then a stop in Shelby to see "the giant stalk"—a towering metal artistic sculpture of corn. There was a small park and nature trail next to the gas station, a suitable spot to give Norway a stretch. Also, it was next to a cornfield. *Funny, this is the first time I got a close look at a six-foot-tall mature corn crop.*

Edge of an Iowa cornfield

Thirty minutes later, we arrived in Omaha, Nebraska. With a general map of the area, we followed some winding roads off the interstate. We stopped at a street beside a stadium, which turned out to be Ameritrade Park, where the College World Series is played each year.

The entire area was empty. I checked one of the parking meters. *Seventy-five cents per hour! What a bargain!* I called Ariel, a friend who lived just outside of Omaha, to confirm a meeting time for dinner.

I put away the phone, grabbed Norway's items, and scanned the area. Ahead was the Bob Kerrey Pedestrian Bridge. This was an ideal spot. I poured six quarters into the meter, and Norway and I started exploring. We walked through the stadium lot and toward the bridge, then reached a fence surrounding the stadium. *Awesome, someone plowed open a three-foot section.* Norway and I squeezed through instead of having to figure out a way around the fence. Then, up a hill. Across a street. And there was the bridge! *That was a fortunate shortcut.*

We ascended the spiral ramp and walked along the bridge, above the Missouri River, with views of the Omaha area. Norway was greeted by lots of kids. Occasionally, we passed other dogs. Halfway across the Bob Bridge, we turned around and faced the stadium and horizon. Beside the bridge was a lovely park area with ground fountains that kids were playing in.

Norway playing in the fountain

We finished along a path with another view of the Missouri River, local sculptures, and OMAR the Troll. OMAR (Omaha Metro Area River), a blue sculpted figure, lived under the bridge, hung around, and welcomed visitors.

When we returned to the car, my stomach began rumbling. Luckily, there was a bar open. Nobody around, but this bar was open. I went inside and got a soda to go and used their facilities. Mission accomplished. *Norway has his way. I have mine.*

On the way out, we did a quick reconnaissance through the town. We saw the old market and other parts as I followed the gridded streets to 7th Street. In front of the ConAgra product development building stood the bronze statue of Chef Boyardee, the premiere face of canned pasta products.

A few blocks away stood a metal fork in a wad of metal spaghetti. Located in Little Italy, it looked like it was randomly set next to someone's house. The fifteen-foot-tall sculpture was named *Stile di Famiglia* meaning "family style." The artist, Jake Balcom, was inspired by the idea of a big family sitting for dinner, everyone talking about their week and enjoying the company. It was a cool piece of artwork.

I took the Omaha side streets to I-480, then followed route 75 north, aiming for Fremont. The roadway turned into a slow road with traffic lights. *Are we going the wrong way?* After a quick turn-around, we resumed heading north on US-75 and eventually found ourselves on Route NE-36. There were turns to other highways. *Do we take I-29 /I-680? Or, stay on NE-36?* Fortunately, one block later I saw a sign: "Fremont - 30 miles." Bingo! We stayed on NE-36, straight to Fremont. *How lucky was that?*

When we got to Fremont, I called Ariel. She helped with suggestions, including a new restaurant to try.

"Is there outdoor seating for the dog?"

She checked. "No, there is no patio for a dog. The only outdoor options seem to be places like Buffalo Wild Wings."

Then I suggested, "On the road, Norway and I will often get takeout. Then, we find a park and eat outside."

It worked! The restaurant had takeout, and Ariel knew of a park three blocks from the hotel.

It was a wonderful picnic with Mitch, Ariel, and their daughter, Aubrey. We talked about a range of topics, including our 29,029' hiking experience in Sun Valley, traveling, his training for a hundred-mile run, growing up in Nebraska, and sights to see. The food was terrific, and Norway enjoyed their company.

After dinner, I asked about dessert suggestions. They recommended Zesto's soft serve. To cap it off, I picked up a cherry sundae for me and a vanilla pup cup and cookie for Norway.

Snacks

We returned to the hotel. The superior Fairfield was unavailable and quite expensive when you included the pet fee. So I had settled for the Super 8 next door. Big difference. At less than half the price, the shabby, run-down Super 8 building had chipped paint, stained carpeting, and smelled a bit of smoke. Our room seemed drenched in disinfectant cleaner. At least the trucks parked in the lot were well-maintained, so the clientele seemed OK. Later, we met a couple of guys. One had caked dirt on his truck—he was a crop worker.

On the upside, the room did have HBO and Cinemax movies. I listened to a podcast and booked rooms for the next three driving legs into the Black Hills area. Meanwhile, Norway finished his ice cream and was lounging in the cool bathtub.

FREMONT, NEBRASKA, to NORTH PLATTE, NEBRASKA

MANY YEARS AGO, I made my first trip across Nebraska. I was moving from Arizona to Chicago, which required a drive through the middle of the country. I remembered Nebraska being uneventful, like Kansas—just a place I wanted to cruise through. Now, I have a much different perspective. From years of road trips with Oscar and Norway, I realized there are sights to see almost everywhere, including Nebraska.

At seven a.m., I walked with Norway around the hotel concrete parking lot. There were some grassy spots by the Fairfield Inn next door. Otherwise, Buffalo Wild Wings and asphalt commercial places bordered the Super 8. Norway sniffed around the area.

"No dumpster diving," I implored him.

Sometimes Norway would pick up a leftover fast-food item or wrapper. If it was a worthy scrap, there was no way to pry his mouth open.

I kept the walking around brief. Time to get out of here and explore Nebraska. We drove south on Highway 77 to Lincoln, pausing briefly to see the big metal "paper airplane" at the Lincoln Airport entrance. It was kind of a nifty sculpture off the side of the road, twenty-three feet high with a wingspan of twenty feet. It did look like a paper airplane. Installed in 2015, this piece of public art weighed 14,000 pounds. *What does a small Cessna aircraft weigh?*

We took the freeway into downtown Lincoln. Navigation to the capitol area was very easy. Not much traffic, plus I could see the big buildings in the distance. On approach, we followed the grid-like one-way streets to the capitol building. Friday morning parking was no problem.

We walked around the block, passing the governor's mansion and some special historical buildings. Also, Norway enjoyed their ornate water sources. He dipped his face in the capitol fountain. Then, further along the plaza, he was enticed by the cool water path of the Missouri River fountain. The entire area was a terrific place for our morning walk.

After a quick stop at the "brick head," an interesting sculpture next to fountains, we went through the University of Nebraska to see the football stadium. Among the sights were Tom Osbourne Highway, statues and championships, and a hall of fame. "Big Red" banners flew everywhere. Pure Cornhusker football.

Back on I-80, we cranked out miles until the Grand Island and Hastings combo stop. At mile 312, we exited north on Highway 281 to see Grand Island. We visited "Fred's Flying Circus," which consisted of mini-cars mounted on poles. The funny cartoon cars demonstrated incredible craftsmanship by the founder of the custom auto shop. I wish viewers could have gone inside, but we could see the sculptures between and over the fencing.

Next, we headed south on Highway 281 back over the I-80 to Hastings. Home of Kool-Aid! Along First Street, we passed statues in the town while visiting the birthplace of the sweet drink. Then, at Fourteenth Street, we stopped outside the Hastings Museum to view several cool statues and history exhibits. Plus the footprints of Kool-Aid Man.

Cooling off next to the Kool-Aid building

After a quick pit stop at Jimmy John's, we drove fifteen miles back to I-80 and started cruising along. We tried the Kearney Archway, but pets could not go inside and they closed at five. Outside were notable bronze sculptures. Also, I liked the nearby maze attraction. We went above to look.

Eying the I-80 traffic passing under Kearney Archway

On the drive out, I saw five high school teens get out of a car, walk across the street, and throw fishing lines into the water. Nebraska summer!

We ended the day one hundred miles farther in North Platte. I had hoped to shorten the leg to Kearney, but I couldn't find a hotel that took dogs. I wondered about South Dakota. *Will I have trouble booking last-minute hotels with Norway? Maybe I need to book rooms a few days in advance?*

NORTH PLATTE, NEBRASKA, to CHADRON, NEBRASKA

I PREFER ROOMS with two beds, leaving extra space for luggage, electronic accessories, and Norway. Sometimes he picks the second bed. Otherwise, he chooses to hog mine. Last night, Norway moved around in my bed. Then, he went into the shower area. Eventually, he returned and settled in the other bed. Nevertheless, we got enough sleep.

I tossed last night's takeout leftovers. Luigi's pasta sampler of manicotti, lasagna, and penne was OK. I sensed the food tasted better in the restaurant. Norway's chicken and rigatoni dish was adequate, but it might have been too spicy for him. I wish they'd had pizza available. *Better luck next time.*

I jumped into the shower and wiped away the dog prints with my feet. The Motel 6 had soap but no shampoo, so I used some that I had collected at other hotels. After listening to part of the War Room podcast, I turned on the television. *Raiders of the Lost Ark* and *Full Monty* were showing on HBO. While letting Norway rest, I caught up with photos, trip notes, and emails. Since there was no complimentary breakfast, I snacked on two oranges and a granola bar saved from yesterday's "to-go" bag.

While Motel 6 lacked some amenities, it provided a game-changer: a rack of tourist brochures at the entrance. I skimmed over the samples and pulled one from Alliance. We were headed there to see Carhenge. At the bottom of the rack was a detailed highway map of Western Nebraska. That was the entire region we were doing today!

We started down the road at the 20th Century Veterans' Memorial. The notable North Platte site was located just south of I-80 on the Highway 83 route to town. It was worth a stop for anyone traveling through, highlighted by a 16x60-foot engraved brick mural depicting the five major conflicts of the twentieth century. The bronze statues and tributes along the walkway were impressive and a noteworthy dedication to military men and women who served.

Norway strolling along the heroes. A salute!

We departed I-80 at the US-26 connection and traveled northwest. Between Lisco and Broadwater, we stopped at a Nebraska historical marker near mile 83. In the middle of nowhere was a roomy pull-off and a plaque to read about the area. This one offered a history about Narcissa Whitman, one of the first white women to cross the continent in the 1830s. She, her husband, and a group of Protestant missionaries passed through this part of Nebraska and continued to Oregon. It was a noteworthy piece of nineteenth-century history.

Bunches of these were randomly placed on the highways. I find historical markers are hit and miss, from inane to interesting. Most are just a quick stop if you decide to check them out.

Norway in the backseat enjoying the view

Throughout the day, I observed the changing landscapes of Nebraska. As we headed west and north, there was a gradual transition from corn crops to plains. Eventually, there would be ridges and even a forest.

We reached Chimney Rock, a cool natural wonder. Reminiscent of Devils Tower and Pompeys Pillar, the formation springs out of an open plain, rising almost three hundred feet. As I took photos and let Norway wander, I noticed a gentleman taking pictures with a professional camera.

"Can I trouble you for a photo of me and my dog?"

"Of course," he replied.

He was a pro and took nice shots with my phone's camera. I learned he was from Lincoln, working for the Nebraska foundation that managed all the region's federal places. He explained that after eighteen months of renovation, they were reopening this museum. He had traveled to Chimney Rock for the ribbon-cutting, which explained why he was carrying giant scissors.

View of Chimney Rock

After talking to the Nebraska museum guy, I weighed going to Scotts Bluff National Monument. Ten minutes later, we were at the crossroads. Left turn would go to the monument twenty-five miles away; right turn would skip it and continue our travels.

Feeling tired, I began driving to the right. Then, at the last second, I U-turned the car. *Ugh. It is a national monument.* Mount

Rushmore is also a national monument. If we were thirty minutes away and I skipped it, only to find out later we should have gone, it would kill me! Norway was fine either way.

On the way to Scotts Bluff, I followed the wrong sign and got lost. I turned around and went into a gas station. Inside, a woman corrected my path. The thirty-minute ride stretched to over forty-five minutes. *Oh well. We are here.*

Entrance to Scotts Bluff

Scotts Bluff was worth the detour, with amazing views, especially when you drive up a road to the top. It was a little nerve-racking ascending the winding hills with no rails, through some bored-out tunnels. But at the top was a sweet panorama.

The ride back down the hills went much easier. At the bottom, we parked in a lot and checked out a stretch of information boards and attractions. Then, Norway found an appealing spot in the shade.

"Come on, buddy. Let's get rolling."

He decided not to get up from his cool, grassy spot. When I tried to lift him, he resisted with an annoyed look. I walked away and came back five minutes later.

"Ready to go?"

He didn't care. He had his spot. I could neither persuade nor drag him. I listened to music. I went to the car to get a drink. Norway did not move.

Shady spot at Scotts Bluff

Oh my gosh. We are not going anywhere until he is ready. Maybe Norway needed to rest his paw pads. The hot temps, mixed with pavement, asphalt, and gravel areas, might have made them sensitive. *Perhaps he was tired of me dragging him around?* In the end, he wanted to enjoy his little shaded grass oasis!

I hoped someone with a dog would pass by and rouse Norway, but it didn't happen. After an hour, Norway was ready to proceed. I offered him water and a treat. Then he climbed into the car.

We backtracked on Highway 26 and connected to Highway 385 north toward Alliance, and northeast to see Carhenge. I missed the turnoff to Route 87 and had to backtrack for fifteen minutes. Late in the day, this was not good for morale. But the detour to Carhenge was worth it!

The attraction was unique as well as the background story behind it. The artist, Jim Reinders, studied Stonehenge first-hand while living in England. In 1987, he created a replica of the world-famous English Stonehenge, constructed of old cars. The Nebraska automobiles were placed in the same proportions as the original stone. Carhenge's mix of old and new cars, with car parts covered in gray spray paint, had aged quite well.

Cruising around Carhenge

Among the crowd of visitors was a family with a five-year-old female husky. When Norway and she crossed paths, it was a good meet-and-greet for thirty seconds. Then, Norway did his growl and posture: tail wagging and wanting to mix it up. While we walked around the fields, he kept eyeing the husky, wanting to play!

At the exit, we recognized two families from an hour earlier at Scotts Bluff. All of us seemed to be on the same western Nebraska route. *Will we see them at Mt. Rushmore?*

We wound our way back to Highway 385 and headed north toward Chadron. The terrain changed suddenly to plush mountainous pine. We had entered the Chadron State Park. It was a preview of the Black Hills terrain we would see in coming days. The elevation was about five thousand feet, and the scenic forest was filled with ponderosa pines.

Ten miles north of the park, we saw the "Welcome to Chadron" marker. I noticed the Best Western emblem right at the entrance to town. I veered off the road into the parking lot. *Excellent: I don't have to look for the hotel.*

The room was a delight, dark and cool with the air conditioner cranking. Two big beds, with a table, cabinets, a microwave, a fridge, coffee/hot water, and more. A nice place to stop for the night. I noticed the clock and was pleased to realize that somewhere we had changed time zones. An hour of travel time was recovered!

I searched the local restaurants, hoping for pizza, but there was no locally owned pizza place. Just Pizza Hut and Dominoes. Upon review with Norway, we went with reliable Taco John's. Oscar and I had gone to a few during previous western road trips, and it worked great. Ten cars were lined up in the drive-thru. Inside, there was no one waiting. I ordered chicken taco salad and a chicken and bean burrito with guacamole and sauce. Norway and I ate dinner in the front patio, finishing our delightful meal as it started to sprinkle.

Back at the hotel, we were greeted by the young receptionist who was sitting with her two friends. *Is this their Chadron Friday night hangout?* They lit up when they saw Norway. I brought him over, and Norway soaked up the attention!

In the hotel room, Norway enjoyed his post-dinner bone. I listened to a podcast, had a candy bar from the vending machine, and looked at tomorrow's route and weather forecast. Hopefully, the light rain would pass.

As I uploaded the day's photos, I was very pleased. Western Nebraska was a wonderful spot to visit. Plus, picking Chadron, just outside of South Dakota, was a terrific springboard to the Black Hills. In hindsight, I wish we had booked a second day here. This was a good place to recharge before the next section of our road trip.

CHADRON, NEBRASKA, to LEAD, SOUTH DAKOTA

I WOKE UP and scanned the room. *Where's Norway?*

I stepped into the bathroom, and he popped his head up. He looked quite content in the cool bathtub. *At least, he didn't tear open the hotel soap and shampoo!*

Norway in the bathtub

While Norway chilled, I went down the hall to grab a banana, juice, and a muffin. When I returned to the room, he greeted me at the door.

"Sorry, no eggs." I handed him a piece of my muffin and a few dog treats.

After packing up, we checked out. A half mile from the hotel stood another historical marker. It displayed an interesting north-western Nebraska story related to local Sioux leaders. I read the multi-board displays, from the Dawes County and Nebraska State Historical Societies, filled with photos, a historic timeline, and mid-1800s settlement maps. Besides the history itself of the Sioux, gold settlers, and fur traders, I appreciated the preservation of these American West stories.

We started today's drive on Highway 385 North toward South Dakota. The Nebraska-South Dakota border did not have a "Welcome to …" sign. Instead, there was a "Casino at state line" board. A random casino appeared in the middle of nowhere. Then, the mile markers began at 2, 3, 4, and on. I guess it was more notice-able—and more profitable—to put up a border casino rather than a "You're now entering South Dakota" welcome sign.

Ten miles further, we reached Oelrichs, SD, and parked beside a skeletal metal rancher statue and time capsule. It was a nifty little sculpture, and the historical society gave a noble effort, embellish-ing the site with a waving American flag, a large plaque describing the history of the town, and a centennial time capsule to be opened in 2089.

We stopped for gas in Hot Springs and discovered a little Western town of murals, history, shops, and tidbits. I particularly liked the old wooden jail built in the 1880s. According to the sign, Calamity Jane had made some trouble at the saloon down the street and spent a night in this jail. During a brief walk along the main thoroughfare, I collected free maps of the Black Hills area.

As we continued through the scenery on Highway 385, I noticed many pull-offs with plaques. I decided to investigate one along Wind Cave National Park. This plaque described the area's prairie dogs. In view were countless prairie dogs to observe, just doing their thing in the open land. An SUV pulled into the area and watched me observing with a camera. Then they saw the little guys peeking out. A few of the prairie dogs approached the SUV. *Cool nature.* Meanwhile, Norway was sitting in the car. There was no way I would let him out there. He would try to chase every one of those critters!

Along Highway385, we made a quick stop in Pringle, SD to see a bicycle sculpture. In a field was a pile of hundreds of bicycles. They were seemingly arranged, with a pathway into the middle of it. *Is the bicycle collection a work of art? A junkyard? Or a huge recycling opportunity?* It was a unique display in Pringle, a town population of 110—far fewer than the total number of bikes. As we returned to the car, two women rode by on bicycles. The second one stopped to take a picture of the sculpture.

At lunchtime, we reached Custer—a launching point to the Black Hills area and attractions. The town was busy with tourists, a carnival, and local offerings. We walked down the road to check out sights and view the painted buffalo statues that were placed throughout. When Norway got his eye on another dog, we followed them into the carnival.

There were small rides, food, music, and games. One vendor asked if I wanted to play the ring toss game to win a chew toy for Norway. I passed. Norway had plenty of chew dolls. And I couldn't win a prize if I spent every dollar in my pocket!

We paused to buy a large lemonade and water. Norway found a shady spot to rest and cool off in front of the Chamber of Commerce and Visitor Center.

"It's a hot one today," I said to Norway.

While he was lying in front of the door, a woman came out of a side entrance to see if we needed anything. She was friendly and answered questions. Even better, the center provided brochures and shop information with maps of South Dakota.

Norway continued to lie in the shade, until a guy with his energetic two-year-old dog showed up. That motivated Norway to stand up. We weaved through the crowds of visitors in Custer while staying in the shade. Occasionally, I stopped to shoot a photo of the scene, particularly the painted buffalo sculptures placed around town. The vibrantly painted fiberglass buffalo were part of a public art project created to give artists an opportunity to showcase their talent. The colorful eight-foot long figures added charm to Custer.

Feeling the heat, we headed back to the car. For some reason, Norway nibbled on the grass. Then, a block later, he puked it up. Mindful of higher temperatures, I monitored Norway. He heaved onto a grassy spot next to the parked Nissan. Back inside the car, I cranked up the air conditioner and directed the vents toward his face.

While he chilled in the car, we drove to view Crazy Horse. The very cool memorial featured the eighty-seven-foot face of the Lakota leader. The carving began over seventy-five years ago and continues today. Since it was quite expensive to go inside—plus, Norway was not fit to walk far at one p.m. in the blazing temps—I took photos of the Crazy Horse Memorial Mountain from a distance. The height was nearly twice that of the Statue of Liberty. When finished, it will be the largest mountain carving in the world.

We traveled sixteen miles north and east to Mount Rushmore National Memorial. South Dakota did a great job with the signs and directions to Mount Rushmore. And they had an efficient parking scheme—briskly funneling the visitors to the parking lots. Since Norway wasn't allowed inside the memorial, I asked a parking attendant where the best spot was to view the monument.

She suggested Parking Lot 6. "And, there is some neat stuff inside. So maybe you could leave him in the car?"

"Nah, he's coming with me." I had the same travel deal with Oscar eight years earlier. Either we both go, or we skip the attraction.

We parked in Lot 6. Norway started out strong. Then, the heat got to him again. He repeated the stubborn "sit in the shade routine" from yesterday, except this time it was in front of Mount Rushmore. I didn't mind the break. I had a rock to sit on, in the shade, with a priceless view of the sixty-foot faces of the presidents.

Mount Rushmore

After Norway's forty-five-minute siesta, we strolled back to the car. We exited and followed the signs into Keystone. We drove past the touristy main street. Since it was still hot outside, I didn't want to drag Norway through town. If desired, we could return tomorrow.

At the other end of town was Dahl's Chainsaw Art. The outside wooden pieces showcased an appealing display of talent, sense of humor, and craftsmanship. The two Dahl brothers, carving since they were teenagers, produced a wide range of impressive wooden figures. I walked around for ten minutes while Norway sat in the cool car. Then, I saw a bench with a wolf carved out of it. *It looks like Norway!* I retrieved Norway and brought him over for a comparison.

As Norway approached, he looked at the figure cautiously. Eventually, he stood next to it.

Norway looking at the wolf bench

After we took the photo, a young man came over and put a price tag on the bench: *$2,300!*

I asked him about the artist and how long it took to make.

"This one took about one day."

"Really?" I thought it would take weeks. "It's a cool piece," I said to him. *But that is a lot of money.*

"And, they can ship it?" I asked. "I live in Illinois."

"Yes, they ship items all over the country. Shipping would be about four dollars per pound."

Transporting it would not be an issue. But, over two grand? Instead, I took home a picture.

We drove to Hermosa to see the giant three presidents display. In an open field by an RV park, fifteen-foot busts of Bush, Reagan, and Kennedy faced the interstate. Meant to complement the Rushmore presidents, Texas sculptor David Adickes made eighteen-ton heads of all the presidents. He sent them to Presidents Parks in Virginia, South Dakota, and Texas. Each outdoor park displayed the sculpted busts of forty-two US presidents, along with their history and biographical information. Unfortunately, poor public response led to the parks' closures in 2010, and the busts were dispersed.

After stretching our legs and getting a closer look at the heads, we got back in the car and doubled back to Rapid City and drove to Lead. Driving on Main Street, I viewed the town while heading toward the hotel. At the end, I saw Glendale Drive, but then it ended?

I called the hotel and spoke to an old guy, who clarified my directions. One minute later, we arrived at Blackstone Lodge. We got out of the car, and Norway immediately paused. Then, he looked up a rocky wall. He just stared upward. *What did he see?* Then, I looked up and could see a deer at the top of the rock wall!

"Great eyes, wolfie," I said to Norway. "Let's leave him alone."

The Blackstone Lodge had a comfortable room and super-nice reception. The old guy recommended Lewie's Burger and Saloon. We drove there, but it was packed with people. Unsure how long the wait would be or how I'd manage with Norway, we returned to town.

On Main Street, I recognized the Stampmill from a prior online search of restaurants. Good news: dogs were permitted in the outdoor seating. Bad news: a pair was sitting with their dog. There weren't enough tables to separate Norway from the dog.

While waiting for diners to finish, Norway and I went sightseeing up and down Main Street. There were murals, a view of the huge gold pit, old buildings, and memorabilia related to Lead's history and mining. Also, we passed a laundromat. While I went inside to get detergent for later, a young woman stepped outside to greet Norway. I learned she had two husky puppies at home! We had a pleasant chat about the dogs and this area.

Norway and I returned to the Stampmill Restaurant and Saloon. The couple and their dog were still there. But a distant corner table opened where Norway and I could sit. Eventually, we moved to another table with a better breeze and view. Now, the sun was down, and it was beautiful and cool outside. *I love travel moments like this: perfect weather, relaxing, and an ideal dog place.* Norway found his spot, and we had dinner.

We started with salad and chicken on top—a large amount that Norway gobbled up. Then, soup and grilled cheese with fries. The soup was OK, but the sandwich and fries were terrific. And, the waitress was great, covering the entire patio. *The town shops overall seem short-staffed.* The waitress was efficient and polite, including her attention to Norway.

At the end of the meal, she commented, "Your dog is so well-behaved."

"Well, at six years old, he's starting to mellow out," I said. "Plus, we had a long, hot travel day. Mostly, we've traveled all over, so he knows the drill."

She added, "He's very good. A lot of people bring dogs that don't behave."

Sometimes it is just recognizing the atmosphere. I would avoid any spot that would make Norway stick out.

In the end, the bill was thirty dollars. I left her an extra tip. She was working hard! When we left, the patio was empty.

Back at the hotel, Norway enjoyed another chew bone. Meanwhile, it was time for some laundry. *Do it while you can. Not when you have to.* I got change at the front desk. They were very accommodating, and since there was a bar/casino next door, it figured that they'd have quarters for the slot machines.

In between wash cycles, I typed up notes and walked around the lobby. I found a Black Hills brochure with locations of wineries, breweries, and distilleries. The map had tremendous detail with helpful routes between towns.

I picked up the pile of clean clothes and returned to the room. While I folded and transferred the items to the suitcase, Norway watched. At home, for some reason, he loved when I folded laundry. When Norway sees me carrying a pile of clothes from the basement, he races ahead to the bedroom. He hops into the bed right next to the clothes that I lay down. I have never seen someone so excited about folding laundry!

LEAD, SOUTH DAKOTA, to SPEARFISH, SOUTH DAKOTA

NORWAY WAS UP—*5:05 a.m. Ugh*. I realized I hadn't turned on the air conditioner. Either too warm or needing to go out, he stood by the door and looked at me. I put on shoes and a light sweatshirt, turned on the air conditioner, and we headed outside at sunrise.

Norway sniffed and squirted in a few spots. It was a worthy trip. Back inside, we enjoyed ninety minutes of sleep in the icy room. Norway lay next to me with his head on the fluffy pillows.

During breakfast, I found an Airbnb for later this week. Unfortunately, I couldn't remember my old account password and info. And I couldn't find it in the laptop files. To reregister, I needed my phone and an uploaded picture ID for a security check. I was tempted to avoid the hassle and give up on the website, but the Airbnb spot in the middle of rural South Dakota looked appealing.

After completing the hotel reservations, we checked out of the Blackstone.

"You're leaving? Can't you stay longer?" The crew at the hotel liked Norway!

"I wish we could." I prefer staying put and leaving our stuff in one place. "But there was no vacancy on the second night." We booked a place in nearby Spearfish.

We drove down the hill a few miles and entered Deadwood. The towns are close, even sharing some services, such as the high school and hospital. We followed Pioneer Way into the Deadwood historic downtown. There were restaurants, saloons, history, and attractions. A huge fan of the HBO show *Deadwood*, I found the history detailing the lives of Wild Bill Hickok, Seth Bullock, Calamity Jane, and others especially appealing.

We walked up the shaded side of the street, passing shops and casinos. I realized we were in an area where gambling was legal, with storefronts advertising live poker and sportsbooks. I could see the party vibe of this place—a cool, scenic alternative to Las Vegas, Atlantic City, and Reno.

As we walked, I shot pictures, and Norway sipped every bowl of water he passed. Countless people asked to pet the dog or commented on how beautiful Norway is. Then, "How is he managing in this heat?"

"The husky coat is better suited for wintertime," I said. "But he likes to come along." Then, I added, "Lots of air conditioning."

I talked to vendors and tourists and received help to get a photo souvenir: Norway and I sitting in a huge wooden chair. It was another Dahl's Chainsaw Art masterpiece. Although Norway was shy in front of the camera, we got a nice memento.

Sitting with Wild Bill Hickok in Deadwood

As we stepped off, a tour bus passed with travelers pointing at us. *I am such a tourist!* Then, several others followed our lead, climbing onto the Deadwood chair. Walking back along the other side of the street, we passed Saloon no. 10, where Wild Bill was shot with black aces and black 8s, the Dead Man's Hand.

We drove to the next destination, Sturgis. *Quite a vibe!* Motorcycles, working-class patriots, tattoos, and friendly people. A few weeks before another big rally, the town had a motorcycle theme and a festive atmosphere. In the summer heat, we took a brief walk. I got several photos of cool statues and monuments, especially the Joe Petrali bronze motorcycle sculpture. Unveiled a few years ago, the life-size figure depicts Petrali, a champion hill-climber and dirt-bike racer, on the Harley-Davidson Streamliner he used during a record 136.183 mph one-mile run in 1937. It is a sleek motorcycle piece, fitting for Main Street in Sturgis.

We headed east out of town on SD Highway 34 to see the sculpture *Flaming Biker with Chainsaw.* The photo online was fierce, something worth going out of our way to see. From SD-34, we turned north on SD-79 toward Vale. Unexpectedly, we hit a construction stop. While some cars turned around, Norway and I waited inside the air-conditioned car. After twenty minutes, the worker gave the go-ahead to proceed.

Five miles further, we could see the flaming biker. *Awesome.* Moreover, there were several other giant metallic sculptures along the road. The artwork showcased a talented artist that had both attitude and spirit. I learned that the location of these works was not random. They were the centerpieces of Full Throttle Saloon. *Totally badass.*

Cyclists and a road warrior

Full Throttle Saloon had a massive bar with a food area and outdoor patio. There were tons of biker and machine memorabilia. *What a place!* It was part museum, bar, and motorcycle pilgrimage. And dogs were welcomed. Since it was midday, we decided to look around, soak in the atmosphere, and have a drink.

I picked an open spot on the side of the enormous outdoor bar. While looking over the bottles and menu of drinks, one of the bartenders nodded my way. She was very cool, with tattoos, tight jeans shorts, and a biker vibe. Fit the place.

I pointed at the house mixes. There was a punch version or a lemonade version. I picked the red one. While Norway rested in the shade, I had a tasty punch/moonshine/something drink.

A couple of visitors were sitting off to the side, looking at the machinery decor. Then they noticed the dog and me.

"How's it going?" I nodded politely.

"Good," they said. "Nice dog. Is he tired out?"

"Yeah. But, after a break, he'll be ready to go again!"

The woman asked, "How is that drink? We thought about trying it."

"It's actually very good." Then, I added. "Strong. One will be enough."

The guy mentioned, "The brews here are terrific. Did you try any?"

"Not a beer drinker." I added, "Just never liked the taste."

"Not even the ales?"

"Naw. I've tried them. Never liked it, not even back in school."

"You never drank?"

"Not really. Most parties only had kegs and beer. Until college. Then, it was mixed drinks."

The couple smiled. "A fine aspect of higher education. We have a son in a fraternity."

"The first week, before classes," I said, "I was a freshman just walking down the dorm hallway. I peeked inside one of the rooms, where some upper-classmen were partying.

"I began to walk away. 'Hey, what's up?' one of them called out. I turned. 'Wanna drink?' One of them held up a beer.

"I walked into the room. 'Thanks, but I'm not a beer drinker,' I quickly added. 'Just don't like the taste.'

"'Man after my own heart,' his friend said. 'What do you want?' On the table was a row of different liquor bottles.

"I had no idea, so I answered, 'Whatever you're making. What is that?'

"'It's a Long Island iced tea.'

"I had never heard of that. 'What does it taste like?' I asked.

"'If it is made right, it tastes like iced tea—with alcohol.' Alan started mixing a batch.

"I thought to myself, *I like iced tea, so why not?*

"'Try this.' He handed the drink to me.

"It turned out Alan's long island was the best I had ever had. And strong. I learned about different types of liquor and quality."

"So you learned something useful in college," the guy half-joked.

"I know." I laughed along. "Funny, I asked what the measurements were. He always said 'I'm not sure. I just do a few shots of each and then add by taste.'"

"True science," he said.

"My friend Alan was a physics major. His buddy was a chemistry major."

I finished FTS's special moonshine punch. Refreshing. The bartender asked if I wanted another. I passed. Not sure if I could finish another. And Norway was a terrible designated driver.

Norway and I did a second tour around the large facility. On the way out, a group approached to meet Norway. One of them had a shirt from East Troy, Wisconsin. We chatted a bit about the area.

We continued north on SD 79 to Highway 212. Then, west to Belle Fourche, a town of about five thousand people. French for "beautiful fork," Belle Fourche is in the tristate area of Montana, Wyoming, and South Dakota. I had read that it was the geographic center of the United States, if you included Alaska and Hawaii. There was a nice welcome center with a giant map and compass beside the building.

In the lot, fifteen motorcycles were lined up. A few of the riders were wandering around the area. Others were cooling their faces in the fountain. *I bet that motorcycle ride was hot!* Norway went to a grassy area under a tree and took his daily siesta. Meanwhile, I walked to the displays and took photos. The group of bikers moved under the tree beside Norway.

"He must be hot out here!" one guy said.

"He definitely prefers the cold weather," I answered. "But he's managing."

"He must shed a lot," the guy said.

"He sheds a little bit," I started. "Except for twice a year, when he drops his coat."

"Really?" the guy responded.

"It's funny. I adopted him in January. And the first few months he didn't shed at all. Then, one day in May, I came home and there was hair everywhere! It was like a snow globe in my house. White hair was floating around the living room."

"Oh my gosh!"

During our conversation, I learned they were from a place near Evansville, Indiana. Eventually, they hopped back on their motorcycles and headed down the road.

At the Belle Fourche visitor center, I spoke to the woman working there. She was by herself, knitting, while sitting in the log cabin. *Apparently, not many visitors.* I asked about the "real" center of the nation. The woman confirmed it was thirteen miles north on Highway 85.

"And it will turn into gravel road about seven miles away." She added, "There's a modest marker off the road near a farm."

That meant about twenty miles each way to see the true center point and traveling on a gravel road. Plus, it was not easily marked. *Would I miss the turn?* It was blazing hot, for Norway and the car. So we passed on that idea. This monument was close enough to the center of fifty states.

Spearfish was twelve miles south from our spot. As we drove into town, a bank sign read *4:15 p.m. 93 degrees.* Time to settle in and relax. I dismissed thoughts of an excursion into Wyoming to see Devils Tower and Hulett—favorites with Oscar. Maybe a stop at Sundance. But we had used up too much time today.

We were in the hotel room before five o'clock. There was time to chill, write notes of today's journey, upload photos, look at email, and watch a show. The Quality Inn was nice. We had a large, cool room with good cable TV and the best internet connection since we'd gotten to the Black Hills area. Although the pet fee was a steep $40 per night, the total room rate was terrific.

"How's pizza sound?" Norway raised his ears.

Online, Dough Trader Pizza looked awesome. But they were closed on Mondays and Tuesdays. *Maybe another pizza place? Or anything with outdoor seating?*

We went into downtown Spearfish. As the temperature lowered, it became pleasant to walk around their Main Street. Where Deadwood and Sturgis are the party places, Lead and Spearfish seemed more mellow. The places closed early, leaving fewer dinner options. After asking where the pizza place was, two women pointed across the street. There was no sign on the roof, just "The Atomic" in red letters with an arrow pointing to a doorway. *Perfect. But where was the outdoor seating?*

During a lap around the block, I spotted wood tables and debris in the back "alley," where a patio was being constructed. It was empty. But there was a cool breeze and no trash odor.

I went inside the Atomic Pizza café and ordered a slice, which was one-fourth of a regular pizza, plus a Boylan soda from the fountain. They had a huge selection of beers and ales too. I took the black cherry soda, collected Norway's stuff, and went out back to wait.

A young teen brought my order. The pizza was good size and different, with unique cheeses. The sauce was tasty and fresh, and the crust was notable: a texture like toast and easy to bite into. Best of all, it was a bargain. Soda and pizza for about six bucks!

Picnic dinner at Atomic

While Norway ate his regular dog food, I went through my dinner. Occasionally, someone would pass by and greet us. Then, a guy with an Atomic Pizza hat came through.

"Does your dog want more water?"

Norway had water, but an ice-cold bucket would be better—plus Norway always likes the other person's water!

When he returned, I asked, "Are you the owner or manager?"

"I am the owner," he said. "Mike."

"The pizza is terrific." I added, "And it's a great price. Glad we stopped here."

We talked about his pizza place, soccer coaching background, trading options, and Huntington Beach, where he was raised. Also, Spearfish, real estate, and building this business around a college town. He asked me about my math tutoring and work in the financial markets, travels with the dog, *RoadsideAmerica*'s destinations,

328

and writing about the journey. Later, his wife arrived for dinner and joined us.

All in all, it was a wonderful encounter. Our conversation lasted almost two hours. I asked a few times if I was taking up his time. But he said it was not a problem. The staff could take care of the restaurant.

Hopefully, we'll be in touch again. I gave him my card and mentioned *Bring Oscar.*If he reached out, I would send him copies of the book. Otherwise, I would keep track of the Atomic Pizza Cafe and the coffee place he would be opening soon. Two new businesses, intending to draw in the college crowd, were hopefully a winning ticket.

Norway and I returned to the car. At ten p.m., I relished the cool breeze and empty Spearfish streets. It was so peaceful and pleasant.

SPEARFISH, SOUTH DAKOTA, to WOOD, SOUTH DAKOTA

AT SEVEN A.M., I felt a paw and a nose resting comfortably on my arm. I could feel the breathing of the tranquil husky next to me. I opened my eyes and saw Norway gazing at me. We got up and took a walk around the premises. Norway had a pep in his step. The combination of sleep in a cool hotel room and mild morning temperatures energized him. Plus, he could sense the animals, wildlife, and other dogs.

Back in the hotel room, I took out the Quality Inn pad of paper and wrote detailed directions for Rapid City. After driving through construction zones two days ago, I realized I could get detoured or lost in the town's layout.

We took I-90 to Rapid City. I found a parking lot in a central location. In the downtown area, we strolled by the murals, attractions, shops, breweries, and restaurants. I noted the South Dakota town was vibrant in contrast to the COVID-mandated locked-down Illinois towns around me. At the Main Street square, parents watched their kids cooling off in the interactive splash patio.

No masks, playing, and smiling. By comparison, the park in my neighborhood was closed, with yellow police tape wrapped around the playground to prevent use.

While browsing around the shops, I recognized the life-sized bronze presidents at each corner. Every president from Washington to Obama was placed in random order around town. While Rapid City offers a walking guide map, many treat it as a scavenger hunt, looking for a favorite. The "City of Presidents" project started in 2000. Each statue was privately funded and required up to nine months for a local artist to create. Later, I read that each statue matched the actual height and weight of its president. These public sculptures of different poses, clothing, and expressions nicely accented Rapid City.

John F. Kennedy and a presidential canine

As the day turned into another hot one, Norway seemed fine ... until he puked up some yellow stuff. I hoped it was just grass or bad food and not heat exhaustion. I offered him water, but he declined. *Gross—some of the yellow puke was on his white fur!* I poured water to dilute it and wash it away.

We rallied and went across to Memorial Park, where we discovered a running creek! This was a big break on a hot day. Norway thoroughly enjoyed wading in the shade and drinking the cold water. After Norway got a second wind, we walked around the park.

Memorial Park was filled with statues, greenery, a pond, and tributes, as well as a Berlin Wall memorial. The interesting exhibit and information area featured a large piece of the Berlin Wall. Installed in 1996, the middle of South Dakota seemed an odd place for this piece of European history. But I enjoyed reading all the panels and viewing the historic photos. Meanwhile, Norway comfortably waited in the grass under a tree.

Enjoying the park

We circled back to the creek, giving Norway a chance to cool off again. After returning to the car, we made a brief stop by the "giant prospector." The colorful statue of Johnny One Feather stood in front of his gold panning attraction and business. Johnny, a former stuntman full of stories, had passed away a few years earlier. But the giant figure and a rock shop next door still stand along US-16.

Departing Rapid City, we visited the giant quarter-pounder with cheese at a McDonald's off I-90. Weighing over eleven tons—or the equivalent of 92,000 real quarter-pounders—the bronze giant was unveiled in 2020. McDonald's picked this spot, claiming Rapid City had the most quarter-pounder-with-cheese fans per capita. Etched in the base was the Latin phrase *calidum et deliciose succosum*, meaning hot and deliciously juicy. And, on the back: "Weight before cooking 4 oz... Statue is not edible. Do not eat the statue." *Just in case someone decides to sue!*

Back on I-90, we cruised along, taking advantage of the eighty-mph speed limit, until stopping at Wall Drug. After listening to Mike last night, I decided to give it a quick try. The fifteen-minute stop at the tourist strip was enough.

We continued to Cactus Flat to see the "giant prairie dog." The twelve-foot-tall, six-ton concrete mascot was a nifty thing standing beside a prairie store and food shop for the prairie dogs. I could see dozens of people in the field feeding the little guys. Of course, I left Norway inside the cooled car. This was not a place for husky games or a prairie dog graveyard. Finally, we cruised over to the Minuteman Missile. I was curious to see what it was all about. Unfortunately, the historic site and museum were closed.

We had much better luck at Murdo, stopping to visit the Pioneer Auto Museum, which featured the General Lee car. I took a few exterior photos, went inside, and got information from the guy in the gift shop—an air-conditioned gift shop!

I asked about the museum. Entrance was $12.50. "Are dogs permitted?" I hoped.

"Oh yeah. They take dogs."

"How 'bout in here?" I added. "My dog would love the air conditioning."

"He can come in here on a leash," the nice gentleman answered. "Just can't go next door into the cafe."

Aside from the museum prospects, I was pleased to walk around, stretch, and get Norway out.

We walked through the air-conditioned entrance, passing a life-size Trump wax figure, a seated Ronald McDonald fiberglass character, and a row of souvenirs.

We found a teenager at the entrance.

"Is it 12.50 for both of us?" I asked.

"Oh yes."

I gave him a twenty-dollar bill. He returned ten dollars in change. "That's good enough," he said.

The museum's online reviews were mixed, but I liked the privately owned style of the place. The nifty site contained a good variety of car styles and models in various conditions. Plus, there were all kinds of other nostalgia items: bicycles, rifles, old toys, as well as sheds and rooms filled with antiques and collectible cars that spanned decades.

We found the General Lee used in the *Dukes of Hazzard*. Also, the Trans Am from *Smokey and the Bandit*. Mostly, it was wonderful just to walk around a spacious place with Norway. The outside exhibits were primarily in the shade, so the temperatures were OK. Norway even found a bucket full of water for a refreshment.

Cruising around the cars

After forty-five minutes and a variety of great photos, we headed for the exit. The young kid was engaging and kindly took some pictures of me and Norway. Then, he pointed out the cooler of water. "You could take one of those cups and give it to your dog," he suggested. And the older gentleman gave us a friendly farewell. Outside, I noticed a sign on the side of the building indicating pets were allowed. *And welcomed.*

After the Murdo auto tour, I found a message from the South Dakota Airbnb. I called Amy and explained that we were at Murdo and on our way. I apologized for running late because I forgot about the one-hour time zone change.

"We're heading out right now. Should be there soon."

"It'll take over an hour to get here," she informed me.

"Really? It doesn't look that far." The map's road did not seem that long. Then, she explained that the road was gravel. *Ugh.* Memories of our drive to Labrador, Canada, came to mind. Tire worries and slow pace. At least the Nissan's recently replaced tires were only two months old.

"Are there any local restaurants?"

She mentioned that the nearest towns, Wood and Winner, were each forty minutes from their place.

"Most people bring food. We have a full kitchen. There should be a few places before you get off the highway."

At the I-90/Highway 53 junction in Vivian, I found a Sinclair gas station with a Pizza Hut Express. Also, Heidi's Deli was part of the facility. Inside, I learned they had closed at four p.m. But they did have premade sandwiches. I bought a wrap, a chicken Caesar salad, an individual pizza, cookies, and a soda. I wanted to be sure we had plenty.

On State Highway 53 South, we cruised at sixty-five mph. In the distance, I saw the speed limit drop to fifty-five. So, I slowed. Then, suddenly ,I realized the pavement was ending! I slammed on the brakes, and the car leapt onto the gravel. *Oh my gosh. That was abrupt.*

The next twenty miles was over slow gravel road. Norway and I enjoyed the rural scenery of ranches, buffalo, crops, open land, and dirt roads.

A gravel road less traveled in South Dakota

I kept on the lookout for our turn at 288th Ave. No car was going my way. Several trucks came from the other direction. I stopped twice for photos, and I paused at a corner to get a closer look at a dusty sign. It was 250th Ave. So, I felt good heading down SD-53. We passed another road, where I missed the sign. I stopped the car. Went in reverse to read the street sign—it was 288th! *I almost missed it.*

I followed 288th Ave. Further ahead, there was another road sign with letters covered in dirt. I kept going, but after a while, I turned around. When I got back, I tried the other side of the sign. It was 258th Street. *My turn!* I passed a batch of mailboxes. *Which house?* The first house had a Ford in the driveway. Amy had mentioned a Camaro. I drove closer to look. *Nope, not it.* I turned back, and I continued down the road.

Suddenly, my phone rang. It was Chuck. "Follow the plow with the hay."

Ahead, I saw someone going down the road. I followed it to the ranch, where I saw Amy waving next to a Camaro.

"Our neighbor called us," she said. "Figured it was someone visiting."

I pulled onto the grassy patch beside the other cars. The setup was great. I discovered that this place—Outlaw Outfitters—catered to hunters who come in the fall. The lodge had several bunks and rooms, and a TV, kitchen, and living space. At this time, Norway and I were the only ones, with the entire place to ourselves!

The air conditioner was cranking, and the atmosphere worked for us. Amy mentioned the stained carpets from winter visitors.

"Actually, I like that!" I told her. "So, no problems if Norway tracks dirt."

When asked about Wi-Fi, Amy explained there was no Wi-Fi on the Airbnb descriptions. She mentioned that I could try the main house Wi-Fi.

"No worries," I said. "Just seeing if I could check my email. But I have no problems being off the grid."

Airbnb in Wood, SD

Outside with Norway, I had dinner in the fresh air and did get internet reception! We stayed out for three hours, enjoying the cool temperatures and listening to podcasts. I downloaded photos, made hotel reservations for two days out, typed some notes, and appreciated the surroundings.

At nine p.m., we went inside. I gave Norway a biscuit and a bowl of cold water from the tap. I plugged in the electronics. Among the many outlets, I picked the one with the surge protector, just in case.

I sat on the couch, turned on the TV, and went with the movie *Friends with Benefits*. Norway sat next to me, got sleepy, and then retired into another room. He picked a spot on one of the beds. Peaceful evening.

WOOD, SOUTH DAKOTA, to MITCHELL, SOUTH DAKOTA

LAST NIGHT, I picked out a bunk and went to sleep. At 1:10 a.m., Norway got me up for a walk outside. The wind was blowing—it was chilly. The motion lights went on, so the flashlight was unnecessary. We encountered their sweet fourteen-year-old dog. She had wandered to the spot where I had spilled Norway's dog food and was nibbling the snack.

Back inside, Norway piled on top of me in one of the single beds. *Twenty bunks to choose from, and he likes mine.* Eventually, he switched to another one.

At four a.m., Norway wanted to do another lap outside. I put on an extra shirt. We walked around again, where he explored and marked territory. Back to sleep. At 7:45, Norway was on the side of the single bed watching me. I got up and wrote a few notes. As I was writing, Norway was at the front entrance, scratching the door.

I took him for a long walk around the grounds. We passed the main house, bales of hay, farm machinery, open lands, and the dog pen, where three dogs were barking for our attention. I wasn't sure if I could bring Norway close to them, so we continued. Along the path, we passed a dead snake—a reminder to stay out of the brush.

Norway exploring the ranch

We reached the end of the fenced-in part of the property. I took in the fresh breeze and beautiful view of the South Dakota horizon.

We trotted back. Halfway, Norway stopped to relieve himself. *Do I pick it up? Or leave it?* It was in the middle of the brush, near a stray piece of plastic. Since there were animals in the area, and it was far from the main house, I left it there.

Back at the lodge, I turned on the TV and listened to OAN news. In the bathroom, they provided mini-soap and shampoo with the towels. I used my own shampoo and conditioner to save them from having to replace them. Afterward, we went outside to pick up the Wi-Fi.

Amy came over to check how everything went. Then she asked, "Do you mind if we let the dogs out?"

"Sure, let's see what happens."

When the five pups came rushing out, Norway got extra excited. Some of the pups were scared off, others wanted to play with him. It was a melee. So they collected their dogs and put them back in the pen.

I chatted with Amy, Chuck, and his son. Chuck was from the area and had inherited the ranch from his parents. Amy was from Texas and met Chuck on Zoosk, an online dating site. Months later, she moved to South Dakota. We talked about the economy, COVID, Biden, businesses, and living out here. It was very interesting to get the perspective from a rancher. The gas price increases had already raised their annual machinery costs by $25,000.

His ranch produced bales of hay for the winter, beef cattle, and some corn. She was starting the Airbnb. In the fall, they maintained the buildings. Then, in the winter, they hosted hunters who stayed at the lodge. Hopefully, they could manage the challenges. I was pleased that we gave this remote place a try.

We hit the gravel road and retraced our way back onto State Highway 53 toward the I-90. With pleasant temperatures, we drove with open windows. Norway kept sticking his face outside to enjoy the cross breeze and smells. He especially got excited when we passed the cattle.

We crossed the I-90, passed Vivian, and detoured north on US Highway 83. Thirty miles later, we reached Fort Pierre and the city of Pierre. At the entrance to Fort Pierre was a statue and round map plaque to get a lay of the land. Alongside was a brief history of the fur trade during the mid-1800s. Then, a colorful bronc-riding statue honoring Casey Tibbs. Born in Fort Pierre, Tibbs was a nine-time world rodeo champion. Later, he would appear in television ads, advise directors in Western movies, and even perform stunts. An interesting bit of local history.

We drove past a colorful huge mural on the side of a building welcoming us to Fort Pierre. We continued down US-83 through the small town, then crossed the Missouri River into neighboring Pierre, the capital of South Dakota.

We paused near the river, along Steamboat Park, to see Pierre's first schoolhouse. Built in 1881, it has been restored, moved, and become a nice landmark. Down the road was the state capitol and

Capitol Lake. The area was spread out with bronze governor statues, the mansion, and the capitol building itself. It was a pleasant place to walk around. Plus, there was a fountain where Norway could sneak in a dousing of water.

Visiting the capitol

We retraced our way back to the I-90 and cruised east to check out a *RoadsideAmerica* recommendation. The site had listed the *Dignity of Earth and Sky* Native American statue in Chamberlain. We exited I-90 and went up a winding road to take a look. *Damn, that thing is huge and impressive.* Near the fifty-foot-tall steel figure was a bicentennial tribute to the Lewis and Clark Expedition, as well as an open view of the Missouri River valley.

We made one last quick stop at a rest area to see the tiny church in back. Near mile marker 301 outside of White Lake, the structure was about eight by ten feet. Inside were pews, literature, a small altar, and a cross for travelers. It was a nifty, well-maintained little site.

In the afternoon, we reached our hotel in Mitchell. The Kelly Inn was a score. Reasonable price, easy to find, and near the Corn Palace. The hotel itself had a wooden lodge look, with some decorative carved bears adorning the exterior. The suite was sweet! It had a lot of space and a big bed, TV, microwave, fridge, coffee table, and sofa. Norway eased himself down and took a rest on the sofa. I placed the laptop on the desk and started checking dinner options.

El Columpio Mexican restaurant was around the corner. It was too hot to sit outside, and their upstairs patio was closed. But take-out worked great.

After ordering, the guy told me, "It'll take about twelve minutes."

I waited in the car with Norway. Then returned twelve minutes later, and the feast was ready. *Tres tostadas y tres fajita tacos; también dos Mexican sodas.*

We returned to the hotel. *At last.* I was ready for dinner. As I got out of the car, I noticed a two-inch tear in the driver's seat. *Ugh. Did Norway rip it with his paw? Or did I have something in my pocket that tore it?* First, a white paint streak on the passenger door. Now a ripped seat. At least the car kept running.

In the room, we enjoyed the flavorful dinner. Afterward, Norway licked the tasty remains of the meal while I watched television.

MITCHELL, SOUTH DAKOTA, to VERMILLION, SOUTH DAKOTA

I WOKE UP in the spacious king bed with Norway sprawled out next to me. I picked up the hotel receipt that was slid under the door. *One hundred fourteen dollars and no pet fee.* This Kelly Inn was the bargain of the trip!

I picked up a clump of white fur Norway left behind on the carpet. At least it was better than the fluff he can shed. I swept up some of the white hairs left in other places. After closer inspection, I saw areas of white hair on the brown comforters. Fortunately, I had packed a lint roller in the car.

We took advantage of the morning breeze, walking across the street to Cabela's pond. During a lap around the park and pond, Norway was quite pleased with the smells and exercise.

Inside, I used the lint roller to make the bedspread look more presentable. Then, I took a quick shower to wash and to rinse away

Norway's footprints. *Norway would be a horrible criminal—leaving evidence everywhere!*

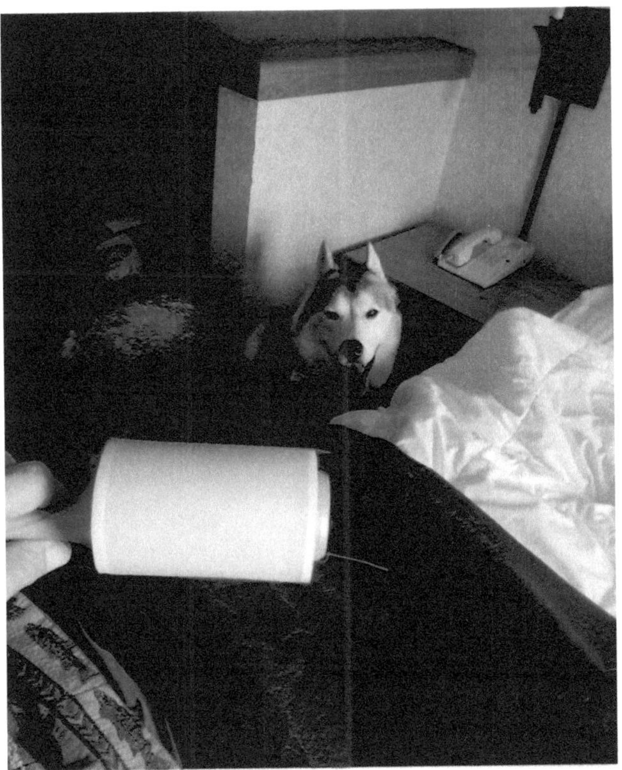

The furry battle

We checked out of the Kelly Inn and drove down the road to the World's Only Corn Palace. There was plenty of parking, less crowded than I'd anticipated. It is a fun place to visit, with its shops, unique history, and regional significance. Mostly, the architecture and murals are amazing—especially when you appreciate how they were constructed. Using twelve types of corn for color, and harvesting the corn from one hundred acres, designers put together countless carved corn pieces, at a cost of $130,000 per year for each new mural.

Eight years after my last visit, dogs were still allowed. Norway and I went inside and toured the building, encountering two other dogs. We watched the fifteen-minute film, a worthwhile documentary about the history of the Corn Palace. Then I bought a caramel popcorn ball. My touristy Corn Palace contribution.

Out front, I took photos of the Moorish-style facade. I found two older guys to get a snapshot of me and Norway with the Corn guy, "Cornelius." They tried working my Samsung phone camera. The photos either came out crooked, or I was cut out of the photo, or half the corn guy was cropped out. I gave him the Kodak camera from my pocket.

"There we go," they said with better familiarity. Old-school, they appreciated the feel of a traditional camera. It took about eight shots, because either Norway was looking away, the photo was off-centered, or I had my eyes closed. But, eventually, we got a keeper!

Hanging out with Cornelius

Norway and I spent time relaxing and enjoying the atmosphere. I went inside the Lemonheads store and purchased a lemonade and a package of s'mores popcorn for later. In a shaded section with a view of the Corn Palace, we watched the tourists before moving to our next sight.

We drove an hour east on I-90 to Sioux Falls. At the Falls Park exit, we followed the signs to a large parking lot. As I got out, fifteen birds were sitting in the shade nearby. A moment later, Norway emerged from the car. The birds briskly meandered away. *Norway rules!*

We walked up the grassy hill, passing a few statues and monuments. Then we stepped over to the falls, enjoying the serene atmosphere. Eventually, we ended up at the Falls Overlook Cafe. Since Norway was going to take his siesta, I set up lunch on the patio. I found one corner table partially in the shade. Norway had a shady spot, and I had a bit of cover and breeze to enjoy the cafe lunch and a view.

I fondly compared this to my South Dakota visits in 2013 with Oscar. Eight years earlier, we had gone to Falls Park in Sioux Falls. Then, we'd stopped at Mitchell's Corn Palace. Today we went the opposite direction. This was a good travel day, with the typical friendly greetings.

Top 5 Norway comments:
"It's a husky!" (especially kids)
"He's beautiful." (particularly seniors)
"Can we pet your dog?" (everyone)
"May I take a picture of him?" (tourists)
"You have such a nice dog! Well-behaved."

Honorable mention:
"Our dog is at home. We can't wait to get back to him."

During the meal, several folks approached. A mother and daughter from North Carolina smiled at Norway, watching him from their adjacent table. A few moments later, a couple from New York chatted with me for ten minutes. They were huge dog lovers, mentioning their fifteen years of volunteer work at a New York animal rescue. Norway enjoyed the steady flow of visitors, all while resting in the corner. Eventually, a German shepherd passed by and motivated Norway.

We returned to the car and drove through downtown Sioux Falls, passing a stretch of displayed artwork and shops. *Nice.* Since we were only an hour from our hotel destination, we had time to go back. But first, a search for a particular statue at the corner of a huge park. The statue was installed in 2008, McKennan Park's centennial. Titled *The Potato Man*, the lifelike sculpture of a nineteenth-century potato farmer was a cool tribute to the Irish of Sioux Falls. Beside the figure were dedication bricks engraved with family names of people who gathered to purchase the statue. The bricks were assembled in the shape of Ireland with the front brick carrying the quote, "May you live as long as you want; but never want as long as you live." An Irish flag was painted on the adjacent brick.

We turned around and drove five minutes back to historic downtown Sioux Falls. As I picked a parking space, I turned south—I like to face the direction I need to go next. If disoriented, I can use the car's positioning to suggest the direction to exit.

Listening to music on my headphones, I followed Norway on the shaded side of the street, looking at the shops, restaurants, and artwork. Sculpture Walk in Downtown Sioux Falls (DTSF) was an enjoyable display. Better yet, halfway was a huge fountain with running water. Norway's oasis was a perfect spot for him to drink and cool his head. Then we turned back and finished the pleasant excursion.

Back at the car, I knew the I-29 was west of us. I started winding through the streets and road construction. The commercial downtown turned into a residential area, turned into regular stores, turned into DQ/Subway/Dollar General stores, and then a casino. Finally, I could see cars racing by in the distance. It was the I-29.

After an hour straight down I-29, we turned onto SD-50 and drove six miles to Vermillion. In the small town, population 10,258, it was easy to find the Red Roof Inn. We parked in the vacant lot and went inside. The young woman at the desk gave us a nice reception. The room was good, with wood floors, microwave, fridge, and TV. And I could see the Nissan out our window. Norway took one of the two beds.

Since it was a small town, it would be easy to get a quick bite. For dessert, Dairy Queen was an option two blocks away. In addition to the local high school, we passed the University of South Dakota. *There should be good eats here.*

After some rest, Norway was ready to go. We drove five minutes past the university campus and into the commercial downtown. Around the street construction was a Thursday outdoor music festival. We found a place on Main Street to park beside a strip of various restaurants and bars. I picked R Pizza, which offered take-out or delivery only. While Norway chilled in the air-conditioned car, I went inside. The manager—the only worker—took my order and phone number.

"I'll call you when it's ready."

Norway and I walked around the block. We viewed the murals, listened to a band playing catchy rock, and observed. I noticed the stores emphasized wearing masks and promoted vaccines—very different from other parts of South Dakota. Also, I saw a flyer for a rally to defend transgender rights, among the liberal campus causes. Although near Iowa and Nebraska, Vermillion seemed more South Evanston than South Dakota.

The order was ready five minutes early, so I returned Norway to the chilled car. I picked up the salad, individual Margherita pizza, soda, and chicken fingers for Norway. Thirty bucks. *Geez. So much for cheap eats at the college.* Maybe it was like Evanston. When parents are paying sixty grand to Northwestern, their kids can afford to spend thirty dollars for dinner.

The Margherita pizza looked and tasted great—all natural ingredients. And the salad was good quality, with fresh greens and tomatoes. Even Norway's chicken tenders had more chicken meat than usual. The Stubborn Black Cherry Tarragon Soda was good. In the room, we were two satisfied customers.

VERMILLION, SOUTH DAKOTA, to HAMPTON, IOWA

AT 7:10 A.M., the room was quiet. Last night, the creatures above us were pounding on the floors after eleven p.m. *What is wrong with these people?* Breakfast was lean, offering a bagel, cream cheese, a granola bar, and Brita water. The vending machines were old-school with cheap cans of soda.

In the room, I still had trouble finding a hotel for tomorrow night. Spending $230 for a Saturday night in Dubuque, Iowa, seemed extreme. We'd barely gotten a reasonable dog-friendly room last night. I had to be creative and extend my search, which led to reserving a room tonight in Hampton, a small town off the main interstate.

At 7:45 a.m., the ceiling pounding resumed. On the upside, our room, next to the hallway side door, was a ten-second walk to the car. I gave Norway a quick, un-scenic lap around the Red Roof Inn. Then collected the laptop, electronics, and Norway's bowl—and washed away the paw prints in the bathtub—then we headed out.

Following an Iowa foldout map, we stopped in Holstein to visit the Ida County Freedom Rock. This one had meaningful images on the sides and a colorful painted American flag draped over the rock.

We continued east on Highway 20 to Sac City. We started at a park near the fire department. There were tributes to military veterans from Sac County and to Judge Eugene Criss, the founder of the town. Beside this Freedom Rock was an information board that described each of the painted images. The illustrations included Navajo wind talkers rescuing a soldier during WW II, two Tunnel Rats in Vietnam, a veteran pilot flying over Europe, and a woman Marine serving the country. The soldiers depicted were veterans from Sac County. And, the painted flag draped over the rock had ashes of two local veterans mixed in the paint. Next to Sac City's historic museum village, their huge popcorn ball sat, housed in its own structure. Rebuilt in 2016, it was over eight feet tall and weighed more than 9,000 pounds. The ball required 2,300 pounds of popcorn, from Noble Popcorn Farms in Sac City, to mix with sugar and corn syrup. The community seemed very proud of this attraction.

Norway sniffed around, settling in a spot under a tree. Meanwhile, I took out my ordinary popcorn ball from the Corn Palace and set it beside the "world's largest popcorn ball"—good photo op. I finished reading the statistics and history of the attraction.

"That's a lot of salt and butter, Norway."

He was delighted to relax in the shaded grass.

Taking a break by the big ball
(small popcorn ball on the window ledge)

We continued to Rockwell City and Fort Dodge, stopping to view more beautiful Freedom Rocks. The presentations varied from modest areas to well-manicured, ornate plazas. Many of them were placed in prominent parts of a town. Finding some was sort of a scavenger hunt, being placed in county spots off the beaten path. We got lost in Fort Dodge but eventually stumbled onto the giant painted silo and Freedom Rock.

Back on US Highway 20 East, we turned north at I-35 and connected to Iowa Highway 3 East, passing acres and acres of high corn.

In Hampton, we pulled into the AmericInn parking lot. Just as we arrived, guests from four cars walked inside to the front desk. Norway and I waited in the lobby as one receptionist checked everyone in. I noticed many hotels had just one person working the desk. *Are they struggling to hire? Saving money?* The hardworking woman moved the crowd through quickly. Then it was our turn.

I gave her my name and credit card. She tried a few times unsuccessfully.

"It's showing that you're not scheduled."

"Really? I'm sure I have a receipt."

After checking my 7/23-7/24 online confirmation, I called BringFido. The phone representative informed me there was a no-show charge yesterday from Lori. Then she gave me the number to Expedia.

"Ask the AmericInn receptionist to call," the BringFido rep suggested.

Fortunately, it only took five minutes to get through to Expedia. It became clear it was their mistake.

The receptionist and I pieced together what happened. I booked my reservation online through BringFido, which guaranteed a pet-friendly room on my date. BringFido checked to ensure it was a pet-friendly space. Then Expedia made the reservation and got their fee, but the agent at Expedia incorrectly scheduled the room for 7/22-7/23.

Since I did not show up yesterday (7/22), they still charged me for the no-show. I was in the system, and the room was mine—even if I showed up at ten p.m. Today, I arrived, and there was no room.

Although Expedia put the reservation in 7/22, I had the BringFido receipt for 7/23. They refunded my money, and fortunately the AmericInn had one room left!

As the receptionist was finalizing the details, Lori the manager arrived. Lori explained that she ran the card through when I didn't show up yesterday.

"The system showed you arriving on July 22nd."

We discussed the hotels and working with some of the worst online outfits. They suggested I just call directly instead. I mentioned a discussion I'd had with the guy at Kelly's Inn about the online booking deals. In the end, we got our room and didn't have to scramble. Norway took it all in stride, resting off to the side.

We collected our belongings and settled in the room. After Norway got up from his comfy nap, we drove down the street to a Chinese restaurant. It had five-star reviews. Granted, there were only seven reviews, but they were all good. We parked, and I went inside to scout the restaurant. There were a few diners inside, and an Asian hostess was by herself. "Cash only" was written on a sign.

"Sorry, our credit card machine is down," the hostess apologized.

"No trouble at all," I said. "Cash works."

From the enormous menu, I selected a few dishes. There was no way that we could finish it all, but I wanted to sample the menu offerings.

"I'll try the Kung Pao chicken, chicken with vegetables, and spring rolls." *Norway is gonna feast on the chicken.*

"It'll be about a fifteen-to-twenty-minute wait."

"Perfect." Norway and I could walk around the little town.

We found a mural, a prominent courthouse, and restaurants. Also, there was a huge block party going on down the street with Latin music and Hispanic families. Above a sign read "Relay for Life."

"Nice dog," I heard as we crossed the street. "We have a husky too," a teenager called out. He was sitting on a porch with his buddy. They stood up and asked if I wanted water for my dog. *That's nice of them.* Friendly people.

Just before twenty minutes, I returned Norway to the car and cranked on the engine and air conditioner. Then, I went inside the restaurant.

"Perfect timing," the Asian lady said, holding a brown bag.

I remembered to ask for utensils and was given two sets of chopsticks. *Wonder what Norway would do with chopsticks!*

Back at the hotel, I opened the bag and began sampling. The food was fresh and delicious, and the spring roll dipping sauce was terrific. Norway plowed through his first round:- white meat chicken and breaded chicken from the kung pao. I gave him seconds. He inhaled a few chicken chunks, and then hopped back on the cool bed next to the air conditioner. He fell sound asleep. *It must be canine food coma.*

I went outside to get my baggage, water, and the s'mores popcorn for a snack. The older woman I met earlier was outside smoking a cigarette at the picnic table. I called it "the cigarette table"—every time I passed there, I would see someone smoking. Butts lay all over the place.

"Where's the dog?" she asked.

"He's in the room, sleeping. Too much to wake him up."

She was from the Minnesota Twin Cities, in town for a funeral. She grew up here until the1980s. I asked about these Iowa towns. *Are they dying? Or did COVID kill them?* Also, I asked about the chain restaurants versus the local establishments.

She told me that two major companies left with most of their employees, and it crippled her hometown. In one case, the owner would fly in and out for business. He wanted to extend the runway so that he could fly a larger private plane.

"He needed some farmland to make room for the longer runway," she continued. "and offered to pay for the land and all, but the town refused."

"Probably didn't like some rich guy changing things."

"Some folks didn't like it," she agreed. "So he picked up his business and left for Des Moines."

"People don't realize that when a millionaire leaves so do the jobs. More importantly, there goes support for restaurants, real estate, and other shops. Like it or not, it's all economics."

"All they had to do was sell him the extra land," she said, "and he would've paid for the construction of the runway."

Who knows: maybe that bigger runway could open opportunities for someone else to build a factory or business? Hopefully, these towns will manage.

Inside, I watched the end of a Hallmark movie while enjoying the S'mores Kringles popcorn. *Damn, it's good.* And, Norway had a chew treat and biscuit to cap off his day.

HAMPTON, IOWA, to HOME

BIG DRIVING DAY. Unable to find a decent-priced hotel, I decided to finish today rather than split the drive in half. While we had about 350 miles to travel to get home, we wouldn't need to stop for sightseeing in Illinois.

Before checking out, I took Norway for a morning walk down the main road, Highway 3. I observed signs promoting the recent Franklin County Fair and an upcoming gun show. A liquor store was for sale. Next to it was a cafe that opened from time to time. At the entrance sign at the end of town, we turned around. We passed a historical farm and a museum section. Then we approached two hotels: ours and the next-door motel. We returned to the lobby, which was pleasantly accented with lodge-like decorations. There was a canoe against the wall and an American flag. Also, some golf pictures and a map with pins placed by visitors from all over the world. *Nice.* On the way down the hall, an older woman stopped to greet Norway.

"You are beautiful." she said.

Norway looked up at her and recognized the adulation.

"My hound girl is at home," she added. "Can't wait to get back to her."

I grabbed a breakfast snack. It was the first accommodation in a while that offered fresh fruit. Plus, a strawberry topping that looked homemade next to the waffle maker.

We checked out at eight a.m. Outside was cloudy. *Finally! Maybe the heat will subside today?* Norway hopped right into the car without persuasion. Perhaps, leading the walk this morning sated his energy.

I followed US-65 south to Iowa Falls, connecting to US-20 East. We made our first stop at Independence, IA, to see the Buchanan County Freedom Rock. Just off Highway 20 and Iowa Ave., we found another vibrant mural. The slanted rock was sleek and naturally different.

Norway and I walked around the adjacent empty lot, where a theater offered five-dollar movies between Friday and Sunday. Across was an interpretive center and museum of old agriculture equipment and other random items. It was a good driving break with just enough space to walk around and enough items to look at to break up the monotony.

The next stop, forty miles east along Highway 20, was Dyersville, population six thousand, and home of the Field of Dreams. While searching for the site, we ran across a car wash—and right beside it was a dog wash! A formal little building with cleaning supplies for dogs.

I looked at Norway. "No worries," I said to him. "You're clean enough."

He just looked at me with his tongue hanging. Norway's not a big fan of bathing. When I do wash him, he just races outside and rubs his face and coat in the backyard grass and dirt! He seems to prefer the smell of nature to aromatic shampoo.

Past downtown Dyersville, we proceeded to the actual Field of Dreams. *This is so cool!* I expected a simple field; just a quick photo of a baseball diamond and corn. Maybe a display with Kevin Costner. Instead, it was an impressive, maintained location.

The recognizable sights from the film were before us: the big house to the right and the field and a snack bar to the left. High corn surrounded the outfield, where kids with mitts and adults were wandering around. Youngsters were engaged in batting practice, while friends and family were watching.

The suggested donation was twenty dollars. "Hey, if dogs are allowed, we're in."

I handed the woman twenty bucks and parked in the huge open lot.

Norway and I headed for the Field of Dreams. "If you build it, they will come." Norway was ready. We passed the infield, where kids were playing and adults were supervising and participating. Then, I walked with Norway in the outfield, taking various photos. I saw a young man with a security shirt just watching from a spot in left field.

"Hi. If possible, could you take a picture of us?"

"Of course."

He followed us over. Then I handed him my small camera.

"Hmm," he said. "Old camera."

"Wait," I said. "I have a phone as well." Photographer's choice. Nowadays, folks seem to prefer using phones over cameras. He took some great shots in the outfield with the corn behind us.

Standing in the Field of Dreams

I noticed the worker had braces, and he looked very young.

"Are you from around here?" I asked.

"Yes, I grew up ten minutes from here."

"This is a cool place," I told him.

"I know. I've been coming here for twenty years. Today is a good day."

"Love the fact they can play on the field. Plus, the tall corn in the background is awesome."

"You're here at a good time," he replied. "A lot of people visit between January and May and leave disappointed. They forget that the corn needs to grow!"

"I never thought of that."

Afterward, Norway and I continued along the outfield, watching kids hitting balls served up by parents. Ahead, I saw a group taking a photo within the corn, reenacting the White Sox coming out of the cornfield. *Clever idea.* I asked one of the players to take a photo of Norway and me emerging from the corn in center field!

Coming out of left field

We toured the grounds and checked out the gift shop. Dogs were permitted. While browsing and preventing Norway from trying on any outfits, we soaked in the air conditioning. Back outside, we went by the information history boards.

"Can I pet your dog?"

"Of course," I said to the boy. "He loves people."

Two more came over. Several followed.

If you bring Norway, they will come!

While we stood outside, about fifteen people streamed over. Norway enjoyed the attention.

After Norway's star treatment, we returned to our car parked in the open field. Then we retraced our driving back to downtown. We walked up and down the street, browsing the shops, mostly in search of the Iowa town mural.

Mural in Dyersville

Across the street was a baseball-themed bar and grill. *The patio might be a good place for Norway's siesta.* The menu was limited, but the older woman server was so nice, I didn't have the heart to get up and leave. So I ordered a cheeseburger, fries, and a Coke.

The woman brought out another container of water, after Norway had drunk—and tipped over—the first one.

The patio was somewhat warm, but we had a spot in the shade. In between the occasional breeze, flies were hounding us. But, not too badly—although Norway was chomping and chasing them.

The burger was huge and tasted like something off the grill. The fries were terrific. Thirteen bucks for lunch. I left the woman an excess tip. She seemed surprised, then pleased. I was happy with her service.

We hit the road and went to our last Freedom Rock of this road trip. Just west of Dubuque, it sat next to the fire department in Epworth. Norway stayed inside the car with the air conditioner running. While I took pictures of the area, a car with Iowa plates pulled up. *Holy cow! It was the first time I had seen someone look at a Freedom Rock.* Usually, only Norway and I took any interest. A middle-aged couple got out. I gave a polite nod. Then we began talking about the Freedom Rock.

"How many have you seen?" the guy asked.

"About fifteen. I went west on I-80 last week. Then east on 20 now. I'm trying to catch them along the way. How about you?"

"About fifty," he said.

"Nice. It is an incredible thing. I learned about it on a website. Then, I realized there's one in every Iowa county. It's fantastic."

"Yes, ninety-nine of them. We live six hours away and decided to drive around and see a few more."

We talked about specific rocks we had seen. I mentioned the Pat Tillman one. And the one recognizing the Tunnel Rats in Vietnam. Plus, we talked about the benefit these rocks bring to each town. He told me a few local stories. "The painter met a person who wanted to spread someone's ashes at the rock, so the artist mixed some with the paint." And he mentioned people he knew personally who were deeply moved by the rocks because they were close to a person honored and portrayed on the rock.

I stepped over to the Nissan to check the inside temperature. "Just making sure my dog is cooled off," I said to them.

"Our dog is in the car too," they said. Then the woman went back to their car. Meanwhile, the Iowa man started taking photos of this Freedom Rock. I said my good-byes and took off.

Another hot day, so we kept driving and driving. We went through Galena, Illinois. Then passed Freeport and Rockford, skipping a couple of suggested tourist sights.

Eventually, US-20 turned into the I-90 tollway. *Sucked.* Tolls. Plus, it was all I-Pass, so I would have to inconveniently go online later to pay. At least the traffic was cruising. Cars were flying at eighty mph. In fact, we were making great time, until…

These road trips never end well in Chicago. With just twenty-five miles to go, we could be home in under thirty minutes. But, in the distance, there were lightning flashes. Five minutes later, the skies darkened. Then it started to rain. Then pour. Then buckets. Traffic built up.

Ninety minutes later, we neared home. A few miles out, the clouds cleared, producing a rainbow. Still, there was a ton of traffic at 5:15 on a Saturday. *Where are these people going?*

At last, we pulled into the driveway. I looked down and saw that the trip odometer read 2,918 miles.

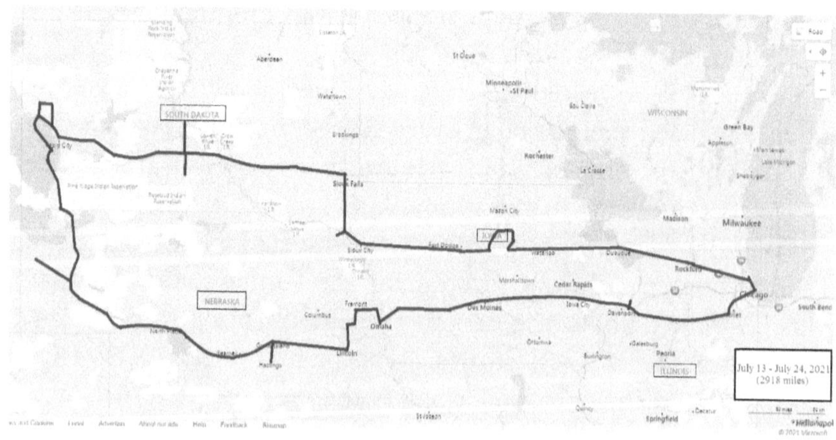

I brought in a few items with Norway trailing behind me. In the backyard, I checked the garden. There was greenery everywhere. Only a few tomatoes were ripe, but eight massive zucchini squash were ready to pick. Vines were climbing everywhere. They would yield cucumbers soon.

While I looked over the yard, Norway sat happily in his grassy spot.

"Good road trip!"

He smiled with his tongue hanging out. *Home sweet home.* Then he jumped up and chased a squirrel.

PART VI

ROUTE 66

A HESITATION I have before road trips is the *beginning*. It takes about five hundred miles to get out of the area. This trip would require back-to-back three hundred-mile drives, from Chicago to St. Louis to the southwest corner of Missouri, just to get to the *good stuff*—places I wanted to see and explore. The route would start through ordinary scenery I had seen or places I had visited multiple times. Mostly, it would take a few days to get to the warmer weather.

EVANSTON, ILLINOIS, to ST. LOUIS, MISSOURI

AFTER TEN HOURS of sleep, we leisurely rose at seven a.m. I showered and finished loading items into the car. Norway walked through the slushy snow in the driveway and climbed into the passenger seat. Rather than wait until nine, we left a quarter to eight, believing the day after Christmas and lousy weather would offset rush-hour traffic.

Heading into downtown, there was no traffic this Monday morning. It was fifteen degrees and gloomy. Chicago looked like Gotham. There was a bit of snow dust but not nearly as bad as two days ago when it was arctic below-zero wind chills.

We connected onto I-55 and motored down, trying to avoid the regular potholes. Talk radio was discussing the 100 billion dollars of aid for Ukraine. *That would have been useful to fix these roads.*

We made our first pull-over in Joliet. Although sixty miles from home, I had never actually visited. I always thought it was a small town that featured rural land and a prison. During the past twenty-five years, the town had developed and expanded.

We stopped along a row of Route 66 sights on Broadway Street. In Route 66 Park, Norway got a nice wintery walk. He enjoyed himself, sniffing and smiling while covered with snow and icicles hanging off his whiskers. *Nobody is around.* Across the street, Kicks on 66 ice cream shop was closed for the season. I took a photo of the Jake and Elwood Blues Brothers figures dancing in front of the overhead ice cream cone logo. Next, we wandered to Dick's on 66 towing, where Norway stepped on an original brick from Route 66.

Dick's on 66

On the way out, we passed a George Mikan statue. Later, I checked to see that the basketball great was from Joliet. Another bit of road trip trivia.

On I-55, we traveled forty miles to Dwight, IL. The museum within an old gas station was closed, but I could peek through the window and see the nostalgic auto exhibits. Outside were more Route 66 colorful signs, information boards, and photo ops.

We took Historic Highway 66 to the next town, Odell, to see another old, restored gas station. This one had fewer features but was worth the visit. Then we continued driving on US-66 to Pontiac. Running next to the I-55, we were able to travel fifty-five mph on the twelve-mile stretch of smooth service road.

In Pontiac, we toured the building illustrations, including some of the best Route 66 murals anywhere. The three-story-high "Route 66 Pontiac Illinois" shield mural towered behind the Route 66 Hall of Fame and Museum. A sixty-six-foot-long portrait and map of the Mother Road extended along Main Street. It displayed the route and notable towns we would pass in the next week.

Around the corner, I noticed a Mexican-American restaurant. *A takeout burrito sounds good.* After considering lunch in the car, I decided to eat *al fresco*. Across the street, I took a bench, with Norway readied in position for some tastes.

Our twenty-two-degree picnic in Pontiac

An old gentleman walked by. "Looks good," he said. "You're lucky. Yesterday, it was much colder." Across the country, it had been twenty degrees colder and windier following a national polar drop. *Husky weather.*

The polar picnic worked. The chicken burrito was delicious. And the chips with rice and beans hit the spot. Plus, the chunks of chicken were easy to pick out and hand to Norway.

After the lunch break, we followed I-55 until reaching Towanda. At the exit, we found a sign pointing to "Dead Man's Curve." Apparently, the hard curve had been the site of numerous accidents during the early days of Route 66. I could see how a car, going too fast, might slide into the neighboring ditch. It was a fun little stop with tourist signs. Mostly, it was interesting to realize how narrow and small the original Route 66 roads were. Across the street was a hundred-yard stretch of original road. It was compiled brick and uneven. Even with a decent car suspension, this would have been a rugged, bumpy ride.

We continued adding miles along I-55. My windshield went from clear to frost, as the cold kept freezing the mist. At least, the traffic was cruising along.

Our last planned stop was to see the "turkey tracks in the road." While paving in the 1920s, a group of turkeys walked through the concrete, leaving their permanent claw prints on Route 66. The road maintenance workers in the remote area just left the prints.

At the I-55 turnoff, I stopped to recheck my map. The road to Nilwood was about eight to ten miles off track. I was having second thoughts. But the *RoadsideAmerica* comments were positive. So we started driving west on Waggoner Road and drove and drove past remote farmlands. Across one barn, "Trump Country" was painted in huge white letters. Others were adorned with Christmas decorations.

We reached Nilwood. *Now where?* I drove around and scouted the area. The printed map began to make sense, matching the road's layout. Eventually, we found a colorful turkey figure beside a road sign!

Norway and I stepped out to get a closer look. In the wintry concrete, we did find turkey tracks.

Norway on the trail

It was worthwhile, I guess. The story of the tracks was better than the tracks themselves. But it's all part of the journey! *Now, how do we get back to the interstate?*

We continued south on IL-4, according to the Nissan's compass, until reaching Carlinville. *Civilization.* I stopped at a gas and liquor store. Inside, I asked the attendee behind the register for local directions. He seemed bewildered. *How can he not know where I-55 is?*

I drove further down the road and tried a crowded gas station. Inside, there were customers and two teen girls working the register.

"Any idea how to get back to I-55?" The girls looked confused and couldn't answer.

"I know it's somewhere east of here," I added. "What road could I take to get back there?"

A fiftyish customer jumped in. "Just continue south past the square. Then turn at 108."

"Keep going down IL-4," I said. "Square?"

"Yes, there's a town square, and 108 is there."

"Great! I know I'm about ten miles away."

"Twelve miles," the guy added.

"Awesome. You saved me a lot of time."

At four thirty, it was getting darker. A downside of winter road trips is daylight ends earlier. The man's directions were right on; it was twelve miles to I-55.

We reached St. Louis around 5:45. It was dark and starting to snow, but thankfully no bad traffic. I followed I-55 to I-44. I recognized some of the street names, and the big Red Roof PLUS+ sign appeared!

While waiting in line for check-in, a young guy behind us gave Norway a bunch of attention.

"He's a terrific dog." Then he added, "He must love this cold weather."

"Yes he does. Me not so much!"

Fifteen minutes later, we got to our room. I checked email, picked out a restaurant, and made a hotel reservation in Clinton, Oklahoma, for two days from now. Meanwhile, Norway was napping in the bathtub.

At seven, I finally reached the restaurant. They were super-busy, especially the day after Christmas when most restaurants were closed. I learned delivery and online orders would not work today. The nice woman on the phone took my order of salad, meatball sandwich for Norway, and pasta pomodoro with basil, tomatoes, and marinara for me.

The restaurant was closer than it appeared on the map. After weaving through the Italian neighborhood of one-way streets in "The Hill" area, I found Anthonino's Taverna rather easily.

I recalled an old friend of mine had mentioned this terrific Italian area. Red, white, and green Italian colors were everywhere. Some were temporary Christmas colors but most were permanently painted.

Although cars were lined up around the block, I found an empty temporary parking area. I ran inside to pay and pick up my order. At that moment, my order came out. *Great timing!* I paid thirty-four bucks and left a tip for their quick, helpful service.

"I'm not sure who I spoke to on the phone, but I appreciate the woman's help," I said.

The guy said, "It's OK. We split the tips."

Anthonino's Taverna was a fine choice with delicious food. Norway gobbled his meatballs, and I devoured the salad and pasta. Norway enjoyed a few slurps of noodles as well. The only downside was no soda. The hotel soda machine would not take change, bills, or my credit card. Oh well. No beverage on this episode of Route 66.

ST. LOUIS, MISSOURI, to JOPLIN, MISSOURI

AFTER A FIFTEEN-DEGREE stroll at three a.m., Norway got me up again at six thirty. While I wanted to sleep more, I also wanted to get a head start. So, up it was. We checked out before eight.

Today was a direct path west on I-44 across Missouri. Because only a few stops were in the plan, I anticipated an earlier hotel arrival.

We began with an hour drive to Cuba, MO. We took the first exit and found the "oldest still running Route 66 hotel." The Wagon Wheel Motel did have some original artifacts. The highways and cars had changed over the past eighty years, yet this place was still open!

Several new cottages were situated along the grounds. *Maybe we can stay here on the way back?* When checking the front office to see if they accepted pets, the doors were locked. I took a few photos and made a note to check later.

I had read about murals in Cuba's downtown. In person, these colorful illustrations were more impressive than the online photos.

It was enjoyable walking around, where Norway appreciated the exercise and husky chill. While browsing, I saw a billboard for a giant rocker located four miles up Route 66. Instead of going back to I-44, we drove up to Fanning.

There we found a giant red chair labeled "Route 66 Rocker—Fanning outpost—World Famous." Standing over forty-two feet high with a seat twenty feet wide, it was the largest rocking chair when constructed in 2008. The steel chair weighed over twelve tons and was surpassed several years later by a fifty-six-footer in Illinois. Too big for Grandma to use or for Norway and me to climb up. Still, it was a nifty sight.

Giant rocker in Fanning, MO

Beside the rocker was a general store stocked with snacks and every possible cane sugar local soda. I picked out a few for later. This was a great find.

Back on I-44 West, we passed numerous Meramec Caverns roadside ads. Since pets were not permitted, it was a moot point. *If*

Norway isn't allowed, I have no interest. We paused at a Stuckey's gas station beside a packed Dunkin' Donuts, pizza, and food court. As I finished filling the tank, I watched a cute black-and-white shepherd mix skip by. No collar. *Is it abandoned? Is it the Stuckey's mascot? Maybe the owner lets it run loose?* It seemed a little scared. Hopefully, it was going to be taken care of. Norway watched the potential friend scamper by his view through the window.

Twenty-five miles further, we stopped at Uranus, MO. I didn't intend to exit, but three miles beforehand, I opened one of the sodas and it overflowed onto me and my seat. I needed to clean up and regroup.

Numerous promotional boards led to the tourist spot. "The best fudge is packed in Uranus" was one of its comical selling points. In Uranus, we viewed the one-time "world's largest belt buckle," paid one dollar to hear a comedy music act from the figurines, and toured the lot.

Route 66 top-notch entertainment by the Uranus Pickers

We drove two hours to Carthage. At the I-49 exit, we got off I-44. *Now, I must figure out where to go.* In town, I found a sign for Route 66 on Garrison Street. We followed the road to a big park. Nearby was the hundred-year-old Carnegie Library, with an *Alice in Wonderland* statue in the garden area. It was an intriguing figure with Alice emerging from a book. Also, down the road stood a Marlin Perkins statue. The TV personality from *Mutual of Omaha's Wild Kingdom* was born in Carthage. *I learn something new every day.*

After a pleasant walk in sunny high-thirties temperatures, we found a connection to Route 66 West. Instead of doubling back to I-44, going to Joplin, and heading north up to Route 66, I attempted to go directly from Carthage.

It was interesting to ride through the rural areas at speed limits of thirty-five mph. We did pass the Route 66 drive-in theater. Otherwise, it was an adventure trying to follow Route 66 as it changed local names and wove through towns. I realized that taking the true Route 66 from start to finish—Chicago to Santa Monica—without getting off would be an incredible task.

We reached Joplin and found the way to its Route 66 tile mural. After a quick look, we arrived at the hotel by 3:45. The sun was still out and shining when we checked into the TownSuites. The suite was sweet! Like a nice studio, it provided a full kitchen and appliances. The room had a couch, a bed, a TV, and furnishings. This was a pleasant upgrade from the hotel last night. I watched TV, listened to a podcast, uploaded photos, and relaxed with Norway.

At five thirty, Norway and I did a lap around the hotel. In the lobby, a bulletin board map posted countless nearby choices for dinner. I settled on a Thai place. We had Italian yesterday, and I anticipated Tex-Mex as we headed west.

We went through the busy traffic around hotels and restaurants and reached the Thai place. Closed. And another Asian place was closed. So we backtracked and were on the lookout for another spot.

We ended up at my backup: Fuzzy's Taco Shop, near the hotel. Inside was a cool sports bar mixed with a family vibe. They served alcohol, yet there were pictures made with crayons hanging on the wall, drawn by kids who had visited.

I ordered a sampler of avocado and veggie tacos, some chicken for Norway, chips, and an enchilada plate. A lot of food for a reasonable price. Then I added two cookies from a local brand that advertised using eggs from pasture-raised chickens.

The food was very good, including the guacamole and chips. I should have added more chicken tacos for Norway. The woman said there were other Fuzzy's in Missouri and Texas. *Maybe we'll try again later in the trip.*

JOPLIN, MISSOURI, to CLINTON, OKLAHOMA

I FELL ASLEEP watching an old movie on TNT and missed the ending. At midnight, I opened my eyes. Norway was by the bed staring at me. Occasionally, he shook, so his collar and tags made a jingling noise. *Is that intentional?*

I put on jeans, a jacket, and shoes. Then, I staggered outside, behind a peppy Norway. As the wind gusted, I felt the thirty-degree breeze whipping, while Norway happily marked random areas around the premises.

After a ten-minute lap, I was ready to go back inside. We went through the lobby, passing the night receptionist. Behind him was a stack of board games. That was a nice hotel amenity, although Norway would never play Scrabble with me.

We returned to the room. I took off the layers of clothes and set them on the couch, next to a pillow with a dog-shape pattern sewn in—a welcoming touch by the hotel. I looked back at Norway. He was in the bed, half-asleep already.

"Geez. Hogging again." I nudged him over and tried to fit into the space.

It took a while to wind down. I kept thinking about the drive ahead. I hoped the old car would make it. We had a lot of miles to cover. And we had to drive all the way back. I shifted my thinking. *Relax and stay present. It's a vacation. Enjoy the moment.* Eventually, I got back to sleep, with Norway's body spilling onto me.

At seven a.m., I scouted the breakfast. There was a small selection, but the orange juice and banana were decent. I grabbed a bit of scrambled eggs in case Norway wanted a taste. I wasn't hungry, so the tasty leftovers of guacamole and chips were tossed. Surprisingly, the fitness room two doors away had two guys working out and using the only machines. I skipped a quick workout and packed.

We returned to I-44 and headed along today's Route 66 itinerary. The wind was whipping from the south. Good news—it would warm up the region. Bad news—the car was countering huge crosswind gusts.

We passed the border into Oklahoma. I saw a sign for a tourist welcoming center. *Excellent! I have good luck with those.* Inside, the woman at the counter was super helpful. On the free maps, she traced routes to Mickey Mantle's home and statue. Moreover, she explained that taking Route 66 only added twenty minutes versus taking I-44. Good intel. While some places had slower thirty-mph US-66 roads, the Oklahoma ones were faster—often repaved, with four lanes.

Using her directions and a map of Commerce and Miami, we aimed for the Mickey Mantle statue beside a baseball field he played on. Along the way, we found his childhood home. I peeked through the window and saw a simple, rustic house with wood floors and old furniture—humble beginnings before Mantle rose to legendary status in New York City. The nine-foot-high bronze statue of "The Commerce Comet" was monumental, constructed behind the high school baseball field. It is a classic piece of history.

Mickey Mantle with a canine legend

I noted Mickey Mantle Blvd. and a "7" painted on the Commerce water tower. We drove through town, passing the Conoco "car sticking out of the wall," an old gas station Route 66 site, as well as a few 66-type stores in Commerce.

We continued to Chelsea, OK, to check out an underground tunnel that passes beneath Route 66. The spot under 6th Street was sort of appealing. The memorable moment was trying to get Norway down the spaced metal stairs. He hates those. When I tried to pick him up, he squirmed, fell out of my arms, and let out a yelp.

We walked across the street, allowing Norway to calm down. Then I grabbed him and trotted down the steps before he could react. After I set him down at the bottom of the stairs, he casually trotted down the pedestrian tunnel. Along one wall was a mural illustrating several portraits that celebrated Chelsea and the Mother Road Route 66. On the other wall was graffiti. Norway led the way back up the stairs.

"See, that wasn't so bad," I said to the happy husky.

We continued along the Route 66 trail, going about fifty mph. Occasionally, I had to figure out where the road stopped and started. But mostly we stuck to OK-66 and minded the signs. As we passed through Catoosa, I searched for a giant blue whale. We missed it and ended up at the Hard Rock Casino and Hotel. It was a majestic building behind a giant guitar with "Hard Rock Tulsa" on it. Colorful guitars were placed around the parking and grassy areas. The casino wasn't too busy. I guess that was a good thing on a Wednesday.

We merged onto I-44 to search for two spots in Tulsa: the *Golden Driller* and the *East Meets West* statue. Both were worthwhile representations of the area. The *Golden Driller* was a mighty exhibit located beside the Tulsa fairgrounds. Originally built in 1966, the seventy-six-foot-tall golden oilman leans against a steel tower. The chiseled figure was an impressive tribute to the men in the petroleum industry.

Nissan next to the giant oilman

On the other side of Tulsa, we visited Cyrus Avery Centennial Plaza. It was an adventure finding the statue near the Arkansas

River and the I-244 overpass. Although there were sparse parking spaces, it was an expansive area to walk around and explore. The featured work of the area is the *East meets West* exhibit. The symbolic sculpture of a horse-drawn buggy encountering a Model T motor car shows the two modes of transportation coexisting as well as conflicting.

Beside the plaza was a stretch of Route 66. From Tulsa, Cyrus Avery had lobbied Congress to build Route 66, as well as direct it through Tulsa. He even suggested the Mother Road use the number 66 because he liked the number. Norway and I took advantage of the historic site's walking and bike paths to enjoy the driving break.

Today's last Route 66 item was the "World's Tallest Gas Pump" in Sapulpa, just outside of west Tulsa. The towering attraction was a well-maintained exhibit next to the Heart of Route 66 Auto Museum. Just over a symbolic sixty-six feet, it afforded a nice giant, nostalgic photo op. Ironically, it did not actually offer gas, but there was a little parking area with two Tesla electric charging stations!

In the afternoon, we continued west with 180 miles of driving ahead of us. Halfway, we crossed through Oklahoma City. Big cities are usually too vast to see in a day and require extra time to find places and cover ground. While winding through Oklahoma City and the mix of interstate highways, I pulled out the tourism maps while speeding on the highway to check whether Clinton, OK, was off I-44 or I-40. Messy. But we guessed right and got through.

At five o'clock, we arrived at La Quinta in Clinton. It was off the road, by itself, but they had signs pointing to the hotel. Since we were on the western edge of the time zone, I anticipated daylight lasting later than usual.

The suite was spacious with a king bed and an entire living room area, including two TVs. One was regular cable TV; the other looked like a Pluto, Netflix, Showtime subscription app version. I was not sure what the basic rooms looked like, but I think I got my twenty dollars' worth for upgrading to this suite. Norway scouted out the comfortable choices available. Then he picked the king bed.

I looked up three dinner choices the woman at the front desk had suggested. Canelo's Mexican Grill and Bar won out. Tonight would be another *Friedman Fiesta Feast*. I ordered samplers of enchilada, tostada, chicken fajitas for Norway, guacamole, and chips. The chicken fajitas smelled spicy, but it did look good. The tostada was delicious, piled high with fresh tomatoes, cheese, and extras. The shell was softened, but it didn't matter—I had plenty of chips to dip into it. The only thing missing was bigger napkins! The guacamole was tasty, and the cheese enchilada had a nice flavor. *Good call by the nice woman at the front desk.*

Following our evening walk, I realized we were locked out. *Ugh, while collecting Norway, my camera, my jacket, and the leash, I had forgotten the room key.*

I turned to Norway. "You don't have your key, do you?"

He looked up at me with a smile. Then he stared at the door, waiting for it to open.

We returned to the lobby, where the understanding woman at the desk quickly handed me a spare.

As we walked by, there were six locals sitting by the bar. I could hear the distinct Texas/Oklahoma accents. Almost a thousand miles from home, we were in a new part of the country.

CLINTON, OKLAHOMA, to TUCUMCARI, NEW MEXICO

IN THE MORNING, I aired *Real America's Voice* on the laptop. I gave Norway a chew bone. He had barely touched his fajitas from last night. And he dismissed the scrambled eggs offered this morning. The exercise room down the hall was huge and worth using. But, hesitant to leave Norway alone, I did burpee sets in the room.

The shower in the Clinton La Quinta was outstanding with massive pressure and flow. It was like showering under a warm waterfall!

I took Norway down the hallway. He sniffed around, especially the area near the kitchen and guests' rooms with dogs. Outside, the temperature was in the low 50s, with a sweeping chilly wind. Regardless, I realized on day two that I had forgotten to pack shorts. I had exercise shorts to sleep in but, no regular shorts or a belt.

We drove out of Clinton and skipped a Route 66 museum in Elk City, since Norway was not permitted inside. Seventy-five miles along I-40, we stopped at the big "Welcome to Texas" sign for a photo. The wind was gusting and tumbleweeds were rolling by. Another driver, with Maryland plates, got out of his car with his puppy, and we greeted.

After battling the winds, Norway and I climbed into the Nissan and continued to Mclean to check out the restored gas station. Not bad. Around the corner, we investigated a barbed-wire museum. The Devil's Rope and Texas Route 66 Museum looked worth a visit, but they were closed until March of 2023. I peeked into the window and saw a sign allowing small dogs. *Maybe I could have gotten Norway inside.* There were a bunch of nifty exhibits.

We passed Groom, TX, and I noticed the leaning tower. The water tower, with "Britten USA" written on it, was a marketing ploy to attract visitors. Deliberately designed by Ralph Britten in the early 1980s, he elevated two of the tower legs, tilting the tower at an eighty-degree angle. It proved to be a clever structure, attracting drivers to his truck stop. Although the truck stop burned down in 1988, the leaning tower has endured.

A couple of miles down the road was a massive giant cross in front of a church. *Biggest in the world?* Almost two hundred feet, or twenty stories high, the Groom Cross weighs over two million pounds. It was rather impressive for a town of five hundred people.

Like parts of Oklahoma, we encountered big wind farms. *Where are the oil wells?*

In the middle of North Texas, we entered Amarillo. The town was much bigger than I thought. We started at Big Texas Steak Ranch, the site of the seventy-two-ounce steak—free, if you can finish it in under an hour. *I bet Norway could get it done!*

The appealing tourist stop included a motel, shops, and the steak restaurant and bar. Outside was an enclosure for folks with dogs. I brought out a five-inch steak sandwich, fries, and a Coke. I took a nibble of the steak and fed the rest to Norway. I ate the fries and toasted bun with a tasty Hawaiian bread flavor.

The weather was windy but finally warmer. While Norway enjoyed his snack, I took photos until my camera failed. All the photos were too bright. I hoped there was a settings fix I could figure out.

We jumped back on I-40 and continued to exit 60. At Love's Travel Stop, I filled up the car and noticed their open dog park, where a bunch of dogs were frolicking. Nice offering.

We went down the road to Cadillac Ranch. Norway and I parked and walked four hundred yards through a windy field to the spray-painted cars. Constructed in the 1970s by hippie artists, the ten half-buried Cadillacs have been decorated, painted, or vandalized—depending on your point of view. It has become a popular stop along Route 66.

Cadillac Ranch

There were several people with spray paint, coloring the cars. Cool activity. It was nice to get Norway out there. He enjoyed the gusting wind. Simultaneously, it was interesting to watch the paint spray into the wind. But the fumes in the area ... *Whew.* We couldn't stay long, but this site was a nice detour, second to Carhenge in Alliance, NE.

We returned to I-40 and headed for the highlight of the trip: the halfway point of Route 66 in Adrian, TX. I had anticipated this photo op for hundreds of miles. When we arrived at the midpoint marker, there were no cars anywhere. The roadside Midpoint Café was closed. And the nearby hotel looked vacant. It was just us. But I was prepared to wait until someone showed up. It would be this trip's first photo of Norway and me.

The population of Adrian was less than two hundred. Luckily, another car arrived a moment later. An older couple got out, and the gentleman was holding a camera and a tripod. They greeted Norway and me. I asked if they would go across the street and take our picture. They gladly agreed. And I got a fine photograph!

Route 66 Midpoint

I learned the couple was originally from Poland. They had lived and worked in Long Island for over twenty years. They were "done with NY" and were relocating to Sedona, Arizona.

When Norway and I left, there was no one in sight. The town was vacant, seemingly closed for the winter. The drive through this part of northwest Texas was quiet and smooth. I-40 coincided with Route 66 throughout Texas. So, detours off the interstate to see Route 66 attractions were brief. An hour later, we crossed into New Mexico.

We arrived in Tucumcari at two thirty, helped by a time zone change. Since the Roadrunner Lodge didn't open until four, Norway and I walked up and down 66 Blvd. past the motels and shops.

Tucumcari was a mellow classic town with a nostalgic vibe. *Is it quiet and closed due to a holiday? Or is the town fading?*

We walked to the donut shop. An Asian guy beside a new car was parked outside. He said, "We're closed till the 1st. I just got back from vacation."

Next, we checked out Watson's BBQ up the street. It seemed like a good dinner option for later. We returned to the hotel and waited.

At three thirty, the owner of Roadrunner Lodge knocked on our car window. "Are you staying here?"

"Yes, I'm the guy with the husky. You helped me out yesterday on the phone."

"I remember," he said. "We'll be open for check-in soon."

"No problem. I know we're early." I asked about the BBQ restaurant.

"You better hurry. They close soon."

I mistakenly thought it was a dinner restaurant. We drove back, and they had closed.

We checked into the Roadrunner Lodge Motel. Good thing the owner had reached me yesterday. The pet rooms were booked. It was very cool! Inside was like walking into a 1950s room with retro décor and furniture, and even an old AM/FM classic radio playing oldies, news, and music. It was the Route 66 radio channel I had seen advertised around Tucumcari.

The room had old-school keys and locks. Area rugs were spread over the old tile floor. Even the shampoo and accessories had the retro Roadrunner Lodge monogram. It fit the entire atmosphere of this town. It reminded me of visiting Las Vegas in the 1970s. *I dig this place.*

They left dog treats from Elvis, one of the owner's three dogs and the "director of canine hospitality." The note card was addressed to Norway, adding a personal touch. Plus, there were two bottles of water and two Moon Pies. I wasn't sure if they were edible. But with social media on the labels, they couldn't be too old.

Using the Wi-Fi code swanky60s, I checked online for information about the local restaurants. Across the street was Del's. It had a substantial history and a #2 listing on TripAdvisor. Most importantly, it had a dog menu. Winner!

I went early for fear they would close too. It was a bit far to walk, especially due to freezing desert air climate. I didn't want to have to wait outside. We drove down the road into a packed parking lot at Del's. Most of the other restaurants appeared closed. Lots of travelers and old-timers were inside eating. I noticed they posted a New Year's Eve steak package. Sold out.

I bypassed the line waiting for a table and went right to the front to order takeout.

"It'll be about twenty minutes."

I rejoined Norway in the Nissan, cranked the heat, and waited, checking photos, listening to music, and hanging out.

When I went back inside, the food was ready. I filled my carton from the salad bar, then headed out the door.

In the motel room, we enjoyed a great meal. Norway cleaned out his bowl, enjoying the doggie burger and rice. My salad dressing was a good topping. And the pasta marinara worked well.

In the evening, Norway wanted to go outside, and I needed to grab stuff from the car. We stepped out of the warm room and into the cool night. Norway went over to the lit dog section in front of the hotel. He sniffed and explored the enclosed, clean area. The festive green, white, and red night-lights lit up their pups' area, and a basket of balls was provided to play catch with the dog. Every detail was taken care of at this motel.

We returned to the room. I gave Norway a biscuit, and he hopped onto the high bed. After enjoying his dinner treat, he went to sleep while listening to the oldies radio music.

TUCUMCARI, NEW MEXICO, to GALLUP, NEW MEXICO

AFTER LAST NIGHT'S nine-thirty stroll, we stayed in the rest of
the evening. Norway switched back and forth between the bed and
the thick floor rug. But, thankfully, he had no desire to go outside
until six thirty a.m.

Following our brief walk, I started searching online for Route
66 sites in New Mexico. Then, it occurred to me: *When did I miss
Kansas?*

I had overlooked the signs and historic sites listing Kansas
among the Route 66 states. I opened a map and realized I had taken
I-44 out of Joplin, Missouri, and bypassed the Galena, Kansas, turnoff, heading directly into Oklahoma, where we started at Commerce
and Miami. *Unbelievable.* I had missed the thirteen-mile section of
Route 66 in the southeast corner of Kansas, six hundred miles ago.
Fortunately, this was a round-trip road trip. We could get a second
chance on the way back through Missouri.

Today, we started at an auto museum in Santa Rosa, NM. I
figured I'd get a few snapshots of the cars outside. *Maybe get inside*

with Norway? When we arrived, I noted a few autos displayed around the parking lot. While taking pictures, I watched a family head toward the entrance. They had left their dog in the car.

I asked inside about bringing Norway into the museum, and the lady seemed OK with it. I offered to pay extra for Norway, but she insisted I only pay the five-dollar entrance fee.

"Just don't touch any of the cars!" she said.

Excellent, Norway was in. *It never hurts to ask.*

The auto museum was fine. It was more of a private collection with restored and vintage cars for sale. I especially liked the old-era memorabilia in the shop surrounding the cars. Norway was happy to be participating. Overall, it was a good, nostalgic excursion.

Cruising around the Route 66 Auto Museum

We continued along I-40 West, briefly connecting to adjacent Route 66 in Moriarty. In view was another Love's Travel Stop with a dog park. Nice. Norway was napping in the back until our next break.

We passed through Albuquerque. Considering it was eleven thirty in the morning, there was a lot of traffic. Quite a big city. We continued through the snow-dusted mountains under overcast skies. Then, we marched past the Route 66 casino to Grants, NM.

In Grants, there was an eighteen-foot-high neon display begging for souvenir photos, including your car. Finished in 2016, it honored ninety years of Route 66 passing through town. Next to the neon bridge was a large park, beside the uranium mining museum.

En Fuego in Grants, New Mexico

During the last hour of driving to Gallup, we went along a beautiful stretch of scenery. I noticed a sign announcing the Continental Divide. *It doesn't hurt to check. If it's nothing, we can pop back on I-40.*

At the turnoff, an excellent sign displayed the Continental Divide town and elevation next to a Navajo gift shop. Mostly, I got a great view of the snowcapped red rock mountains!

Norway at the Continental Divide

We reached Gallup and checked into the La Quinta Inn. We entered a nice suite on the second floor, which included a bed with a living room area. There was a big table for my laptop computer and electronics. Norway hopped onto the bed while I checked email, uploaded photos, and wrote notes. I also tried to figure out why my camera was messed up.

After an hour, we headed out to visit the Gallup sites. Traveling down a busy Route 66, we found the Code Talker statue. Located outside a cultural museum, the ten-foot statue honors the Navajo code talkers who served in World War II. We parked and walked around the town. I noted lots of murals and Native Americans wandering around. After going up and down the historic downtown streets, it was time to search for the Galoop statue and pick up dinner. We drove west for a while to the end of town. I completely misjudged the map. I searched for gas, settling for a run-down gas station. I filled up the tank, paying with cash since the pump kiosks would not accept my card. Then, we backtracked ten minutes east into town.

On the way, we unexpectedly ran into Ford Drive—the street I had been looking for in the first place. We followed it up the road over the I-40 and back down to the turn. We turned left and on the side was the thirty-foot-tall Galoop statue. Named for Gallup + Loop, the cool piece looked like a cutout from a Hot Wheels loop. Officially, the sculpture is titled *Paso por Aqui*, meaning "pass through here"—a tribute to the groups of people who contributed to Gallup's history. Unfortunately, there was no place to park for a closer view. Maybe that was intended to prevent graffiti.

We continued maneuvering through traffic, figuring this road would lead to the pizzeria. When I spotted Fratelli's Pizza Bistro on the other side of the road, we turned around and parked in the crowded lot.

I went inside to order pizza, salad, and a soda. Back in the car, I sat with Norway and checked email while waiting for the pizza.

When I returned twenty-five minutes later, the order wasn't ready. No surprise; they were busy! The young kid remembered taking my order. I gave a woman my name: Friedman. She said there was a mix-up in the back. Then she asked what I had ordered. I repeated the items.

"Wait, are you Lance?" She figured out that I had given the wrong name.

"Oh, I'm so sorry." They were busy, and I was not helping their situation. "My bad."

I appreciated the courtesy and awareness of the woman and the young kid handling the large dinner crowd.

I got the food and returned to our hotel, which was on the other side of town. It took a while to get back. Also, we had a room on the second floor and had to use an elevator. And the items required two trips between the car and the room. I had to leave Norway in the car and bring the food upstairs, then return to the car and get Norway and his dog bowls and dog food. My stomach was growling. Norway was so anxious to get to the room, he raced ahead into the hotel lobby and straight to the elevator. Then, on the second floor, he led me right to our room.

At last, we could enjoy the pizza dinner, watch TV, and relax in the huge suite!

GALLUP, NEW MEXICO, to PHOENIX, ARIZONA

AT SIX THIRTY, I prepared for a morning stroll, wearing a thermal shirt, sweatshirt, and jacket. Norway had his coat. We were set for the whipping arctic wind. I patiently followed Norway around the La Quinta grounds. In back, we found the pet area, which was clean and enclosed but had no grass. It was adorned with lava rocks, boulders, rocks, gravel, and a bare tree in the middle. Lots of scents for Norway! Meanwhile, a few other guests were outside in the dark with their dogs.

After twenty-five minutes, we returned to the room. I jumped in the refreshing shower. Nice and warm, with high shower head and great water pressure. Then, I put on my jeans for the sixth day in a row. They passed the smell test. I layered up, anticipating a wintery drive through northern Arizona and Flagstaff.

I ran downstairs to drop off a bag in the car. On the way back, I collected watery orange juice and a banana from the breakfast area. Hot chocolate would have been a better option. When I returned to the room, Norway was at the door. At some point, he had gotten up from his cozy spot on the bed.

After scanning the room and leaving a five-dollar tip for maid service, we headed out into the chill to begin our sixth leg to Phoenix. We went onto I-40 local, which was Route 66, then merged onto I-40 toward Flagstaff.

Due to time and the overcast weather, we skipped the Petrified Forest and Painted Desert. These are wonderful places to visit another day. The focus of this trip was Route 66 and surprising the family. An hour later, we reached Holbrook, AZ., stopping briefly to peek at the longest Route 66 mural. It was huge. Plus, another wall carried a mural of the Petrified Forest attraction. Although not the most colorful or artistic, it was an impressive effort by the steakhouse across the street.

We returned to the car and continued thirty miles to Winslow. At the first opportunity inside the eastern city limits, we exited to Route 66. There were a few photo ops and a dog park. *Perfect.*

Winslow Bark Park was huge. After ninety minutes of driving, this was a terrific break for Norway. Since it was enclosed and empty, I cut Norway loose. While he explored, I went through photos on my camera.

Ten minutes later, a woman from New Mexico pulled up with a large dog. I reached for Norway's leash and gathered him.

The woman asked, "Does he get along with other dogs?"

"Sometimes." I hesitated. "He's friendly, but sometimes, he gets overexcited and can play rough."

"That's OK," the woman said, looking at her dog. "She'll be fine. And will be submissive if needed."

I released Norway, and, with enthusiasm, he plowed into Hazel. But they worked it out, and Norway had a sweet, new canine friend!

Fortunately, the weather was chilly but not brutal. And Norway got rid of a lot of energy. After thirty minutes outside, we packed up and headed down the road to see the "Standin' on the Corner" Park.

Standin' on the Corner in Winslow

Winslow had a pleasant downtown and historic district and Route 66 themes. Aside from some homeless stragglers, it was rather clean and not too crowded. The shops seemed nice. We took photos, walked up and down the streets, and found an area with free Arizona maps.

I considered lunch but preferred to add miles. I had no idea what the road conditions in Flagstaff would be. I handed Norway a treat. Then I grabbed a bag of pretzels and a wild cherry Marilyn Monroe soda purchased a few days ago at the giant rocker in Fanning, MO.

Oh, it is not a twist top. And I don't have a bottle opener. I used a hammer from the trunk to pop open the top.

We passed through the mountain area and high elevation of Flagstaff. The visibility varied, as snow came down sporadically. But the roads were decent, and traffic flow was great. We departed I-40 West and turned onto I-17 South. Roughly eighty percent of the way to Santa Monica, CA, we stopped tracing Route 66. Not enough time. Someday we'll return and drive the remaining portion of the Mother Road. We reached our final planned stop in Camp Verde to visit Montezuma Castle. It was much different than I remembered—especially the towering hotel and casino atop a mountain.

At the park entrance, there was a moderate crowd. I left Norway in the car to check about fees and dog policy. A uniformed park ranger said they were closing. "We want to get out for New Year's Eve." It was only 1:45.

I thought they would at least stay open until three o'clock. The entrance sign indicated closing at 4:45. Oh well.

It seemed like a cool spot to wander. Instead, I took a few photos of the distant castle. Norway and I walked around the parking area.

While leaving the historic area, a sign caught my eye: "Fry Bread." *I remember that!* As a kid, Indian Fry bread dusted with powdered sugar was a fantastic treat. It's like funnel cake but lighter.

We U-turned and pulled into the gravel lot. A friendly guy was selling Apache and Navajo trinkets, as well as fry bread.

"We're out," he said.

"Really?"

"I have to make another batch," he said. "It'll take twenty-five minutes."

"Great! We'll wait."

We had traveled two thousand miles over six days. We could spare a few extra minutes for fry bread!

While Norway and I hung out, we watched other tourists pull in. We chatted with a college coed who grew up in Camp Verde. She loved Norway, and it was a nice conversation.

"Norway, it looks like you have another friend," I said.

"I love dogs," she replied. "Especially huskies. Does he talk?"

"Sometimes," I said. "At night, he'll bark at me when he wants his ice cream."

"Ice cream? I bet he likes that."

"I give him a treat each night. Sometimes, I'm doing work. He'll show up, look at me, then bark to let me know. So, I get him his snack." Then, I added, "And yes, sometimes, he'll do the husky talk. It is funny."

"He's so pretty," she said while petting him. "And so well-behaved."

"He might be waiting for the fry bread," I joked. "But he has calmed down. When I first got him, he tore up the house."

"Really?" she said.

I gave a few examples. Then, "A long time ago, I met a woman who raised huskies. She told me that in about five years, he will mellow out! Five years? That's a lot of damage." I laughed. "But now it's five years later, and Norway is so much mellower and better behaved. Such a fantastic companion."

The vendor handed out the next batch of fry bread. I got the traditional powdered sugar and a cinnamon sugar one. The Camp Verde coed got a fry bread taco, which had beans, tomato, and lettuce on it. Yummy snacks.

Eyeing the fry bread

I offered Norway some of my fry bread. He took a piece and buried it in the dirt. That amused a bystander watching. Norway did sample a few pieces, but he preferred the chew bone I gave him instead.

We continued down two more exits and went into Camp Verde to see the world's largest Kokopelli. The thirty-foot-tall figure stood in front of a Starbucks and a fast-food joint. It was a cool giant statue. I wondered if people knew who Kokopelli was and what the fertility significance of a giant Kokopelli might represent!

I jumped back into the car, and we cruised the last eighty miles on I-17, descending in elevation, racing to Phoenix. The Saturday traffic was minimal, so we arrived at the hotel in no time.

Across the street was a bank sign that stated the temperature was sixty-two. I watched a guy in shorts and a T-shirt jogging with a stroller. This was much different than what I'd seen back home and during the trip.

Best Western Inn Suites was located two blocks from my dad's house. There was plenty of parking and an easy check-in. During the reception, a couple enjoyed meeting Norway.

We got our room at the end, next to a wall bordering Northern Avenue, but traffic noise wasn't a problem. The comfortable suite included a full entry living room with counter, fridge, microwave, couch, desk, and TV. Then, through the doorway, was a separate bedroom area and another TV. Lots of room to set up and take it easy.

After watching the end of the Michigan vs. TCU football game, it was time to surprise my dad. I walked a few blocks down the road with Norway to my dad's house. He was taken aback and pleased to see us at his door. His dog Cooper and Norway began scouting each other out. To avoid confrontation, they took Cooper into another room. I felt bad that we were invading their dog's place. I offered to sit outside, but my dad felt it was too cold. It's possible that sixty degrees was a desert chill by Phoenix standards.

After a couple of hours, we walked back to the room. Time for some dinner at eight thirty on New Year's Eve. I intended to search up 16th Street to Camelback, down to 7th Street, up 7th Street, and back to the room. Just one-fourth of the way, I opted for Jimmy

John's. It's a franchise I can get anytime. But I was too tired to wait for a busy restaurant to prepare our order. I picked up a sub sandwich in three minutes. Fast and cheap. God bless the young guys working on a Saturday New Year's Eve. I appreciate that work ethic.

The parking lot of the hotel was still rather empty. *Are people staying downtown? Or are they staying at more upscale resorts?*

In the room, Norway gobbled down his regular dog food. Then, he fell asleep on the couch. After dinner, I sat beside Norway and watched TV. We were enjoying our New Year's Eve in luxury.

PHOENIX, ARIZONA

HAPPY NEW YEAR! To celebrate, Norway rang in 2023 with a one a.m. walk around the hotel. We slept great until seven thirty. It was drizzling outside. I tend to sleep well when it's raining or snowing. It was the same for Norway. Many times I have seen him peacefully sleeping out back in the rain and snow.

Since we had to visit my friend Linda before ten a.m., I allotted enough time for a shower, a quick breakfast, and the forty-minute drive.

The shower was out of shampoo. *Two televisions, but no shampoo. I'll take that trade-off.* I pulled out my extras from other hotels.

After dressing, I took Norway for a walk. Despite a slight sprinkle, it felt warm considering where we he had been one week ago.

In the lobby, I sipped orange juice and collected a muffin and hot chocolate packets for later. On the way back, I ran into a housekeeper who was checking rooms.

"Hi. I'm staying in Room 163. Do you clean that one?"

"Sorry, in Spanish," she replied.

I utilized my rusty high school Spanish.

"In *cuarto cien, sesenta, y tres.* [I hoped that was room 163.] *Dos días, so no necesita.*"

She nodded. "No need to clean."

"*Sí,*" I said, satisfied with my communication skills.

As Norway and I headed to the car, the rain was picking up. *What happened to sunny Phoenix?*

The drive to Linda and husband Brent's home went well. Without traffic, we got there as planned. We stopped for gas at a remote station, near a Rosati's Pizza—just like the ones in Chicago. Someone probably saw the desert light and moved to Arizona.

Linda and Brent lived on the edge of town. Their large spread included a ranch home, animals, and land. It was incredible how much Phoenix and Scottsdale had grown. Open desert had been replaced with housing developments, restaurants, and shopping plazas. And it was still growing.

We enjoyed two hours of catching up and reminiscing. Meanwhile, Norway made another wonderful friend: Murphy, their two-year-old dog. While they played endlessly, we talked about common friends, elementary school, and the changes to Arizona.

With more places to visit, it was time to go. Plus, I became concerned that the continuing rain would flood the dirt roads to their house. I didn't want to get stuck.

We retraced our way back toward Phoenix. Unable to reach another friend, Roger, I stopped at a place called Habit to grab a veggie burger, sweet potato fries, and a Coke. Then we headed back to connect with my dad at the hotel suite.

We chatted for a couple of hours. Meanwhile, Norway enjoyed his treat, some of my burger, and just napping on my dad's lap.

After my dad left, we took an hour of rest while it kept raining outside. This was a good reset day halfway through our trip. I tried Roger's home and work numbers. No luck. At six thirty, we got into the car and drove ten minutes to his house. *Maybe he's home?* Otherwise, we would pick up dessert and call it a day.

We arrived and found Roger, his wife, Cece, and two of their three daughters at home. Plus, their two dogs. They put the dogs in another room, allowing Norway to come inside. I apologized for Norway pushing aside their dogs. But it was OK. Norway was a big hit with the daughters. He wasn't shy about climbing onto the couch with them. When you're handsome, you get away with it!

Norway making himself at home

We stayed for a few hours updating and recounting stories from high school and college. Meanwhile, Norway wandered around inside and outside their house. By ten o'clock we left. It was a good day catching up with friends. Good day for Norway socializing!

Following a sweep through a McDonald's drive-thru for ice cream, we went back to the room. After treats, Norway was asleep on the couch.

PHOENIX, ARIZONA, to SIERRA VISTA, ARIZONA

EXCITED TO GET rolling, we were up at seven thirty. I grabbed another packet of hot chocolate, checked messages, and prepared for departure. While walking around the hotel grounds, Norway and I ran into the Best Western maintenance guy. He stopped us to chat for a few minutes. *Another Norway fan!*

After departing the hotel, I did a quick drive down memory lane. We went by the 115 Lawrence house, where I grew up. They had changed the entire structure and front yard, removing the grapefruit trees—now unrecognizable from my childhood. Towering behind was the Madison Meadows Elementary School's second floor. It seemed modernized beyond the 1970s architecture I remembered.

We drove a few miles along Central Avenue, passing Brophy Prep, where I attended high school. Then, we went past the Valley Metro Rail, up Indian School, to the 51 Highway, and south to I-10 East. Since Norway was sleeping in the back, we continued straight to Tucson, cruising around eighty mph. We passed Tucson then onto AZ-90. Then we traveled thirty miles to Sierra Vista.

When the car stopped, Norway popped his head up to scan the surroundings. He was fresh and alert after a three-hour nap. Meanwhile, I called my sister, Kelly.

"We're in town."

"Where are you?" she asked.

"At the Sierra Suites. But we haven't checked in yet," I said. "Is Mom there?"

"She's on her way over for lunch." My mom lived within walking distance of my sister's house.

"Perfect. We'll come over now."

My sister gave quick directions, and ten minutes later we were at her front door.

I knocked quietly. Kelly opened the door. When I entered, my mom lit up, surprised to see me standing there. Then, Norway came from behind, wagging his tail.

"Oh my. You drove all the way!"

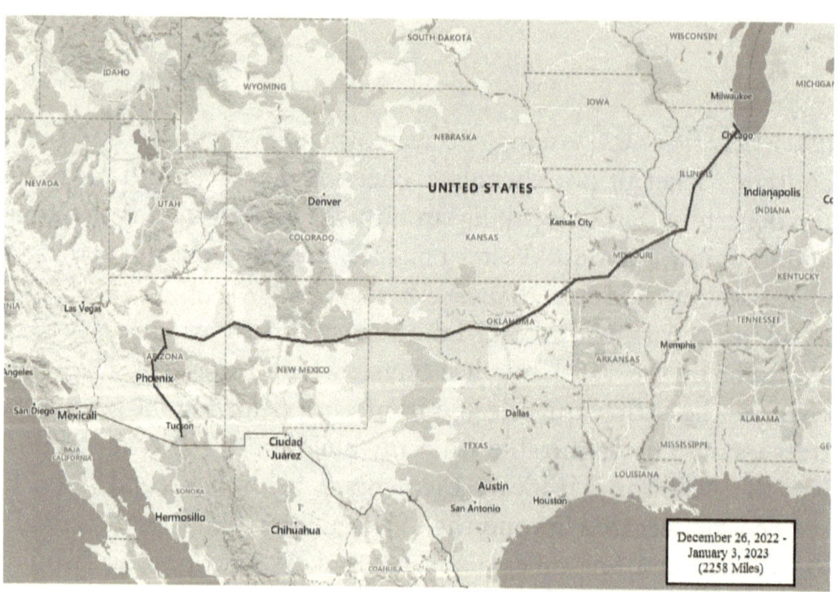

We had lunch outside Jersey Mike's and MOD Pizza in their open seating area. The temperature was a chilly fifties, mixed with wind and sun. Although Sierra Vista is one hour south of Tucson, near the Mexico border, its climate is cooler due to the elevation and nearby mountains. When the sunshine was blocked by clouds, we wrapped up lunch quickly.

While my sister and mom returned home, I took Norway to Veteran's Park down the road on Fry Drive. In the huge park, lots of people were using the temporarily constructed ice rink. Meanwhile, Norway and I enjoyed the windy, arctic walk. To the left were a series of festive Santa billboard paintings. In the distance, I could see the snowy mountains.

Two miles down the road, we checked into the Sierra Suites. There were only a few cars in the parking lot. Inside was an appealing place with a Southwestern motif, tile floors, and Native American decor. We were greeted by the nice management.

Our huge double-bed suite had a full table, desk, two beds, TV, lounge chair, and kitchen area. The beds were higher than ordinary. When Norway hesitated and looked at me, I walked over and gave him a boost. He popped up, circled around, and found his spot in the soft bed. Meanwhile, I watched a show on the giant-screen TV, went through the daily cryptic crossword, and relaxed.

Following a two-hour Norway nap on the lofty bed, we headed over to Mom's for dinner, laundry access, and hanging out. A good reset.

Anticipating a tasty dinner

SIERRA VISTA, ARIZONA (day 2)

DURING A LATE-EVENING Norway tour around the premises, we ran into a young guy.

He greeted us. "Nice dog."

"Thanks!" I responded. *Too bad the nice dog likes to roam in the middle of the night.*

We continued the sidewalk route around the quiet area. The rest of the night, Norway was on and off the bed, but I still managed to get a decent bit of sleep. The good news is we'd have all day to do whatever we wanted.

The hotel had a fantastic dining room with several breakfast options, centered on three egg dishes of different Southwest/Mexican flavors. The bananas were fresh. And the peeled oranges were sweet and tasty. Arizona is a citrus state. I sampled one of the vanilla pancakes. It had good flavor—a little thick, but not bad. I was very pleased with the hotel choice. And we were set for breakfast tomorrow.

Today's plan started with the dog park. My sister and mom had mentioned the spot. On the map, it was a 1.3-mile trek from our hotel. We welcomed the exercise. It had been ten days since we'd done our usual three-to-four-mile morning routine. The temperature was in the forties, but it was bone-chilling with the wind. I wore four layers and gloves. Norway was delighted with the sunny, cold environment.

Starting down 7th Street toward Tompkins Park, we walked and walked, passing residential neighborhoods, Circle K, and a disc golf park. On the way, a guy went by in shorts and a T-shirt. Then, I saw a lightly dressed cyclist pedal by. *Crazy.* Ahead of us was a view of the snow-capped mountains.

We reached the enormous open public park. On the other side were enclosed dog areas. In one section a guy was playing fetch with his thirty-pound pointer. The dog saw Norway and stopped to watch as we approached. The pointer and Norway inspected each other with the fence between them. Then, Norway began his playful run-back-and-forth game with the dog.

While the two dogs interacted and engaged through the fence, I got to know Warren, from Minnesota, who had been living the last sixteen years in Sierra Vista.

"You can let your dog in," Warren offered.

"Maybe in a few minutes." I wasn't sure if Norway would trounce Sarah, the ten-month-old pointer. I had hoped to let Norway run free in the adjacent small-dog section, but a woman with her little dog was inside.

We said good-bye and started back. Suddenly, Norway and I spotted a couple approaching with their white-eyed husky.

They asked, "Is he friendly?"

"Mostly. He sometimes plays rough. He is just playing, but he does scare off dogs."

"He does too," the guy said.

The huskies crouched and danced around each other. It seemed harmless. So we followed them back to the dog park. The couple stepped inside and let their husky go. It ran up to Sarah the pointer.

Oh well. May as well see if Norway can run along. I cut Norway loose inside the large area. He raced to the other two dogs. They introduced themselves with a few sniffs. Then, for thirty minutes, Norway happily ran and played with his friends.

When another showed up, the pack went over to greet it. Then, the four dogs ran.

Norway running with the pack at Sierra Vista dog park

The owners appreciated the dogs having fun and expending energy. I learned about Brendan and Hayley and Steel, their eleven-year-old white-eyed husky. Eighty pounds and lean!

"Damn, your husky looks fantastic," I said. "I thought he was three years old. What do you feed him?"

The guy laughed. "Good dog food. But, mostly, we run him. A lot."

I was encouraged. *Hopefully, Norway will be that spry when he's eleven.*

I learned they had driven from Portland, Maine, to Sierra Vista. She had a five-month health-care job in this area. I offered my card. "If you have questions, just email. I'll pass along my sister and my mom's contact info."

During the walk back, the clouds passed and the sun emerged, opening up a wonderful view of the mountains.

We returned to Sierra Suites. Norway took a big gulp of water. Then he wandered to the high bed and stood there.

"Alright. A little boost." I helped him onto the cozy bed. He sat for two minutes, content with the morning activity. A minute later he was out!

Power nap

While waiting for lunch and giving Norway some downtime, I watched TV, stretched, and had a cup of hot tea. Just a routine vacation day. Up, WarRoom podcast, walk Norway, cryptic crossword, lunch, check messages, watch TV, exercise, run Norway, dinner—except in a hotel rather than home. Still, I was glad we took the road trip. Exploring hundreds of miles is a much different way to occupy time.

We were ready for lunch. According to my mom, it was Taco Tuesday at 143 Street Tacos. Hopefully, it wouldn't be too crowded at one thirty, following the usual work crowd. If outdoor seating was unavailable, or, it became too cold, we could return to the hotel room and use the dining table and chairs.

From the hotel, we walked four blocks down Fry Blvd. to Fab Ave. and to the taco place. The food looked terrific. I ordered a sample of tacos: chicken, carne asada, and combination. Plus beans and rice. I would give Norway the meat and I would eat the tortillas with beans, rice, and guacamole. The owner was running the register, and his wife had prepared the fresh sauces. Interestingly, the place looked like a chain restaurant with Sesame Street colorful decor. Forty bucks for everyone's food—a bargain when you consider it would easily feed four of us. As my sister and I filled our soda cups, they called us.

We looked at each other. "Did they just call our number?"

They had prepared the entire food order before we had collected napkins and gotten our drinks. Although a line of customers kept them busy, this place was filling the fresh orders incredibly fast. It seemed they had a consistent daily lunch crowd. We sat outside at tables in the crisp sunshine. The food was quite good.

Afterward, Norway and I walked back to the hotel, where we took a long siesta. Exhausted, but we were enjoying the day off from driving.

After six o'clock, we rallied to visit my mom and sister. On the way, I stopped at Julie and Sammy's 33 flavors Ice Cream shop. It was Thrifty ice cream with candy, video games, and novelty items. Inside, a young guy was minding the place alone. He was about to sit down when he saw me enter.

"Hey, can I grab some ice cream?" I asked, not wanting to trouble him.

"Sure, what would you like?"

I looked over the flavors and picked out cherry chocolate chip. "And regular chocolate chip."

"We're out."

"OK, cookies and cream."

It was $4.00 for one scoop and $6.50 for two scoops. *I remember when Thrifty scoops were twenty-five cents.* He stuffed about a pint of ice cream into the Styrofoam cup. So it was a big size.

We chatted while he filled the order. Then I left a tip. *Tuesday night, by himself, serving ice cream.* I appreciate and admire people who are friendly and put effort into their job.

I drove over to my mom's place with Norway, eating ice cream, and we spent a few hours there.

Back on the road tomorrow.

SIERRA VISTA, ARIZONA, to LAS CRUCES, NEW MEXICO

AFTER WATCHING TV, I climbed out of bed, showered, packed a few things, and grabbed breakfast. I picked out another sweet orange and a banana. Instead of vanilla pancakes, the Sierra Suites offered a mango crisp. I gave that one a try. *Pretty damn good.*

In the room, I shared breakfast with Norway. Unexpectedly, there was no Wi-Fi connection. Fortunately, I already made screenshots of maps and sites, and I had arranged tonight's hotel. Outside, the weather was cool, crisp, and calm. I anticipated easy driving conditions. From the parking lot, I admired the beautiful silhouette of mountains surrounding Sierra Vista.

We left town on AZ-90, until merging onto I-10 East. Following a dozen roadside billboards advertising "What if?" and "The Thing," I decided to pull over. Even if it was a tourist trap, the car did need gas. I took Exit 322 into Benson. Next to the museum entrance was a big stretch of tourist items for sale. After pumping gas and walking Norway around the premises—a Dairy Queen and fast-food place—I went inside to browse the Southwest trinkets and ask about the attraction. The woman said it was pet-friendly, which was good enough for me!

For five bucks, Norway and I strolled through the touristy "Twilight Zone" history museum. At the end, there was a "thing" that looked like a sci-fi creature. Apparently, it was found sixty years ago in an Arizona mine.

Norway eyeing the Thing

I wasn't sure what to make of it. Regardless, I got to stroll around the shop with Norway. He seemed to like it.

We drove an hour to Bowie, AZ, to see a very colorful Rambo mural and the Earth traveler signpost. The cartoon mural was a tribute to the fictional Vietnam veteran, Rambo, who was born in Bowie. *Some movie trivia.* Nearby, a signpost for earthlings stood, with an odd list of places, including the moon. Behind it was Dwayne's Fresh Jerky trading post, selling a variety of local goods, including honey, jerky, dried fruit, and more. I purchased samples of fudge, toffee peanuts, and caramel candies. A few snacks for the road.

Our next I-10 pull-off was Deming, a town of fifteen thousand people in southwest New Mexico. Their veterans' park contains several appealing monuments—especially a granite Bataan Death March engraved memorial. Very haunting. I learned that New Mexico had a large percentage of veterans in the Pacific theater during World War II.

In the afternoon, we arrived in Las Cruces. We detoured to the "world's largest red chili," a forty-seven-foot-tall concrete vegetable displayed in front of the Red Chili Inn. *I'm starting to think everyone has a "world's largest" something!*

Norway and a giant red chili

After a photo and a few moments walking Norway, we headed through town. I noticed a lot of random people walking around. *Are they homeless? Veterans? Illegal immigrants?* It was a sketchy, strange vibe. Nevertheless, the mountain view surrounding Las Cruces was very pretty.

We reached the hotel at two o'clock. The woman at the Drury said the room wasn't ready. But she kindly left a note for maid service to do our room next.

Norway and I roamed around the Drury, Hampton Inn, Golden Corral, and McDonald's. It wasn't the most scenic, but Norway enjoyed it. He was just smelling things, with little regard for the sights.

"No grazing!" I yanked him away from a chicken piece lying at the curb.

He trotted along to the next area.

"Shall we return to civilization?"

We went back to the lobby at 2:45. I brought my laptop in to occupy the time. Five minutes later, the woman said our room was ready.

"I heard there is a dinner tonight," I said.

"Yes, the Drury has the 'kickback' at five thirty."

"What are they serving tonight?" Maybe the hotel's offer is a dinner-worthy option?

"Usually it's nachos and hot dogs and such. But today is Wednesday. We serve salad, pasta alfredo, chicken strips, chili, and potatoes."

"Fantastic," I said. "That's like a real meal."

Two senior ladies were listening and waiting to check in.

"He'll like that," they said, pointing to Norway.

"Oh, yeah. He'll go for the chicken strips."

Upstairs, the suite was huge. The entry area was a sizable living room with couch, TV, desk, and open space. Then, a hallway with full kitchen that included a sink, refrigerator, microwave, and counter space. Past the bathroom on the left was a king-size bed with a large-screen TV at the end. This was an apartment!

While I was working, Norway started on the couch. Five minutes later, I turned and saw he was gone. I peeked in the bedroom, and he had picked the king bed for his spot.

For dinner, I fed Norway his dry and wet dog food mix. Then, I headed to the lobby to check out the offerings. Popcorn was set out, and a few guests lingered around with drinks. *I wonder if they're as hungry as I am!* The buffet was pretty good. I had chili with a potato. Then, I scooped some fettuccine noodles. I added chicken strips and a hot dog for Norway. The complimentary meal worked.

Oddly, our giant hotel suite had small trash cans without plastic bags. Fortunately, a garbage can was placed in the hallway, right outside my room. I opened the door, took two steps out, and tossed the snacks and dinner scraps in the garbage can. Also, the fitness room and business center (with computers and printers) were conveniently right outside our room.

For dessert, I tried the Dwayne's fudge I'd picked up this afternoon. It was very good, sort of chewy. A worthy purchase.

"Sorry, Norway, no chocolate for you."

Instead, I handed him a doggie treat. He trotted away with his tail wagging.

LAS CRUCES, NEW MEXICO, to ODESSA, TEXAS

AT ONE A.M., the husky invited me for a walk. I climbed out of bed, dressed, and followed Norway to the stairs. He stopped, looked over the edge, and turned around. *Still need to work on steep steps and gaps.* I led him to an elevator, where we went down and stumbled outside. Into the chill, I followed Norway as he eagerly took care of business.

While out there, lit-up semi trucks went by on I-10 above us. One after another. *That seems like a rough job. How long have they been driving? Do they have a deadline?* This was night driving through open New Mexico. For two weeks, I had been driving three hundred miles per day with Norway. *How long could I do it?*

We returned to the room and slept until sunup. For breakfast, I tried an apple and a cup of orange juice. Although they looked good, I passed on the eggs and salsas. After the "kickback" dinner last night, I was plenty full. I filled Norway's water jug and handed him a morning treat.

We left our Drury palace and checked out. I was very pleased with this suite. I had been paying up at every hotel. If it had an upgrade option, I paid extra. At the same time, I considered the pet fees. They ranged from free to outrageous.

We resumed on I-10 East. Adding to a long driving leg, we were making up for a one-hour time zone change. We left southern New Mexico and crossed into the western tip of Texas and began going through El Paso. The roads were crowded at ten a.m. On the right were the mountains and brown air. *Is it smog or dust settling between the mountains?* I could see Mexico in the distance. I think we passed over a dry part of the Rio Grande.

As we headed deeper into El Paso, I could see the metropolis blend of El Paso with Juarez, Mexico. We passed by a turnoff south to the border and proceeded through the busy town. Outside of El Paso, the speed limit in Texas cranked up to eighty mph on the interstates.

In Sierra Blanca, we paused at the rest stop at mile 99. It was a good spot for a leg stretch. The scene of mountains in the distance and giant concrete teepees offered a nice Southwest flavor.

Chief Norway at the rest stop

At the interstate fork, we departed I-10 and headed northeast on I-20. A lot of the drive was remote. I even saw a sign that read: "Toyah - Population 61." Tomorrow, going through middle of Texas, I expected more of the same.

On the way to Monahans, TX, we stopped in Pecos for gas. *Why not check out another small town?* Inside the gas station was a Hunt Pizza. They had a few remaining slices under a heat lamp. That would work: two slices of pizza and a Dr. Pepper snack.

We went around the corner to Veterans Memorial Park. There was a nice seating area next to an airplane and in front of the Pecos, Texas, water tower. The sun was shining with a cool breeze. It was a pleasant January afternoon.

Across the way was an enormous public park. Norway had his eyes focused on little dogs in the adjacent dog park. After the snack, we went there to investigate. The new Maxey dog park was a great spot. The large dog park was occupied, so we didn't enter. But Norway did meet another dog.

Following the thirty-minute break, we continued east on I-20, where pumping oil rigs started appearing. I didn't mind them too much. Unlike giant wind farms, the rigs didn't destroy the skyline.

After forty miles, we entered Monahans to check out the Million Barrel Museum. When we arrived at the area, a woman came outside. During the introduction, I learned she was the caretaker. Originally from Cleveland, she had happily settled in Texas, where she'd lived for the past twenty-five years. I could see her dogs in the distance.

"Yes, you can take your dog in any building except these."

Norway and I walked around the campus. In the background we came across a huge area that used to hold oil. During the West Texas oil boom in the 1920s, there was so much crude being pumped, they didn't have enough barrels to store it. So, Shell Oil Company built this massive concrete container to hold it. Unfortunately, the weight of the million barrels of oil eventually cracked the concrete foundation, so oil soaked back into the ground. Decades later, a man sealed the cracks and filled it with water for recreational activities. But the weight of the water cracked the foundation again. Eventually, the Ward County Historical Commission was gifted the property by the owner's widow. The giant crater has become an area for the town's major events.

Beside the open expanse sat a historic area. Inside the heritage museum, an extensive display gave tribute to the World War II contributions by men and women from this area. An entire section presented stories from the county. Outside, Norway and I browsed alongside a historic house and railcar.

We met two missionaries living in the area. They took a liking to Norway and proceeded to ask if I would like to meet with one of their sisters in Odessa. "No thanks. Wrong religion," I said. "But I appreciate what you're doing."

After an hour, I made a small donation to the museum and said good-bye to the caretaker. We headed down the road to the next exit to see the white sand dunes. Very cool. I wished we had more time. It would be fun to take Norway running up and down those dunes! Instead, we raced to the Permian Basin Museum in Midland.

At 4:40, we reached the museum, twenty minutes before closing. I went inside to scout out the exhibits. It was intriguing but too much to see in a short time. After five minutes, getting a gist of the layout and history, I retrieved Norway and we explored the interesting stuff displayed out front.

We kept the tour short. Norway was having problems with the thorns getting in his paws. After fifteen minutes, we returned to the car. I drove to the back of the museum, where tons of old drills and equipment lay next to the oil patch. A unique collection. Mostly, I could appreciate the area—this was oil country!

Canine oil tycoon

At five thirty, we backtracked westward to Odessa. Unfortunately, there was construction. Worse, the sun was setting. I drove fifteen miles with the sun beaming through the windshield. A brutal and blinding light. But, at least, I had come that way, so I was somewhat familiar with the stretch of road.

Eventually, we reached Exit 121 and headed north. I surveyed the area until the road ran out of buildings. *Too far. I missed it.* I turned around and found the hotel on the way back. Also, I spotted the Chris Kyle statue just down the street. Perfect! We would return tomorrow morning.

After a long day of driving and covering the miles and sights, we landed at the La Quinta Inn and Suites, a giant complex with two buildings.

I walked into the entry. "I'm here to check in."

"What's the name?"

"Friedman. Lance."

"It's not here," the man answered.

I knew there were several La Quintas in Odessa and Midland. I didn't want to get back into the car and try another.

I checked my email again. "It's the one at 4122 Faudree."

"Oh, that's the other building." He pointed across the street.

We moved to the other part of the lot. After checking in, Norway grabbed a ninety-minute nap on the bed. Then we rallied and went two blocks away to Rosa's Cafe for tacos. It had a franchise-homemade feel, located in a crowded retail area with Chick-fil-A and a Texas BBQ in the center. There were pickup trucks everywhere.

I snatched a parking space in front for the to-go orders. Five minutes later, we left with a bag full of dinner: avocado and bean tostadas for me; two tacos, topped with beef and chicken, for Norway. Nothing fancy, but the ingredients were fresh. Their chocolate cake was pretty good too.

Today was a fine, long day—we'd driven over 360 miles, which included passing Odessa east, seeing the oil museum in Midland, then turning around and backtracking west to Odessa. Every travel day is an adventure.

ODESSA, TEXAS, to WICHITA FALLS, TEXAS

AT SIX A.M., I heard an alarm go off a half dozen times. Perhaps one of the construction workers staying at the hotel. Or a traveler on a tight schedule. We were on a schedule, needing to get back to Chicago before work resumed and my mail hold ended. Although both were flexible deadlines, I wanted to stick to six days to drive home.

Today's itinerary was a morning walk to the Chris Kyle Memorial. Check out of the hotel. Then three hundred miles zigzagging north and east through Texas. Online, I scanned *RoadsideAmerica* and could not find a Texas attraction until Wichita Falls. I found a website called "The Texas Bucket List," with two guys posting videos around Texas. It included a map marked with places they had visited. There were numerous clusters across their online Texas map. But not much on the route today. I even tried a search for "center of Texas." I was close: Brady, TX, was in the region, but it would add 130 miles of detour driving to see it. *That's a lot of driving for a photo op.* I decided we would just drive and see what was out there.

At eight a.m., we visited the Chris Kyle Memorial. Norway enjoyed the morning walk, but he didn't like having to stop and have me dig thorns and burrs out of his paws. The dry Texas ground was not kind to his tootsies.

I had wondered why the memorial had been placed in this empty area. Then I saw the other side of the wellness center: the Permian VA hospital.

Chris Kyle American Sniper

Unveiled in July 2016, a granite and limestone plaza with the bronze statue honored Navy S.E.A.L. Chris Kyle, born in Odessa, and featured in the movie *American Sniper*. The privately funded memorial contains quotes and powerful tributes to Kyle and other fallen American heroes. It is an impressive and inspiring memorial.

Norway and I walked and trotted back to the La Quinta. In the lobby, we received a friendly greeting from the female receptionist. Then, in the hallway, two housekeepers spotted Norway and gave him an enthusiastic welcome.

We took our time packing. Heading east, I was unsure how much the sun would be glaring in my eyes. The later we left, the higher the sun would be from the horizon.

After collecting the electronics and Norway's items, I left money and a thank-you note for housekeeping. Then, we were out the door at nine a.m.

As we drove east on I-20, I noted the surroundings. Oil rigs were pumping. On the road, trucks were hauling equipment and goods. And residents were driving big pickup trucks. I was one of the few driving a sedan. We cruised past Midland. Massive windmill farms appeared near Stanton, TX., dwarfing the oil rigs and wrecking the scenery.

We made our first stop in Sweetwater. At Exit 240, I followed signs to the National WASP World War II Museum. Two cars were parked beside a pair of big airplane hangars. Nearby was an open space that appeared to be an old airfield. I gave Norway a walking break around the entrance and parking area.

Although it was seventy degrees with a nice breeze, I cranked up the air conditioner in the car.

While Norway waited inside the running car, I entered the lobby. The woman at the front gave a welcome greeting.

"No fee," she told me.

"I'd like to check it out, but I'm traveling with my dog."

"Not a service dog?" she asked. "Or small?"

"No, he's a husky. He's eight years old. And we travel all over. So he's OK in public places. I don't like to leave him outside for long."

I scanned the museum. The ground was concrete without any carpet. Norway would not cause any damage.

"Sometimes I'll let dogs in," she confided. "But my boss is here today."

"That's fine. Some places let him in. Some don't. I just wanted to check it out."

The woman provided a brief overview of the facility. WASP training for female pilots did indeed take place here. The second hangar with airplanes was original. The place contained a lot of authentic items and history. Plus, there was a tribute to the thirty-eight servicewomen who perished during the war.

"Yes, there are five veterans living in this area between the ages of ninety-five and one hundred and five," she informed me. *Very interesting.* "Very few people visit, because it's off the highway." The lobby was empty.

"I know. I happened to catch it while online."

I asked the woman about the Rattlesnake Roundup.

"No, there's nothing to see. It's a three-day event in March. They gather the snakes and bleed out the venom for antivenom medicine." She went on, "And, yes, there is a BBQ. It's a good way to moderate the rattlesnake population."

On the way out, the woman confirmed my directions to Wichita Falls. I returned to Norway, who was in the front seat, listening to the radio and resting comfortably in front of the air conditioner.

We went up TX-70 North onto the backroads of Texas. Numerous posted signs made navigation better than expected. The roads were well-paved and most had a speed limit of seventy-five mph. With no trucks and few vehicles, we covered a lot of miles fast. The one downside: there wasn't much in terms of civilization. We passed many farms, windmills, oil rigs, and some cattle. But very few towns.

Soaking in the sights

Norway joined me in the front. Sitting in the passenger seat, he looked out the front window.

"You wanna drive?" I joked.

He looked at me with a smile.

"That's OK. You have one job only," I said. "Your job is to look pretty!"

He was good at it.

We turned northeast onto TX-57 and cruised along. The Big Spring Refinery was interesting.

Then we headed east on TX-92, then north on TX-277. I noted "Goree - pop: 162." And another town celebrating their Texas high school 2013 football champs. We stopped at Haskell, population 3,059. We found a park to walk around, followed by a drive through the main street. A few businesses, a couple of restaurants, and a Sonic.

Exploring a park in Haskell, Texas

TX-277 flowed directly into Wichita Falls. We arrived before three o'clock. The two sights we wanted to see were on the eastern side of town. So we pulled into the hotel from the west side. In the lobby a group of basketball players stood around with their coaches. *Perhaps they're waiting for rooms?* Alarmed, they distanced themselves from Norway. *Wolf!*

We headed up to our room on the third floor. Inside was a TV and dresser on the left and a desk at the far end, along with a king-size bed, couch, and coffee table. It was a huge studio with kitchen appliances. As I set my bag down, I saw another doorway. I peeked over and discovered an entire bedroom! The extravagance of another king bed, lounge chair, and TV for just a dog and me seemed ludicrous.

Norway grabbed a spot on the main bed. As I checked messages, I watched him get up and jump off the bed, then walk to the other room and leap onto that bed. The other room was cooler. Ten minutes later, he returned to the first bed and sprawled out. *Norway was living large!*

For dinner, we tried takeout from Asian Kitchen, located around the corner. It was a score with lots of choices. I appreciated the simple dishes—the chicken and broccoli consisted of just chicken and broccoli. I ordered sweet and sour chicken, vegetables deluxe, and chicken lo mein. I was sure I could put together dishes for Norway and me. *Another Friedman sampler.*

While waiting twenty minutes, we scouted the area and ran errands. I noticed a painted mural horse in front of the grocery store. It looked like part of a city project, like the cows in Chicago, IL, the horses in Ogden, UT, or the little sprouts in Blue Earth, MN. I sensed there were others throughout the city. At the gas station, I grabbed a soda and filled up the tank. When we returned to Asian Kitchen, our takeout order was waiting, steamy hot.

In the suite, I unpacked the dinner. The bag was filled with lots of fresh, yummy food. Norway devoured his chicken from the sweet and sour and the lo Mein. Three servings. My sweet-and-sour sauce, mixed with lo mein and veggies, was tasty. Dinner in our castle was at six thirty, leaving lots of time to relax.

After channel surfing for a while, I took Norway out at eight p.m. I grabbed my bag out of the car, along with treats for Norway. Outside was cool but not freezing! *It is so pleasant.*

WICHITA FALLS, TEXAS, to CLAREMORE, OKLAHOMA

IN THE OTHER room, Norway jumped off the bed. He strolled through the doorway, then hopped onto the bed next to me. He stared, wagged his tail, and let out a few husky words. *Time to get up.* Downstairs, I collected breakfast: juice, apple, banana, mini bottle of water for later, and cinnamon rolls to try. It took extra effort to transport items to our room on the third floor, but we were enjoying the penthouse.

This morning, we intended to visit the Lucy Park waterfall and a "mini-skyscraper" in Wichita Falls. At nine a.m., we departed and headed up the road, past the Lucy Park/Falls turn, and into the downtown, empty on a Saturday morning.

We found the "World's Littlest Skyscraper." The forty-foot-high building was constructed on the edge of town in 1919. Legend has it that J. D. McMahon came to town and presented plans to build needed office space in the growing area. He provided blueprints and raised $200,000 for the building. Unfortunately, the blueprints were scaled in inches rather than feet! By the time construction was underway, McMahon had fled with the money. So the owners had an ordinary building, rather than a state-of-the-art forty-story high-rise. And they could not legally get their investment returned because the construction did match the blueprints.

The modest building was fully occupied during the oil boom until the Great Depression. Then it was boarded up. Decades later, the building was purchased and remodeled rather than demolished. Now this simple building, with its humorous title, showcases a historical structure with an interesting story.

Norway and I went along several streets. We spotted another painted horse, like last night's figure. This one, titled "Choose Your Side," was illustrated with several comic villains and heroes. I learned these horses began appearing in 2007 as part of "The Mane Event" public arts project. Besides the painted fiberglass horses around town, Wichita Falls had quite a few colorful murals. It was a nifty place to walk around.

We returned to the car and headed to Lucy Park. The ten-minute drive was easy. Wichita Falls provided plenty of blue signs with directions. Lucy Park was enormous and clean. In the winter, I didn't expect many people. But it seemed like they kept the place maintained, providing a nature area, jogging paths, playground, and more. The only disappointment was that there were no falls. It was dry! I had looked forward to the beauty and sound of water flowing—but no water on this winter day. Regardless, it was a nice stop. Plus, Norway and I did some jogging to and from the empty falls.

We left Wichita Falls and crossed out of North Texas and into Oklahoma. We traveled on I-44 East for ninety minutes until pulling into Chickasha to see the giant lady leg lamp. The forty-foot-tall fiberglass piece on top of a ten-foot crate made an interesting photo op. Unveiled in November of 2022, it was the centerpiece of a park and downtown plaza. If it was built to draw tourists like us, it worked.

Norway and the lady leg lamp

Later I learned that local Chickasha resident Nolan James made the first lady leg lamp as an art project. Then a producer from the 1983 *A Christmas Story* was inspired to use it in the movie.

After we checked out the giant lady leg lamp, Norway and I walked up and down the quiet, empty streets. *Another historic downtown with no one around. Because it's winter time? Or is the town struggling?*

We walked past a few open shops. A pretty woman with stylish streaks of gray hair was taking a smoking break. She saw Norway.

"Pretty dog," she pointed out.

"Well, on his behalf, thank you!"

She laughed.

The woman was attractive, wearing a sexy, stylish black goth outfit. Very cool. *Oklahoma fashion?*

On the way back to the car, I noticed a pizzeria with an intriguing colorful red, white, and green storefront. *Maybe get a couple of slices for the road?* Only three cars were parked in front. I liked supporting the local stops.

Norway waited in the car while I went inside Ben and Jay's Pizzeria. The menu had a variety of items, including burgers, sandwiches, and salads. I ordered a small pizza, cookies, and a Dr. Pepper.

"It should be ready in about fifteen minutes."

"Sounds good," I said. "I'll be back."

Outside, Norway joined me at a bench in the sun located in front of the restaurant.

A few moments later, the female manager walked out.

"I had to see your husky. It looks just like mine!" She glowed. "Same color, except ours is smaller." She reached down to meet Norway. "How old is he?"

"He's eight. I've had him for six years."

"What's his name?"

"Norway."

"Great name," she said. "Hang on. I have to get my husband! He'll kill me if I don't let him know."

A moment later, a man wearing a Ben and Jay's pizzeria shirt came outside.

"Doesn't he look like Avon?" she said to him.

"How old is your husky?" I asked, while looking over digital photos of their happy pup.

"She's two years old. We got her as a puppy."

We compared stories—especially about the shedding. "It's like a snow globe in my house twice a year," I told them. "It just floats around the room."

They nodded. "Yes, her entire coat comes off every summer and winter."

"Funny, last year, I watched a bird pick up Norway's white hair off the ground and carry it to its nest." I added how ironic it is that Norway chases birds and critters yet provides material for the birds. Cycle of life.

"Lots of energy and tears up the house." They laughed.

"They are such smart dogs."

"More like mischievous," I added. "They'll sneak off with anything."

He said, "Yes, they are smart. But it doesn't mean you can completely train them! Avon will do whatever she wants."

"I'm OK with it. Because, in the end, they are super with people and kids."

"I know," the guy said. "The kids pull on her ears and she doesn't care. She is so sweet."

A young woman appeared with my lunch order.

"Wow, that was fast," I said. "Thank you so much for bringing it out to us."

They had to return to their customers. I wish we'd had more time.

Back on I-44, we headed toward Oklahoma City. I missed the turnoff to Norman to see the James Garner statue and perhaps the Sooner Stadium of the University of Oklahoma. Instead, I kept driving and eating pizza.

Just east of Tulsa, we turned onto Route 66 toward Catoosa. I recognized turnoffs we had taken last week. Then, in the corner, I saw a blue object. *Aha, that was the part I missed last time* .I U-turned and went further down the road until we encountered the giant blue whale.

We walked around the pond and onto the whale, which provided lots of nice photo ops. Beside the cool blue attraction was a small souvenir shop, next to blue signposts that listed several places along Route 66—many Norway and I had seen.

Big blue whale and Norway

We continued down Route 66 and arrived in Claremore at four o'clock. I passed the hotel and continued into the downtown area. When I saw the Will Rogers newspaper statue, I found a parking spot. It seemed like a nice town to walk around a bit. A chilly wind was blowing, and the sun was setting. Still, it was winter nice. We found a couple of statues and sculptures for interesting photos. Also, a couple of murals to highlight our tour.

Norway was a rock star. As we walked along the street, three young women looked in our direction and pointed at Norway. On our drive out, Norway sat in the passenger seat, tongue hanging out and smiling. A beautiful blond woman looked directly through the Nissan window and smiled at him. *Oklahoma kindness.*

CLAREMORE, OKLAHOMA, to CUBA, MISSOURI

NORWAY STOOD IN front of the bed and made a sound at 6:45 a.m. It was still dark. We were on the western part of a time zone—late sunrises. (Also, late sunsets, extending the daylight for us.) On the eastern parts of time zones, it reverses. This is noticeable when traveling east-west, especially in the wintertime.

When I got up to check messages, Norway jumped into the bed, taking my spot. I guess he just wanted to get me going.

"I like the enthusiasm, but we have lots of time today." The 270-mile travel day went along I-44, through northeast Oklahoma and Missouri, mostly places we toured last week. Our principal stop would be the twelve-mile Kansas stretch of Route 66 we'd missed.

I flipped through the cable menu, picking the middle of the film *Point Break*. I enjoyed a comfortable shower with high shower heads and glass doors (instead of curtains). *Is this for La Quinta Suites? Or in every room?*

I swept through the breakfast room and brought back delicious oranges and an Otis Spelunker muffin to go. When I set out scrambled eggs for Norway, he looked at them and walked away. No interest. *Maybe I should have added ketchup to them? Or perhaps he's waiting for something better at lunchtime?*

We headed east on I-44 for about seventy-five miles. At exit 313 near Miami and Commerce, we exited and followed my hand-written directions from the online maps.

10 east to 137 north to Quapaw, OK. Then, 69 North/Main Street.

US-69 coincided with Route 66 and Mickey Mantle Blvd. in Commerce. I made a quick stop at Quapaw to fill up with gas. This part of the country had some of the cheapest gas prices. I noted the familiar area beyond Commerce. Eventually, US-69North ran into the Kansas state line.

The sites listed on *RoadsideAmerica* provided a terrific outline to view this Route 66 section.

In Baxter Springs, there was a 1930s gas station and a welcome area. At ten thirty on Sunday morning, the tourist office was not open. Norway and I walked around the vacant area to stretch our legs and view the colorful murals. Baxter Springs was using Route 66 to its fullest to attract travelers.

Norway surveying Kansas

We proceeded to Riverton to see the curved bridge, a nice piece of history. The Rainbow Curve Bridge, constructed in 1923, was the only remaining one of that type from the original Route 66. *Still here after one hundred years.* Then, a big Route 66 Kansas sign provided a good photo op. Across from it was an extensive kiosk with history to read. Plus, open space and smells for Norway.

We finished the town trifecta with a pause in Galena, browsing Main Street, highlighted by Pappy Litch Park, a classic gas station, murals, and a US flag made from Kansas license plates.

We veered southeast, down Route 166, to the "Tri-State Marker." Without detailed directions, it was almost impossible to find. We followed the road toward Downstream Casino. Then we took an unmarked left turn onto a steep gravel road. No markings. Rough road. At the bottom we found a concrete section and a graffitied border. *Another random geographic attraction.*

"Here it is!" I said to Norway as we approached a marker for where Kansas, Missouri, and Oklahoma meet. I took photos of Norway standing on all three states, walking around the area, and other shots. Then, he settled down for a nap on the marker. *Traveling through three states is exhausting!*

Norway resting in three states

Unexpectedly, a pickup truck came down the road. *Is it another tourist?* The Native American driver circled past us and left. *Is he checking us out? Or is he lost?* Otherwise, nobody showed while we were there for fifteen minutes.

We finished our detour through the southeast corner of Kansas. The twelve miles of Route 66 was well worth the return. I couldn't believe I'd missed it the first time. We were only a few miles from Joplin, where we were last week!

We had about two hundred miles of driving ahead of us. Cruising at eighty mph most of the way, we paused in Marshfield, Missouri, to see their mini-Hubble telescope. In the hometown of astronomer Edwin Hubble, we stretched our legs and looked over the telescope replica next to the courthouse. On the way out of town, I picked up an Impossible Whopper snack for the road. Norway was not interested.

"Not even the fries?" I offered.

Norway took a sniff and dismissed them. *Must be on a health kick.*

Along I-44 we passed Missouri places I remembered from last week: Uranus, Lebanon, Fort Leonard Wood, Rolla. We did make one stop: Redmon's candy shop. There were countless signs counting down the distance—35 miles... 32 miles...All the way down to 0 miles. It was remarkable. The candy shop was filled with goodies. But more impressive was the "world's largest gift shop" next door. Inside the massive warehouse were rows of toys and souvenirs. For a few minutes, I glanced through a section of puzzles, one of Ty dolls, one of Route 66 trinkets, and on and on. I liked the logo of an excited boy with the R (for Redmon) hat. But it wasn't enough to get me to buy anything.

We were winding down our drive through the Ozarks. In Fanning, we passed the giant red rocker. The trading post with the popcorn and sodas was closed—not surprising at 4:15 on a Sunday in January. We continued into Cuba, past the downtown area, and to the Wagon Wheel Motel. The place was closed, but the phone number was posted.

I reached the owner, Connie. "Yes, room 17."

"Oh, I thought it was 18," she responded.

"Either is fine with me."

"And pets must be off the beds and not in the bathtubs," she emphasized. "Guests have not been listening. It ruins the white linens. And it's fifty dollars to replace them."

I wondered, *Why use white linens, then?* Part of me wanted to say, "Just charge me fifty dollars so my dog can roam free."but, that might have sounded obnoxious or disrespectful.

"If you can't keep your dog off the beds, I'd prefer you just go to another hotel."

Not the sweetest welcome, but I could see her point of view. Besides, I didn't want to switch hotels. Open since 1938, this was the longest continuously running hotel on Route 66. I wanted to see if we were up to the challenge.

The room was like an individual cottage. Inside was a double bed and single bed, across from an old 1950s fridge, red microwave, and small TV. It was a modest and well-maintained place. The table with two chairs crammed on the side would be a good dining spot.

The grounds sort of gave me a Bates Motel feel, mixed with old-school motel. Since the woman was feeling sick, she sent her grandson to give us the key. The young man was an Ozark-type looking guy. He politely showed us the room and offered some restaurant choices. We would go with the popular BBQ place, conveniently next door.

In the cottage, I put my bags on the beds to block Norway. I laid out his blanket, his pillow, and an extra blanket on the floor between the beds. *Hopefully he will figure it out.*

Outside, we started walking to the Missouri Hick BBQ. A guy unloading bags from his truck greeted us, "He's a good traveling companion, isn't he?"

"Yes, a great pal. He never complains when I change the radio station," I joked.

The guy laughed and nodded in agreement. Then, he introduced himself.

"I know. I travel a lot by myself. My wife doesn't want to go. So I drive alone."

We chatted about backgrounds. Dave had an Army hat on. I learned he was retired.

He mentioned driving to Alaska. "Where did you go?" I asked him.

"I drove to Skagway."

"Really? I went there with my other dog! About seven years ago."

We talked about the Alcan Highway. Plus other traveled places. He was exploring around Route 66 right now.

"We're on our last day," I told him. "We left Chicago and went all the way to Flagstaff. Then looped back through New Mexico and Texas."

Dave compared his travel route. "I wanted to see more. But it takes too long."

"I know. I really wanted to go from beginning to end. But it would take a month using only Route 66."

"Yes," he agreed. "Plus the road starts and stops in strange places."

It was a pleasant conversation about traveling with Norway.

"Are you a reader?" I asked.

"Yes, I have more time now. So I do a lot of reading."

"Hang on." I went to the car and pulled out a copy of *Bring Oscar*. I handed him the book.

"No way, Lance. This is great."

"It covers the four trips I took with my first dog. Including to Skagway."

"So you kept a journal?"

"Sort of. I took notes about places, people, and observations. I like to keep track in case I return. But, mostly, I can go back several years and pick out a day. When I look at the photos and notes, the entire day is crystal clear. I totally remember the moments."

"That's great. I kept a journal when I was going through Alaska by myself. I need to do that again."

"Everything in that book is ninety-nine percent true."

"Thanks," he said. "You gotta sign it."

"Definitely. Glad to."

I wrote a message to Dave, ending with *enjoy the journey!*

"Hope you like it."

"Oh, I'm sure I will," he said. "Wow, you wrote this."

"It took a lot of work to get it published."

"Have a lot of people read it?"

"Nah," I said. "But some have. It's very hard to sell books. But I did it for the experience. And to remember the trips with Oscar. Sort of a tribute to him."

"I've wanted to write a book," Dave said. "I have material from my time as a war strategies officer. But who's going to want to read that?"

"You never know what people want to read. Besides, it's more important to write something you're proud of," I said. "Seeing the final printed book makes it all worthwhile."

Norway and I continued to the BBQ place. I ordered ribs and chicken, mashed potatoes and gravy, salad, and bread. It was fantastic, especially the sauce and chicken. Afterward, I used the Wi-Fi to check messages. While I sat on the only open bed, Norway picked a spot next to the bathroom door.

The room became very chilly. I realized the thermostat temperature was set to sixty degrees. I increased it to seventy-five. Later in the evening, the room was toasty, but it became too much for us. So I dropped the thermostat to sixty-five and opened the door a minute to drain some of the heat out of the room.

CUBA, MISSOURI, to HOME

IN BETWEEN THERMOSTAT adjustments, we went outside a few times last night. Each walk was in the deep dry winter cold but no wind. I walked around with Norway wearing shorts and two coats—a fashion wreck.

Inside the cottage, I managed to keep Norway off the bed. Once he popped partially on, but I pushed him off. Eventually he figured it out and slept on the blankets between the beds. I felt a little bad. Two nights ago, he was hopping from comfy king-size bed to king-size bed. Now he was relegated to the floor. But the husky will survive.

* * *

At 6:45 a.m., I flipped on the TV and found a rerun of *Two and a Half Men*. On my laptop, the Wagon Wheel Wi-Fi option was missing. I guess it was fitting: we were at a decades-old motel. I didn't mind taking a step back in time.

The ol' cottage had plenty of great hot water spraying from the nozzle shower. With no breakfast offered, the Ozark grandson suggested a place down the road that had "the best biscuits and gravy." But that was a pass for us.

As we dropped off the key and loaded into the car, Dave was outside packing up. We had another nice chat. He was headed to Oklahoma to visit his son. Then he would return to Dayton. He offered me a bottle of water for the road and mentioned he would reach out after reading the book. We departed at eight a.m.

Norway and I got to St. Louis around 9:15. The town was full of patched roads and random potholes. *Our gas tax dollars at work.* We switched from I-44 to I-55, to head directly toward Chicago.

We drove straight through until a pause for gas in McLean, IL, another Route 66 town. Fifty miles later, we checked into Pontiac, IL. Following a long walk and a few photos, we returned to the Mexican restaurant there. We enjoyed the same lunch, on the same park bench, as two weeks ago. This time the temperature was twenty-five degrees warmer, providing a better picnic setting.

Since Norway passed on all the chicken, I gave him the last chew bone in the trunk. He was pleased. We left by one thirty—early enough to beat rush hour in the Loop.

Enjoying the homestretch

We reached the Chicago Loop a few minutes before three o'clock. The traffic flow was decent. We were home by quarter to four. We had traveled 4,246 miles in fifteen days.

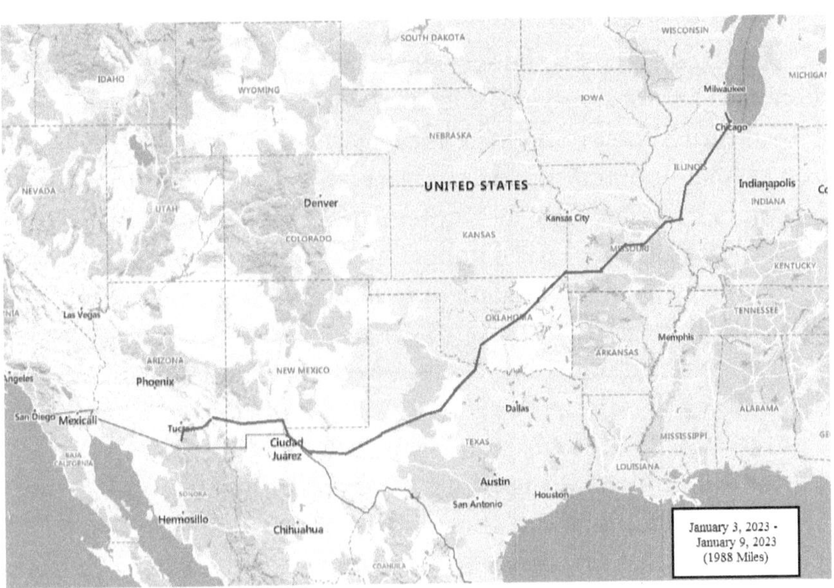

I drove up the driveway, climbed out of the car, and walked into the house. At the doorway, my mail had been piled on the front entrance. The cumulative delivery was scheduled for tomorrow, but the post office missed it by a day. *I guess it was close enough for government work.*

Norway headed to the backyard to take care of business, and I went out front to begin transferring items from the car into the house. It would have taken ten minutes to unload the car but, on the third trip, Norway had come inside and bolted through the slightly open front door. *I didn't latch the door.* He was down the road in a full sprint.

"Ah F$%#K!" After a long day on the road. I was not thrilled to chase after Norway.

I grabbed my phone, car keys, and his leash, then began my search.

Where the hell did he go? Looking for his canine friends? Did he want to tell them about his two-week road trip?

After fifteen minutes, he had disappeared. I went home to check phone messages. Then I did another lap, driving up and down the streets, asking people along the way. I tried the spots he and I walked every day. I double-checked his favorites: the park and Timber—another husky who lived down the street. No luck.

I returned home to check messages again. Nobody had found him. Then, another lap. At the very end, I did one more lap of Norway's favorites. When I got to the southern part of Church Street near the school and Timber's house again, my cell phone rang.

"I have your dog," a woman with a South African accent said. "He's playing with my dog."

The phone number location showed Glenview, a town over five miles away. "Where are you?"

"I'm at 3715 Church Street," she said.

I was in my car sitting fifty feet from her house!

"You're kidding. I'll be there in a second."

I pulled into their driveway. The woman was standing in front, and the two dogs were having a blast chasing each other around.

"Thank God you found him. I've been looking for an hour."

"Sorry, I would've called sooner. But I couldn't get him to stop to read his tag."

We chatted as the dogs raced around the yard.

"Well, this is a blessing." She was pleased. "I've been telling my husband we need to get play dates for Zach."

"Well, Norway will be happy to play any time."

Norway and I returned to the house. He was delighted to have made a new canine friend. And I was happy that we had completed another memorable road trip.

PART VII

MINNESOTA 2.0

"WHAT'S YOUR FAVORITE place?" is often asked when folks learn about our travels.

"Well, it depends," I answer. "If you want the ocean, Hawaii. If it's the mountains, somewhere out West. Maine has great spots. I'm from Arizona and love that area." Then, I add, "I can tell you my least favorite travel spot: Minnesota."

The winter darkness, snow, and cold are notable. But Minnesota summers are no bargain. *The land of 10,000 lakes has ten billion mosquitoes.* Plus, the humidity is not pleasant. I like Prince, MyPillow, and Fran Tarkenton. But I always seem to encounter shady characters, terrible traffic, crowds, and road-rage drivers.

Is it bad luck?

* * *

At a July 29029 Everesting event in Jackson, Wyoming, I got to know one of the volunteers and alumni participant. Aandrea was down-to-earth, pretty, adventurous, and generous. While connecting, I asked, "Where are you from?" She had mentioned the Midwest.

"Minnesota," she said.

"Really?" I wouldn't have guessed that. "What part?"

"Just outside of Minneapolis." Then, she added, "In more of a rural area."

Hmmm. There's a chance we'll pass through there on a future road trip.

Weeks later, I was considering a quick ride to finish the summer break. Norway and I could go west into Iowa, or we could go east through Ohio, or we could go north to the Upper Peninsula of Michigan. The last option was the Twin Cities.

I had confessed to Aandrea that of every state I had visited, Minnesota was the most trouble. "Except for a two-hour lunch in St. Cloud, where I encountered wonderful people," I hedged. "But, mostly, Minneapolis evokes road-rage driving, construction, mosquitoes, and humidity."

I had terrible luck in Minnesota. At the same time, it would be fun to visit her. And maybe if I changed my mindset, it would be a more positive experience? Or, at least, a less negative one.

I decided to give it a try. Aandrea welcomed visitors, offering to meet up when we were in her town of Delano. So I booked the only hotel in Delano for two nights. It was located thirty minutes from Minneapolis. *Perhaps I'll get to know this area better.*

EVANSTON, ILLINOIS, to EAU CLAIRE, WISCONSIN

ON MONDAY MORNING, Norway and I packed up and left at 11:20 a.m. Since the drive went north, we avoided downtown Chicago and construction on the Kennedy Expressway. Thankfully, the route was without traffic. And the car enjoyed smooth roads and no construction sites.

I decided to hopscotch our route to Eau Claire. We skipped Kenosha (already been there) and Milwaukee (been there multiple times to see the Bronze Fonz!). We even went via I-894 to bypass the Milwaukee local I-94.

After ninety miles, we landed at Oconomowoc, WI, before one p.m. Oconomowoc was a nifty town off a couple of small lakes. In the pleasant downtown, we focused on city hall and the *Wizard of Oz* statues, mural, and tribute to the movie debut shown eighty years ago. From there we explored, finding a nice walking area, an old ice cream shop, murals, and more. I picked up a milkshake at the ice cream shop. *Why not? This is dairy country.* The cherry chocolate chip shake was very good.

Norway following the Yellow Brick Road

We skipped Madison (been there), and headed to the Wisconsin Dells. I had visited there with Oscar, but we never went through the town. After driving a hundred miles from Oconomowoc, we reached the Dells by three thirty. It had a touristy, Branson feel. Also, there were many Trump signs and "Let's go, Brandon" T-shirts—a huge contrast from lefty blue Madison fifty miles away.

We parked a few blocks from the main downtown strip. In one of the old-school parking meters, I poured in ten quarters, which gave us two and a half hours. Plenty of time to check out the area.

Norway and I started along the riverwalk. The paved path, lined with placards, provided bits of Wisconsin Dells history. Also it offered views of the Wisconsin River and landscape.

Back on the main strip, an old photography shop stood out among the attractions for visitors. We stopped at Dells Distillery. Inside, I asked the bartender if there was any place I could eat with my dog.

"Sure, you can go up to the patio," he offered.

"Do I go in the back?"

"You can go right through here, if you'd like." He pointed to the indoor stairs.

"Perfect."

I retrieved Norway and guided him inside the cool bar and up the stairs to the second-floor area. Dells Distillery had a patio, but we opted for air conditioning inside.

Naomi, a young cute waitress, entered, welcoming us with a smile that revealed braces. I learned she was a lawyer from the Dominican Republic, working in the Dells for the summer. She loved to travel, having spent time in South Carolina last year. She became very interested in Norway and the places we had traveled, as well as the book written about Oscar.

"He has a great smile," she said, looking at Norway with his tongue hanging out.

"Happy dog," I said.

"He has a pleasant vibe," she added.

"I know. When he was younger, he tore up one of my favorite sweatshirts. I screamed at him. But he just smiled and thought I was playing with him. Then, I frustratingly yelled louder until he scampered outside. After a few minutes, I felt bad. This was not the way to bond with a dog. And there are better ways to teach him. None of it mattered. A minute later, the husky walked back inside. He sat beside me holding his ball. Just smiling."

"Such a sweet dog," she said.

"At that point, I realized reprimanding him was useless. He doesn't care. And he's very forgiving. Everything gets forgotten!"

She commented, "Well, you have a great friend. And he's a lucky dog."

"He's the best."

During our conversations, I munched on the tasty lunch: veggie bean burger, waffle fries, and a soft drink. Norway enjoyed the chicken fingers mixed with his bowl of dog food.

We left the Dells at five thirty and drove two hours for the last third of today's drive. Due to my slight misreading of the map, five minutes on the I-94 turned into twenty minutes hunting for the Eau Claire hotel. At least I chose the parking space closest to our room.

The hotel itself was located amid a mall, with lots of food options in view. This was something to note if we passed through again. Following a quick check-in, Norway and I had a snack and relaxing evening. I watched a *Die Hard* rerun on HBO. It was a good travel day. And, I looked forward to the short driving leg tomorrow.

EAU CLAIRE, WISCONSIN, to DELANO, MINNESOTA

LAST NIGHT, NORWAY took me out for three walks: at ten thirty, *right after I took off my shoes.* Then at eleven thirty. *Again, Norway?* Then he tried at four but waited until five thirty. To his credit, he efficiently did the same lap around the Best Western. Each time, he marked territory and relieved himself. *Better here than some nice town's sidewalk.*

We left the hotel at nine a.m., ensuring no chance of traffic. *We should reach Minneapolis/St. Paul by ten thirty.* The Wisconsin I-94 was smooth sailing with good roads and low traffic flow. As we approached the Minnesota border, the traffic became busier. Around the St. Croix River, the roads turned crummier with bumps and potholes. Then, construction appeared, resulting in narrow lanes and congestion.

I spotted a Welcome to Minnesota rest stop that advertised vending machines and maps! It was a timely break before driving into St. Paul. At the St. Croix rest stop, Norway and I did a lap around the spacious area. It wasn't too hot or too humid, and there were no mosquitoes. This was unusual for Minnesota in August. I read a few info boards presenting local history. Then I darted inside to grab a free Minnesota fold-out map and brochures.

We continued twenty miles into St. Paul, looking for the Snoopy and Peanuts bronze characters somewhere in the city. I couldn't find them. But, while looking, I noticed a huge domed building and a sign for the capitol. *St. Paul must be the capital of Minnesota!*

I drove in the direction of the standout ornate building. Navigating numerous one-way streets, I just aimed for the building in the distance. Finally, I reached a street near the capitol with a row of metered parking.

As I attempted to pay, an African man politely asked, "Can you show me how to use this?"

"I'll try," I said. "The first one over there didn't work. I'm going to try this meter." It didn't work either. *Maybe the sunlight and weather fried the unit? Or the units are obsolete, only permitting app or internet for payment?*

I went to plan B: ask someone.

When two local workers came along, I asked, "Any idea where there is parking? These meters don't work."

"Just go around the corner to the Sears lot."

"OK," I said. "How much is that?"

"It's free!" the worker said.

Two blocks farther away was a huge parking lot beside a closed Sears. And it was free.

Our improvised adventure continued as Norway and I walked to the capitol building. I listened to music and held Norway's water, as he led the way, husky style, excitedly walking around the spacious grassy area. Meanwhile, I took photos of Minnesota historical figures, the buildings, war memorials, and pretty scenery. This open and immaculate area was a substantial contrast to the city area, sprinkled with garbage, homeless people, and dense crowds.

After ninety minutes, Norway found a shaded, grassy spot to rest. Fortunately, it was forty feet from five food carts. While Norway chilled, I got us lunch. One of the carts had a turkey and cheese Panini, fries, rings, and soda. *Perfect time for a picnic.*

While I ate, folks passed by and watched Norway. Some kids approached to greet him. A few local workers stopped to meet us.

A stroll around the capitol

After our one-hour lunch siesta, we visited more monuments in the area before heading back to the car.

We resumed our tour of St. Paul, trying to find the bronze Peanuts characters. Since the Peanuts creator, Charles Schulz, was from the area, I anticipated a few dedications. Born in Minneapolis, Schulz grew up in St. Paul and began a career in art, comics, and illustrations, including the popular Peanuts strip. In 1958, he moved to California.

A resident we met at lunch had said to look for Rice Park in downtown. I headed in that direction and just drove around, sight-seeing with Norway in the air-conditioned car. Suddenly, I saw a sign pointing to Rice Park. A few blocks later, I spotted two of the bronze characters. *Time to park.*

The street parking was difficult, even on a Tuesday. Instead, I found a parking lot. The rate was $6 an hour. Cheap by Chicago standards. The downtown was quite appealing, aside from the homeless scattered throughout the area. Around Rice Park and Landmark Plaza, the Peanuts statues were blended into the scenery. Marcie was on a bench reading a book, with Woodstock over her shoulder. Lucy was with Schroeder playing the piano. Sally and Linus, with his security blanket, were at a street corner watching traffic go by. Peppermint Patty was kicking a football in the grass. And Charlie Brown sat with his best friend, Snoopy, resting on his lap.

Norway finding his beagle friend

Created by Trivoli Too Inc. in 2003, these bold, four-foot-tall sculptures had a nostalgic appearance, reminiscent of old metal toys from the 1940s.

At two o'clock, Norway was done. So we concluded our Charlie Brown and Snoopy pilgrimage.

It took forty-five minutes to get to Delano. I just followed I-94 into US-12, which went all the way to Delano. We found the hotel on the north side of the highway, near the entrance of town.

GrandStay Hotel and Suites was an excellent place! We had a living room, bathroom, and sleeping area. There were two TVs, a sofa, and plenty of room to relax.

We enjoyed the air-conditioned spacious area and found *Magic Mike—Last Dance* with Channing Tatum on HBO. That was a fine time killer. Ironically, I had watched the first *Magic Mike* in a hotel in Idaho, during the first road trip with Oscar in 2013.

In the evening, Aandrea offered to pick us up at the hotel. Norway leaped into the back of her SUV as I went into the passenger seat. On the way to the restaurant, Norway peeked his head between us to enjoy the front window view. We traveled fifteen minutes to Wayzata to have dinner inside the Hotel Landing, at ninetwentyfive. We enjoyed great conversation and a terrific meal. Norway was a rock star, welcoming the people and staff who wanted to meet him.

MINNEAPOLIS, MINNESOTA

LAST NIGHT, WE went to sleep around eleven p.m. Fifteen minutes later, Norway was standing beside the bed looking at me.

"Really?" *I just got comfortable.* Sometimes I think he's playing with me.

"Alright." I put on an extra shirt and shoes and grabbed his leash.

We went down the elevator to the warmth outside. *It's going to be a steamer tomorrow.*

Norway went to his familiar spot in the grass.

"Nice." He had to go. "Just wish you had done that earlier."

We woke at six a.m. Back to sleep. There was no hurry. Ninety minutes later, while Norway kept sleeping in the soft king-size bed, I checked various regional maps, attractions, and distances. I considered travel options: west to Sioux Falls, south to Des Moines, or through southeast Minnesota. Each added up to two hundred miles to our trip. Moreover, we had been to all those places already.

I decided to add another day in Delano. The good news: the hotel still had rooms for Thursday night. The bad news: we couldn't stay in our jumbo suite. Instead, we'd have to move to a standard two-queen-bed room. Norway would have to live without the palace furnishings we had enjoyed so far.

At nine a.m., we left Delano for Minneapolis on US-12 East. I was pleased to see no traffic, and we got there in thirty minutes. Unsure where to go, other than downtown, I followed an exit to 4th Street and parked next to the Target stadium.

We started walking. I hadn't brought a map, but I had a rough idea where the main places were located: the Prince mural was around 8th Street, the Mary Tyler Moore statue on Nicolette, the sculpture gardens southwest of downtown.

I carefully noted the parking area and space so I wouldn't lose my car's location. Carrying water for Norway, I followed him onto 2nd Ave at 5th Street. Around the corner was a huge mural of Bob Dylan. I recognized that from travel articles and a page in *RoadsideAmerica*.

After a few photos, we continued sightseeing—Norway leading the way. The variety of scents and discarded food were attracting his attention. The town was relatively quiet without a sporting event; among the tourists, there were homeless and vagrants, as well as business people working.

I came across a Black cop positioned on the street. Over the music of my headphones, I could hear him say, "Nice dog." I stopped, chatted with the friendly officer, and asked about the Prince mural. He pointed me back in the other direction. We easily found the cool mural, as I got my bearings on the layout of downtown.

Prince and canine royalty

I sent the photo and message to Aandrea—*proof of life in Minneapolis!*

She replied, "Norway is so regal!" *Indeed.*

We walked to Nicollet Mall and spotted the Mary Tyler Moore statue that honored the popular TV show actress whose character resided in Minneapolis. Then, Norway and I started south on Nicollet. I noticed a public map of the area.

It seemed about one and a quarter mile to the sculpture park. *The car is the other direction.* Instead of going back, Norway and I continued to the park, understanding it would be a two-and-a-half-mile round trip. As the walk got longer and hotter, I wondered if we should have taken the car to the park. *Would there be parking there, anyway?* At last, we found the bridge over the highway to the sculpture park. Following a break and some photos of the artwork, we marched back to the car.

At noon, we left the parking lot and went directly onto I-394 West, which went straight into US-12 West to Delano. *Wow, smooth sailing.* Thirty minutes later, we passed the Delano hotel to scan the downtown. It seemed worth a visit tomorrow.

We picked up takeout from a Mexican restaurant and settled back in the hotel room. The fajitas were delicious, as I cleaned my plate, and Norway cleared his bowl.

While I watched TV, Norway walked in and stood beside me.

"Ruh, ruh ruh ruuuuh," he said in husky talk.

"Norway!" *What does he want?*

"Ruh, ruuuuh, rah rah," he cried out.

"Ruh, ruh, ruh, rah, rah," I repeated.

He paused and looked up, "Ruh, raaaah, rah, raaaah," he howled and wagged his tail.

"Ruh, raaaah, rah, rah," I mimicked.

He stopped and tilted his head.

"I know. I am not sure what I said either."

Then, Norway came up to me and planted himself on my lap.

"When did you become a lap dog?" *My seventy-pound lap dog.*

Following a four-hour siesta, I got in touch with Aandrea, who finished work early. We went for a quick hike along a trail at Rebecca Lake. It was fun going down the trail with Aandrea, her ten-pound pup, Martha, and Norway. Unfortunately, the mosquitoes came out midway to join us through the walk. Also, the heat wore us down quickly. Before it became a mosquito massacre, we retreated to the cars.

We considered trying the sixteenth annual Taste of Delano, but, due to the heat, we thought it might not go well for the dogs. Instead, Aandrea ordered takeout from the King House. The ravioli, pasta, and salad were delicious. Mostly, it was a nice change to spend time at her home instead of on the road.

DELANO, MINNESOTA

AFTER YESTERDAY'S HOT trailblazing in Minneapolis and Delano, Norway slept well. In the morning, I went down and got another hot chocolate and two Danishes from the breakfast bar. The early work crews were in the lobby. I headed back upstairs to Norway.

Today was a non-travel day. We could hang out, relax, and enjoy the end of summer vacation. One mile away, I scouted the area and parked in the middle of downtown Delano. *Free parking. Love the small towns.* I grabbed the music player, and Norway and I went up the three streets of downtown Delano. It had painted mural banners, small shops, a few bits of art, and historical markers sprinkled around the downtown.

We walked past old residences to the baseball diamond, water park area, and public fields. After Norway took a drinking break, we circled back to the downtown shops and had a breakfast burrito from Wilbur's Cafe.

For an hour, we lounged at the outdoor table, watching cars and people go by. Several greeted us, particularly a retired couple who stopped for a pleasant ten-minute chat. They lived down the street in the condo building. She was a former teacher, which she revealed after I explained what I did for work and why we were on vacation. Meanwhile, Norway lay on the shaded sidewalk trying to stay cool.

Delighted in downtown Delano

Because the Nissan's interior was a furnace, I started the engine, opened the windows, and ran the air conditioner. After a minute or so, we stepped into the car. Following a lap around town, I decided not to drive to Rebecca Lake. We turned around, passed the crowded ice cream shop, and headed back to the hotel. The bank sign across the street showed ninety-three degrees. It was time for our one o'clock siesta in the air-conditioned hotel room.

I picked up the bag, grabbed Norway and his stuff, and walked toward the hotel entrance.

"Your dog is super cute," said a young landscaper. She was super cute too.

"Well, on his behalf, thank you!" I replied. "He's a good one. A bit hot right now."

"Yes, I'm hot too," she said and smiled. Then she picked up her supplies and walked toward the lawn.

We took the elevator to the room. The housekeeper greeted us. "Can I pet your dog?"

"Of course," I answered. "He'd like that."

While she petted Norway, he leaned into her, soaking it up. "He leans like my dog," she said.

"You have a dog?" I asked.

"I have three. All big dogs."

"They're the sweetest."

"I know," she said. "Especially my giant St.Bernard."

That made nine encounters this morning. Norway is a true magnet, attracting attention.

We had dinner with Aandrea in nearby Maple Plain, where she grew up. The Iron Exchange had outdoor seating to accommodate Norway. They offered tasty cocktails, ales, and drinks. I had a sangria cocktail that tasted like a refreshing orange juice drink. Also, we tried the Detroit-style margherita pizza, with a rectangular shape and slightly smaller crust than pan pizza. The meal accented a great evening to end our trip—and to end the summer break.

DELANO, MINNESOTA, to EVANSTON, ILLINOIS

IT WAS A straight path home—approximately 440 miles. There were no easy, cheap hotel options to divide the drive into two days. I had checked a quality place near the Wisconsin Dells. Online, the headline price was $89, but Thursday's rate was $169. Then, Friday night: $269 plus a pet fee! *I am not paying $289 for a place to sleep in Mauston, Wisconsin.*

We left at nine a.m. to ensure we'd miss traffic going through Minneapolis/St. Paul. More importantly, we were driving east toward the rising sun. By nine, it was high enough over the horizon to avoid being blinded.

Since we were retracing our route back, maps weren't necessary. We'd head through Delano past the rural towns of Orono and Wayzata into Minneapolis. At nine thirty on Friday, it was rather clear. We wound through a maze of turnoffs into St. Paul, and although we encountered road construction and narrow lanes on I-94, the traffic flowed. Soon, we were in Wisconsin and cruising along.

I saw a truck lose its front tire from a blowout, maybe from the heat and wear and tear. Then, I watched a sedan go over the blown tire. Moments later, fluid was gushing out of that car's underside. I could smell gasoline. It looked like the tire had put a hole in the gas tank or tore out the lines. She had to pull over. *That sucks.*

After two hours, we stopped in Hixton to get gas. Following a brief walk, a photo of their fish sculpture mascot—Fishy McFishface—at the travel plaza entrance, we were back on the road. Norway was a champ, mostly sleeping in the back. Occasionally, he would emerge. One time, he climbed to the front and placed his paw on my arm.

"OK." I rubbed his back and face. When I set my tired arm on the armrest, he pawed at my arm again.

"Alright!" I laughed and lifted my non-driving arm to give him a chest rub. He soaked it in with his tongue hanging out and eyes closed. When satisfied, he returned to the backseat to rest.

Resting in first class

At twelve thirty, we stopped for lunch just past the Wisconsin Dells downtown exit. Norway woke and stepped onto the armrest to have a look. Restaurants were mixed among the malls and outlet stores. I pulled into one and spotted a place with outdoor seating behind a giant fiberglass cowboy. At McCallister's Deli, Norway sat in the shaded table section, while I went inside and got us a veggie sandwich, potato salad, lemonade, and a side of chicken pieces. Plus, a s'mores cookie. The lunch was quite good. While portions were on the small side, the lemonade was huge. A good place to fill up and rest in the shade.

We plowed through the second half of the trip with expected maneuvering and congestion around Milwaukee. But, overall, it was fine.

After crossing into Illinois, we chose the tollway over Route 41. The information sign displayed "23 minutes to Lake Cook," which meant no traffic. I could pay all the tolls later. As we flew down the road, traffic was building up in the other direction. It was four thirty on Friday afternoon, so people were heading to Wisconsin for the weekend.

We pulled into the driveway at 5:15. The eight-hour drive completed a terrific five days. *Maybe Minnesota isn't my fiftieth-favorite state anymore!*

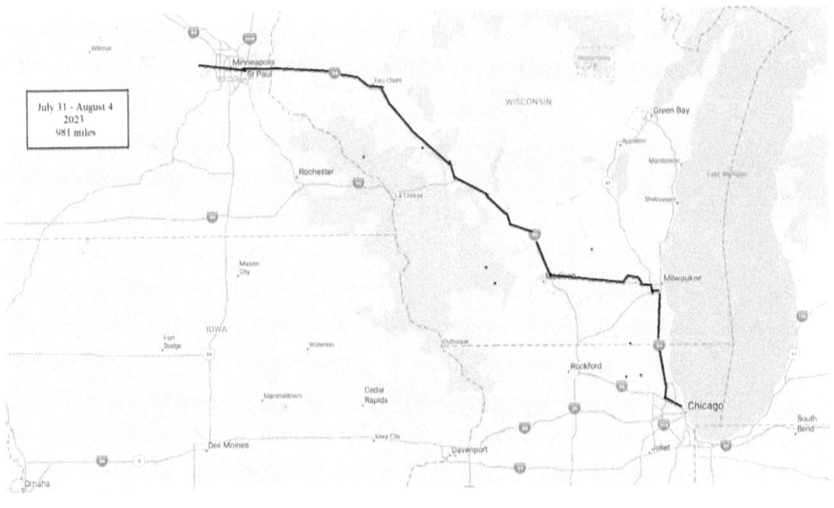

We went inside the house. I dropped off a few items, made sure Norway didn't run away to his friends again, then looked at the backyard. After one week, the garden was filled with several giant zucchini plants, some ripe tomatoes, and a few cucumbers. *A nice yield.*

I started to unpack and acknowledged I had done a horrible job packing! Due to the high temperatures, the packed sweatshirt, blue jeans, and a few other items were unnecessary. Examining two extra shirts, I discovered one had a hole and the other had a stain. Most of Norway's stuff went unused. The canned dog food, regular dry dog food, and treats remained. He got a nice fill of chicken and other people's food instead. Regardless, the brief trip included the essentials: Norway and the car!

Norway passed through the doggie door into the backyard. He weaved his way through the garden and began digging in a shaded spot under the eave. When satisfied with the smooth, carved-out ground, he rested comfortably in the cool dirt bed.

Epilogue

Travel is like surfing or mining for gold. It can take a lot of time and effort to get to that "moment" or "payoff." While attending undergrad school in California, we were about an hour from the Orange County beaches. A buddy and I had Wednesday afternoons free from classes. So we would borrow a roommate's beat-up car and a couple of boogie boards and drive to Huntington Beach.

Would there be good surf? Would the overcast clouds burn off, the sun come out, and warm up the day? We tried calling places near the Huntington Pier to ask about the waves and weather. They proved unreliable. This was long before the internet, instant access to weather forecasts on a smartphone, or surf webcams.

My friend and I would drive over to the coast, often finding a spacious beach and sets of waves. After picking a spot, we would battle the cold water, walls of waves, and wind. Then, finally, it was the "moment"—an awesome set would come down. And we would get an outstanding ride!

During one memorable occasion, a group of dolphins appeared. They were swimming and playing in the surf around us. From the shore, I could see silhouettes of dolphins in the rising waves. Decades later, I remember *those* moments—more than the lectures, textbooks, and formulas I learned in my advanced math classes!

Like treasure hunters looking for another gold nugget, Norway and I continue to explore. We travel at every opportunity, spending time and effort to get to that "payoff" at the end. In between visits to our favorite spots, we discover new places. Each is an enjoyable adventure with countless possibilities. Try it!

2024 and beyond

At the time of this writing, my favorite husky and I are still travel-ing. Here are some photos.

Warming up with Larry Bird in Terra Haute, Indiana

Sweet…World's largest watermelon slice, Mississippi River, Muscatine, Iowa

The Badlands, South Dakota

Resting in the hotel room, Kimball, Nebraska

Highest point in Nebraska

Lance Friedman

Doing time in Rawlins Prison, Wyoming

Volunteering at Snow Basin, Utah

Beautiful… The Big Easel, Van Gogh painting, Goodland, Kansas

Resting on Route 66, Atlanta, Illinois

Ordering a cold one at the Boozehound, Chicago, Illinois

The greatest thing since sliced bread! Chillicothe, Missouri

Mammoth March twenty-mile hike, Kettle Moraine State Forest, Wisconsin

Norway and all the kind canine companions out there are a blessing!

482

Like any road trip, there were turns, detours, and rough patches. I hope you found this true story worth reading. If there are incoherent or unsettling parts, imagine them in the most positive light.

CREDITS

Transforming notes about events, sites, and observations into a memoir was a substantial project. Thanks to the following people who helped in the process of this book:

Susanne Lakin at www.livewritethrive.com who corrected grammatical and style errors, pointed out ambiguities in the manuscript, and streamlined my writing to produce a better flow of events. I'm grateful for the effort, critique, and expertise.

Al and Ian for providing final proofreading remarks.

And, the book design team at Jetlaunch for their fast, efficient, and enthusiastic service.

With their outstanding help, I could produce Norway's story!

This book was a labor of love. One hundred percent of any profits will be donated to Norway's and Oscar's favorite places.

www.ingramcontent.com/pod-product-compliance
Lightning Source LLC
Chambersburg PA
CBHW021333150726
47989CB00005B/1964